Mandela, Mobutu, and Me

D O U B L E D A Y

New York   London   Toronto   Sydney   Auckland

Mandela, Mobutu, and Me

A Newswoman's African Journey

Lynne Duke

PUBLISHED BY DOUBLEDAY
a division of Random House, Inc.
1745 Broadway, New York, New York 10019

DOUBLEDAY and the portrayal of an anchor with a dolphin
are trademarks of Doubleday, a division of Random House, Inc.

Library of Congress Cataloging-in-Publication Data
Duke, Lynne.
Mandela, Mobutu, and me: A newswoman's african journey /
Lynne Duke.—1st ed.
p.   cm.
1. South Africa—Politics and government—1994–   2. Congo
(Democratic Republic)—Politics and government—1997–
3. Mandela, Nelson, 1918–   4. Mobutu Sese Seko, 1930–
5. Duke, Lynne.   I. Title.
DT1974 .D85 2003
968.06'5—dc21   2002073365

ISBN 0-385-50398-9

Book design by Lisa Sloane

Printed in the United States of America

February 2003
First Edition

1   3   5   7   9   10   8   6   4   2

For the Dukes and the Fortiers—

my parents, my grandparents, and their struggles

Contents

Author's Note

 regarded Africa through the eyes of a journalist. That is what I am. I also looked at Africa through other eyes, those of an African American and a woman. Armed and advantaged with these many ways of seeing, I roamed Africa and gathered its stories of the profane, the sublime, and everything in between.

Born in Los Angeles, schooled in New York, sharpened as a journalist in Miami and Washington, I have written of many subjects since I entered journalism in 1984. But never has a story gripped me as Africa's did. The four years I lived and worked there were the most confounding, exhilarating, and engaging of my career. That is why I write this book.

It is based on my reporting from South Africa in the early 1990s, followed by a posting there, from 1995 to 1999, as Johannesburg bureau chief for the *Washington Post*. From Jo'burg, I covered much of the continent south of the equator. I chronicled President Nelson Mandela's South Africa rebuilding itself after the ravaging years of apartheid, and I chronicled the tragedy of Mobutu Sese Seko's Zaire, now named the Democratic Republic of Congo, tearing itself apart in back-to-back wars. Those two stories were the bookends of my African travels, the bittersweet crosscurrents I navigated.

This impressionistic reporter's memoir does not claim to cover the length and breadth of the continent. Nonetheless, it amplifies some of the broad dynamics unfolding among Africa's 800 million people in their disparate regions, nations, and cultures. Many Africans share similar traditions and beliefs about family, society, and spiritualism. These infuse much of the continent with a collective sense of Africanness, as does the long history of conflict with and ultimately conquest by an outside world based on that pernicious invention called race.

The concept of a shared African experience can also be found in the dynamics that have defined Africa since the wave of independence from colonialism in the 1950s and 1960s: the conundrum of the colonial legacy; the onslaught of misrule and autocracy; the resort to violent repression and war; the machinations of the global Cold War and the realignment of power in Africa after its end; not to mention the ongoing push and pull of the global economy.

Some readers will rush to pin a label on this work, for American discourse on Africa tends toward stereotypes. But I am neither an Afro-pessimist nor an Afro-optimist. If you must call me anything, call me an Afro-realist. I write this book with an affectionate concern for and loyalty to the African struggle. I am guided by the legions of African people whose lives are built on extraordinary fortitude, unwavering hope, and profound humanity, despite immense odds.

1

Finding My Way

I hated it when the lights went out. I still had a dispatch to write, for Washington was awaiting my daily file. But there I sat, foiled again, fumbling for my flashlight and candles as the whole of Kinshasa, capital of the Democratic Republic of Congo, was reduced to the darkness of a village. It was August 1998, in the midst of yet another Congo war, and those damned rebels had done it again. They'd seized the country's main hydroelectric plant and taunted Kinshasa, and me, with another nightly blackout.

I fumed to myself as I lit a candle and welcomed the eerie glow it cast over my room. I lodged up on the fourteenth floor of the Hotel Intercontinental, and down below, as far as the eye could see across the sprawling metropolis, cooking fires and candlelight speckled the darkness like stars fallen to the ground. My people, African people, were suffering again. And my people, African people, were the cause. This was getting pathetic.

I pored through my notepads, jam-packed with days of scribbled shorthand, and raced against time as I wrote. I could only hope my laptop battery would outlast the night's power outage; only hope I'd make it through another Washington deadline. Night after night, my dispatches grew more ominous. The rebel juggernaut pressed closer to the capital. Food shortages deepened. Ethnic cleansing swept through the streets. Massacres unfolded all around the country. President Laurent Kabila's regime girded for a fight that his splintered army could not win. The United States, France, Belgium, and Britain evacuated their nationals but had no intention of rescuing Kinshasa itself. So African leaders stepped into the void, assembling a response of their own to the bloodbath that many feared would consume the city's 5 million people.

That was my fear too. The days ahead would be dangerous. I didn't know how I'd make it through. I had a fever and needed sleep. I needed a hot bath in clean water that wouldn't plant strange bacteria on my skin. Sick with the bends from the hotel's lovely display of a faintly rancid buffet, I craved fresh food. And what I wouldn't give for a doctor to do something about the infected boil on my face. It bulged from my cheek like a third eye. It assaulted my vanity each time I looked in the mirror, and disgusted my colleagues as they watched the boil grow.

Strangely, it reminded me of my mother back in Los Angeles. If she could see me now, I laughed to myself. Mom thought mine such a glamorous profession and regaled friends and relatives with tales of my travels. But I am certain she never imagined that a foreign correspondent for the famed *Washington Post* could look as worn and diseased as I'd become—on the road, in Africa, at war.

There was no way out. The borders were closed. And even if I could have gone, I'd have opted to stay. I had a job to do, a mission to fulfill. A certain degree of misguided heroism kept me going, as if Congo needed me to be there to write its latest chapter. It was a delusion, I know. But I'd placed myself fully inside Africa's unfolding story.

Change and upheaval roared through Central and Southern Africa in the 1990s, and that was my territory. Some of it was inspiring. After decades of white-minority rule called apartheid, South Africa had turned to democracy under President Nelson Mandela in 1994—a change that freed southern Africa as a whole and opened the prospect of South African–led peace and development. But farther north, the Central African region reeled from the 1994 genocide in Rwanda that left some 800,000 people slaughtered.

Rwanda's blood spilled throughout the region and was the spark that ignited two wars next door, in Congo.

I'd written through the first war, the one in 1997. That conflict unseated Mobutu Sese Seko, the infamously grandiose and corrupt dictator when the country was called Zaire. And now, only fifteen months later, Mobutu's disastrous successor, Laurent Désiré Kabila, seemed certain to meet the same fate. Kinshasa, again, was the epicenter of events shaping my notions of Africa.

During the day, free of the nighttime curfews and power outages, it felt strange to venture through a suddenly silent city. Kinshasa, normally, is a place of high-decibel noise—loud conversation; loud music, rumba and *ndombola*; loud traffic. You could hear old cars banging down the road, parts scraping against each other, bouncing along crumbled, potholed streets choked with exhaust fumes, honking horns, shouting people, and, of course, the loud music. But all that was gone. No sashaying women, their hips draped in garishly gorgeous cloth; no market women with necks taut from the loads they bore on their heads. Even the ragtag, malnourished children who hawked soap, cigarettes, and facial tissues on every corner were scarce.

Instead, angry troops were on the prowl, including those twitchy teens with guns, the child soldiers. I'd become all too familiar with the barrel of the AK-47, having had so many pointed in my car window by these power-mad juveniles. Nationalism had exploded. Ethnic chauvinism became deadly. Kabila's brutish regime stoked it. The army rounded up all Tutsis—or any tall person with angular features that fit the ethnic Tutsi stereotype—and detained, tortured, even killed them, on suspicion of complicity with the rebel force spearheaded by Rwanda and its Tutsi-led military. As rebels infiltrated the city, some civilians took matters into their own hands. On the streets, they burned suspected insurgents to death, no matter their ethnic background. I worried about Alec, my friend from Kigali, who'd come to Kinshasa for the sake of a renewed pan-Africanist unity he thought would take hold after Mobutu's ouster in 1997. Alec was Tutsi, and that put him in danger. I hoped he made it out alive.

For thirty days, I clenched my teeth. Dodging soldiers and roadblocks, I moved through the city interviewing local people, known as Kinois, as well as foreign diplomats. I worked the cell phone as I drove around with Tom Tshibangu, my translator and tireless assistant, and Pierre Mabele, the driver and strategist of Kinshasa's mean streets. Both had become true friends in a pinch. During much of that month, I teamed up with colleagues including Marcus Mabry of *Newsweek* and Jennifer Ludden of National Public Radio. Marcus was based in Jo'burg and I knew him well. I'd met Jennifer on earlier Africa travels, and, on this assignment, we had run into each other while catching the flight from Nairobi to Kinshasa. Colleagues provided a security blanket. The duress of Kinshasa's tension, plus the expense of drivers and translators, made it unwise to work alone.

But unlike Marcus, an African American like me, Jennifer was white, and her whiteness became problematic. Whether American, French, British, or Belgian, whites were particular targets of Congolese who were angry in their belief that the West was in league with the rebels. Angry mobs attacked foreign journalists routinely, though usually without severe injury. Jennifer got caught one day while trying to interview people at a street rally. Some young toughs descended on her, threatened her as a white person, and hit her as she jumped into her car and sped off with her driver. I had no such incidents. I could easily blend in with crowds. I wanted to keep it that way.

One day I needed to go out to La Cité, a jam-packed and vibrant slum, without attracting attention. I told Jennifer I'd have to separate from her for a while since her skin color made her a magnet for trouble. My tact, no doubt, wasn't very diplomatic. I felt edgy amid the city's insecurity, and that made my manner pretty brusque, even with friends. Ditto for Jennifer, who exploded at me outside the Intercon, as the Intercontinental was called. She said it seemed racist for me to go off without her because of her white skin. She accused me of being disloyal, while I tried to convince her I had to get my work done the safest way possible. As Tom, Pierre, and I drove off toward La Cité, I called Jennifer via cell phone to apologize and we continued our silly debate. We got over it, in coming days, for there was much more to be concerned about than the nuances of race and reporting.

The war roaring toward the city had me pumped with adrenaline. I attacked it, journalistically, like an obsession. Seeing Congo facing yet another setback made me passionately angry, for I knew that Congo was on its own. No matter how bad things got, I feared there'd be no rescue, no intervention to save the thousands of African lives being lost. The West would watch and warn combatants to retreat, but nothing more. Hell, even during the Rwandan genocide a few years earlier, the international community had sat on its hands and let African blood flow. So fine, I thought. With my dispatches, read in Washington but also around the world, I could at least rub people's faces in it day after day after day.

This sounds less than objective, I know. I was there ostensibly to observe and tell the story, not to get emotionally caught up in it. But in the best of times, I am a true believer that journalism should comfort the afflicted. And in these, the worst of times, my sensibilities could not withstand the daily onslaught of fear and death, of sources and friends living under the gun, of people I knew being targeted for death. I felt swept up in a storm far larger than journalism, a storm of history's cruel and unfinished work in Congo.

It all seemed to blend together in my mind, from the fifteenth-century plunge into slaving with Europeans who brought the depopulation and ruin of the ancient Kongo kingdom, to the brutish colonialism of Belgium's King Leopold II, to Patrice Lumumba's briefly valiant 1960 prime ministry as the first elected Congolese leader, to the CIA connivance that helped kill him and paved the way for Mobutu's 32-year dictatorship, to the chaos that followed Mobutu's demise, when Kabila stepped right into Mobutu's shoes.

When mortar blasts rocked me awake one morning toward month's end, I was actually glad. Whoever was bombing whom, I was willing to bet the endgame had arrived. Angola, Zimbabwe, and Namibia, Kabila's allies, had been planning for some days to help save the capital, and as I sat straight up in bed that morning, I hoped that was what they were doing. Luckily, I slept fully clothed. It took only a couple of minutes to slide into my shoes, do some quick ablutions, and grab my gear before running down the stairwell (yes, fourteen flights) to find out what was going on.

To my relief, I learned from diplomats around the city that the allies were fighting rebels out in the city's crowded eastern neighborhoods, toward the airport. From the city center, we could hear the fighting that raged for three days, though journalists couldn't get anywhere near it. But we lined our balconies one night and witnessed a terrifying sight. Near the fringes of the blacked-out city, the sky exploded over and over in the silent white light of huge magnesium flares sent up to help Kabila's allies flush out the insurgents. Out there, in that light, people were dying—rebels, troops, and ordinary people—in what I assumed was brutal street combat. I hated the thought of it, but this was war. And with gunfire raining all over the city from soldiers in celebration in following days, the siege of Kinshasa ended; the bloodbath we'd all feared had been averted.

Leaving the Intercon, a pack of us foreign correspondents, about a dozen all told, headed to the Congo River. The airport remained closed, so a river ferry was our only way out. It would take us to Brazzaville, capital of the Congo Republic, and from there we could fly out on a British or French military transport. But the first attempt at a river crossing failed, for the ferry did not cross from Brazzaville. We spent the night in another Kinshasa hotel, the Memling, then awoke early to caravan back to Ngobila Beach, the port, where our ferry was waiting.

We weren't the only ones trying to flee. When we got to Ngobila, crowds of local people with their bags and children in tow milled about near the rotting docks and jetties. They looked forlorn, but they'd remain stranded. Apparently, ordinary people wouldn't be allowed to board our ferry. The people watched us. Their gaze seemed resentful, or maybe my guilt made it look that way. I would be getting out. They would stay. They would have to endure more of a city with no electricity, no water, dwindling food supplies, and legions of trigger-happy teens.

An armed gang of immigration officials, soldiers, and plainclothes security men swarmed among us. They shoved and shouted angrily. They snatched up our luggage for thorough searches, as if we foreigners surely had some incriminating possessions. Any papers or documents would only bring interrogation, or worse, so I'd hidden mine in my pants and in my suitcase lining. Sweat dripped down my chest. My boil had begun to ooze. My nerves seemed about to snap. But soon I'd be on my way. As we lined up to board, the crowd of locals heaved forward, dragging their bundles and children toward us, toward the gangplank. Soldiers lashed out to keep them at bay, whipping the crowds with long knotted ropes as we boarded.

The light. That's what I remember of my view from the ferry's bow, how daylight suddenly seemed so much brighter, how sunlight dappled the river's swells like diamonds tossed down from the sky. Ten miles across at its widest, the river's broad vista unfolded before me, promising to take me away. So mighty and meandering, this river, this vein of life. It entranced me, whenever I had time to ponder it. So much history was written on its banks, so much misery. It filled me with regret to be leaving this way. I'd come to love Kinshasa for its vibrance, but I felt tingly, almost light-headed, that my escape was finally at hand.

But—*BAM!* The troops opened fire. The *ratatatatatat* ricocheted over the river. It seemed to come from everywhere. I hit the deck, crouching low. My traveling colleagues did likewise. I didn't know who was shooting or why. I chanced a quick glance up to the port in time to see the troops spraying their AK-47s like water hoses to stop the desperate locals who'd rushed the boat. The throng of bodies and bundles hit the ground. Oh God, oh Jesus. Don't let them be dead. Please don't drop another mass killing at my feet. I wanted the entire scene to go away. I wanted no responsibility for it. Emotionally exhausted, I did not want to care. That's what it had come to: massacres could be inconvenient. The port fell silent. I stood up to get a better look, feeling guilty that I'd momentarily lost heart.

How many times had I prayed and cried over African suffering? How many times had I given what meager help I could offer to those in desperate need and bemoaned my inability to do more? How many times had I written so fiercely, even angrily, of the world's injustice? I'd imagined myself the champion of the ordinary African, but was that just a lie? Was I some armchair advocate who, when the bullets flew, got spooked?

I thought people were dying that morning, but the thing that upset me more was the fact that they were dying on my watch. I was, so I thought, bigger than that, stronger than that. But I could not take any more.

The people stood and dusted themselves off. The cacophony of their patois filled the air once again, as if to mock my panic, as if to ridicule me. One of my colleagues, Sam Kiley of the *Times* of London, announced in his officious way that no one had been hit. The troops had fired only in the air, it turned out. As best we could see, no one was dead.

The ferry churned into the current. I watched huge tangles of sickly sweet-smelling hyacinth drift past, headed where the brown waters took them. Silhouetted against the sun, men stood in their wooden dugouts called pirogues, navigating the river with long poles, as people had done for centuries.

Shouts rose up from somewhere on board. A stowaway had been found. The soldiers threw him to the deck and stomped him, kicked him. A photographer in our group raised his camera to record the brutality, but the troops angrily stopped him. The soldiers stuffed the poor stowaway into a narrow ship's storage compartment and slammed the door, muffling his moans. I felt sick to my stomach. I stood at the railing, ready for an upchuck. The spray of the river trickled down my face. It would be elegant to write that the river's mist camouflaged my tears. But I had no tears left. I was stone cold. I was spent.

* * *

I'd called myself "Duke of Africa" once upon a time. Back when I felt expansive and full of wonder at the start of my tour as a foreign correspondent, I'd made up the name to sign off e-mails to my editors back in Washington. I liked its dashing sound and knew they'd get a kick out of it too. Eventually, we shortened it to "DOA." In Congo-Zaire, my acquaintances called me "Madame Duqué" when I'd sweep in to write another chapter of their nation's story. Spoken in French, "Duqué" had a wacky, imperious ring. Some of my traveling pals, especially Marcus and Dele Olojede of *Newsday*, made a sport of mocking the grand persona they claimed came over me whenever someone uttered my new name.

And I did feel grand. I loved my work. I loved living in Africa—the way it felt, so foreign but familiar; so much another world, and yet a world that was my heritage. I was, after all, rare: a black American woman foreign correspondent. I was seasoned in my field, arriving in Africa at the age of thirty-eight after eight years with the *Washington Post*, and the independence of foreign journalism, the freedom to roam and write, ranked for me as the most privileged perch a reporter could find. I milked it to the fullest.

I descended deep underground in South Africa and Zambia, into gold and copper mines that kept economies afloat. I lunched on a Congo River speedboat cruise with diamond merchants from Britain and Belgium and felt the sting of the first world's long tentacles manipulating economies of the third world. I jousted with cabinet ministers in interviews that became debates, sometimes exposing my own frustration with African policies that made no sense, other times commiserating with the awful hand that Africa had been dealt. For no good reason—yes, there were times when I had no mission—I paddled the Zambezi River, dodging its hippos in a comic fiasco I will never forget and in which others less fortunate than I have died. On another journey, I slept in a pup tent in a remote Namibian village where crops were plagued by elephants, and cattle were targeted by lions.

At times, I seemed pulled in so many directions that I struggled to make sense of it all. But when I sat one strange day in 1997 before Mandela and Mobutu together, the heroic statesman and the venal dictator, I found some clarity to my African odyssey. They were Africa's archetypes, symbols of what Africa had been and what it yet could be. They represented the African hopes and African horrors that were the bookends of my personal journey.

But I found myself most fulfilled in that space between the archetypes, that place of normal Africa, where people lived with their hope, their horror, and every conceivable state of being between those extremes. Inside their humble abodes, complete strangers served me tea and biscuits or, if they could afford it, full-out meals. Gladly, they shared with me their aspirations and struggles. Women called me "sister." Elderly men called me "daughter." Children in dusty, rough-hewn villages gathered round just to watch a foreigner and giggle. Their delight was mine. I was the American, the black American, a source of fascination, answering as many questions as I asked. People wanted to know about our civil rights struggle. Our jazz and rap. Our American racism. Our superstars. I felt like a messenger from the other side of the vast ocean that separated us physically but also linked us.

Africa presented me with legions of faces that looked like mine, in places that were ruled by my kind, where people could recite their ancestral line way back to its beginning and walk with the power of knowing whence they came, with ritual and tradition to steer them, plus ancestors ever ready to guide, protect, or foil them, as is the ancestral way. I absorbed Africa's generous humanity and fell in love with it. On a continent whose demise is so often rumored, I felt fortunate to meet many ordinary people committed and working hard to better their lives, their nations, especially human rights workers who toiled against all odds in places where humanity had been defiled.

I thrived on the power I spiritually attached to African blackness, especially in South Africa, where the black majority had finally won its rightful place at society's helm. I felt the strength of their victory. It was a welcome contrast to the ever-shifting weight of the "minority" status that is a fact of life in the land of my birth, where the presence of blackness seemed to trigger an American urge to hem it in or squelch it or regard it as something strange. But I've always kept an inviolable place in my soul that contained my special identity, my culture. My people had survived. Sold, shipped, broken, beaten, lynched, spat upon, sent to the back of the bus—but we are still here. And it is the same for Africa, where my bloodline began: plundered, depopulated, and repressed in European colonialism. The beginning of all mankind and still surviving: for that alone, I held Africa in awe. As I traveled, I felt as if Africa reached out and claimed me as one of its own. That sensation was brilliantly clarifying for who I am in this world—part of a bridge between continents, and connected as much to America as to a vast African narrative that resonates within me like an ancestral whisper.

But sometimes the whisper was a scream, for I also had to grapple with ugly Africa, the Africa of horror and unspeakable brutality. The Africa that sometimes made me question the existence of God. The Africa that I could not ignore if I was to claim the continent as my own. I witnessed a terrible warping of the human spirit and I loathed it. I loathed the thieving of the likes of Mobutu and the legion of bribe-seeking bureaucrats his government begat. I loathed the repressive leaders who did as much damage to their people as the colonialists they replaced, and the warmongers whose aggression bred little more than chaos and turned back the clock on progress.

I saw inhumanity on a grand scale. In Rwanda, I could barely comprehend what I was witnessing when I encountered the mummified remains of thousands of hacked, bullet-riddled bodies, in various poses of terror, in a church-compound-turned-killing-ground during Rwanda's 1994 genocide. In the bombed-out towns of Angola and the scorched countryside, hungry victims of the 25-year war literally scratched the earth for food, for seeds fallen from international relief sacks, while their wealthy countrymen in the oil-drenched capital lunched on lobster.

On my journeys, people begged me for money, for help, for food. It unnerved me, always, to stand in the midst of such suffering and be unable to offer relief. I tried to help in small ways when I could, and I harbored the naive hope that, at the least, my dispatches could bring understanding to a world that so often viewed Africa grimly, so wrongly. I could only watch and write and try to explain what seemed inexplicable.

Always, a nagging fear lurked inside me—a fear that maybe Africa would not, could not, right itself. I feared for Africa's fate, and oh, how I hated that fear. I hated having to acknowledge it. I wanted to simply embrace Africa, to write Africa, to be its advocate. I wanted to deny the terrible mayhem and brutality that goes hand in hand with ordinary life in too many African locales. But I had to accept the raw fact that Africa at times could be profoundly brutal and maddeningly dysfunctional.

I seemed always to be wrestling with myself about Africa as I worked and traveled, and that is where I found myself yet again as I stood at the bow of that ferry churning across the Congo River: trapped by Africa's wonder and its woe as I watched the river's swells.

A faint popping sound caught my attention. Somewhere aboard ship, someone hit a flat hand against the taut animal skin of a drum. I turned and walked toward the center of the deck. A half dozen boys were setting up an array of congas. I hadn't even noticed the boys when we boarded, though they wore colorful sweat suits. A Brazzaville drumming corps that had been stuck in Congo because of the war, the boys were fleeing Kinshasa too and heading home. They were lighthearted and gay as they set up their instruments. All of us on deck gathered round to watch.

Standing in a line, they pounded slowly. They swayed and danced as they drummed into a deep African funk that pumped faster and faster. One of the smallest boys flipped somersaults with his drum clutched between his knees. He drummed as he landed and never broke the rhythm. I found myself bouncing to the beat. I felt relaxed, almost revived. Back in my early years of college at UCLA, I'd performed African dances with a campus dance troupe, and now I felt the urge to jump up and surrender to the beat.

I felt silly for my earlier bout of spinelessness. I thought of all the people, so many, many people, who had every reason, every right, to lose hope in Africa but did not. So who was I to feel beaten down, to feel weary and morose? I had no right. I thought of the old Zulu man, Johannes Ndlovu, who welcomed me as a descendant of one of the mythic black people he thought were lost on the other side of the ocean. Thinking of that sweet old South African man always made me smile. Whatever hardship and heartbreak Africa had offered me, it had dished up an equal amount of humbling marvel, of inspiration.

The boat heaved across the river while the boys from Brazzaville pounded furiously. With each beat, they pulled me back from despair. Theirs, for me, was a rhythm of salvation, a rhythm of the African humanity I could never forsake. Watching the soldiers to make sure they could not see me, I pulled out my small tape recorder. I needed to capture this moment, my personal sound track of a Congo River crossing that took me from confusion to clarity about what Africa meant to me.

2

The Dream

ZOLANI, SOUTH AFRICA, APRIL 1990

apsy's hands felt so soft for one who'd lived so very, very hard. She'd take my hand in hers protectively as we walked down the rutted dirt roads of tiny Zolani, a township for blacks in the shadow of the Langeberg Mountains near the Cape's wealthy wine estates owned by whites. Or she'd take my hand in hers inside the spartan, candlelit room where she lived as she talked of freedom and justice and the stirring South African times to come.

Gertrude Bapsy Magoqoza was her full name, pronounced with a click of the tongue on the q in her Xhosa language. She was a mother. She was a fighter. But most of all, she was a survivor. We met during the nine weeks I spent traveling South Africa for the first time, to witness a nation suddenly turning from utter tyranny to a new hope. And through the years to come, Bapsy remained, for me, an icon of the heroic South African liberation struggle that pierced my conscience and lured me back again and again.

The South African system of white-minority rule known by that ugly word "apartheid" (pronounced, appropriately, *apart-hate*) had tried to break the spirit of people like Bapsy, had tried to break the back of black resistance. But the more brutal and harsh white rule became, the more it fired the resolve of ordinary, everyday people to fight, to resist, and to win.

In Afrikaans, one of South Africa's many languages, "apartheid" literally means "apartness." But in practice, it meant that the Afrikaners, those descendants of South Africa's seventeenth-century Dutch and French settlers, believed it their God-given destiny to lord over Africans as a master race. Building on the segregationist tradition of the British colonialists who ruled before them, the Afrikaners who won power in 1948 ushered in a crushing program of racial engineering. Not only did blacks have to carry passes, but they had to live in areas designated for their own group, absorb the most inferior education, earn wages a slight step above slave labor, and enjoy none of the rights the world came to know as human. Even their hair was examined for its quality, straight or nappy, to decide tricky cases of racial classification between black, mixed-race "colored," Indian, and white.

For a time, it worked chillingly. So many territorial enclaves were carved out as dumping grounds for blacks, called Bantustans or homelands, that the map of South Africa seemed physically pocked by its racism. For decades, people like Bapsy had been humiliated and hounded, jailed and tortured, murdered and dismembered, day in and day out. Bapsy herself spent a few years in political imprisonment for agitating against apartheid's draconian security measures.

Resistance to apartheid came in ways passive and personal, but also in collective waves of protest and violence. After the 1960 massacre at Sharpeville, when security police fatally gunned down 69 people and wounded 186 others who were protesting against the pass books that blacks had to carry to circulate in their own country, Mandela convinced the African National Congress, the leading liberation movement, to launch an armed campaign against apartheid. They called it Umkhonto we Sizwe (Zulu for "Spear of the Nation"), known by most as MK, with a mission to violently sabotage the apartheid state. But the campaign was short-lived. Mandela was arrested in 1962, followed by the dragnet that swooped up his movement's leading comrades in 1963. For plotting to sabotage and overthrow the apartheid regime, Mandela and his conspirators were convicted in 1964 in one of the world's most infamous political trials.

Facing the death penalty, Mandela uttered a statement of his principles that spoke to the heart and soul of his liberation movement: "During my lifetime, I have dedicated myself to this struggle of the African people. I have fought against white domination, and I have fought against black domination. I have cherished the ideal of a democratic and free society in which all persons live together in harmony with equal opportunities. It is an ideal which I hope to live for and to achieve. But if needs be, it is an ideal for which I am prepared to die."

Instead of the gallows, Mandela and six of his codefendants—Walter Sisulu, Govan Mbeki, Raymond Mhlaba, Elias Motsoaledi, Andrew Mlangeni, and Ahmed Kathrada—were locked away for life in a maximum-security prison on a rock out in the Atlantic called Robben Island, surrounded by treacherous seas. Their one white codefendant, Dennis Goldberg, received less harsh confinement, in a prison in Pretoria.

But a new generation eventually rose up to take their places—the generation of Soweto in 1976. This time, the protest movement targeted an educational system that taught blacks in the Afrikaans language, the language of the oppressor. Students—children and teens alike—surged through the streets of Soweto in a rally against that system, and once again met the barrel of the apartheid regime's guns. Hector Petersen, a child of thirteen, was the first to fall. Carried through the streets of Soweto by a screaming friend, his body became the signal image of black resistance that sparked months of rioting all over South Africa in which roughly a thousand blacks were killed.

Young blacks began streaming out of the country that year, to join MK in its bush camps in newly independent black countries and prepare for a real war. Their countrymen back home were also foot soldiers in the struggle. Ordinary people—mothers, sisters, brothers, fathers—manned barricades and mounted protest marches, strikes, and boycotts in a relentless push, which would last nearly two decades, to make the apartheid state ungovernable.

There was a certainty for many black South Africans that victory was inevitable. Their aspirations could not be stamped out, no matter how long the struggle took. After all, this was Africa, this was their land, and the tide of independence that had ended European colonialism across the continent since the 1960s could not be held back from South Africa's borders. As I traveled South Africa that spring of 1990, I thought often of my favorite quotation from Martin Luther King, Jr.: "The arc of history is long, but it bends toward justice." And that is precisely what happened. Justice finally arrived. In February 1990, Nelson Mandela, the messiah of the liberation movement, walked free at last from prison.

He had not been seen in public since his 1964 sentencing. His likeness had been banned for all those years. No pictures of him could be published in South Africa, nor could any of his words. Publication of either was a criminal offense. Apartheid leaders tried to make Mandela a nonentity, and yet the more they tried to squelch him, the deeper his symbolism grew, the taller his mythic stature.

When he emerged from those twenty-eight years of political imprisonment with that famous walk through the prison gates near Cape Town, Mandela set South Africa and the world afire. Hope and anticipation raged as his stunning new liberty heralded the last lap of a struggle for black liberation. It had taken the better part of a century, at least since the founding of the liberation movement, the African National Congress, back in 1913.

In setting Mandela free and unbanning all the resistance movements, Frederik W. de Klerk, the last president under apartheid, astonished the world and rudely shocked his own people, the Afrikaners. But his back was against the wall. South Africa's economy was in a severe nosedive, and black resistance had rendered the state progressively unworkable, just as the ANC hoped. De Klerk also faced tremendous pressure from economic sanctions imposed by countries that prohibited trade and credit with a regime defined globally as a pariah. His actions were motivated by far less than a concern for democracy, but suddenly that's precisely what was on the table: democracy, reconciliation, majority rule—which meant black rule. Everything the Afrikaner had been hell-bent against was suddenly up for negotiation. And South Africans who believed in justice could see their dream taking shape with each passing day.

Which brings me back to Bapsy, for she was one such dreamer. The promise of liberation was her sustenance. Despite her desperate situation— no job, no money, and no prospects for either—she needed only to look up at her wall to conjure the sweetness of the victory she was certain would come. Bapsy was a die-hard ANC acolyte, and she'd splattered her water-stained wall with a huge poster of Mandela, smiling down on her. She wore a T-shirt emblazoned with the logo of Mandela's party, the ANC. Owning such a poster, wearing such a shirt, would once have landed her in jail. But now they were acts of sweet anticipation.

Bapsy had already conjured the "new" South Africa in which she would live. She dreamed of it at night and thought of it during the day. She'd pinned it down to the last detail and could recite its features one by one. She was not after the moon and the sky, only a secure life of dignity. One day that April of 1990, as we sat at her little secondhand wooden table, Bapsy's words, though stilted, painted a picture so vivid that I could see it too. She smiled that broad smile that made her slanted Xhosa eyes squint, and she swept her hands through the air as she began.

"I dream my house is big; veeeery pretty. I must have got everything, like beds to sleep and furniture and TV and electric. And my kitchen must be nice—kitchen furniture like fridge, stove, ironing board, washing machine. I feel laaaazy [tired] of washing with my hands. And I must have money to put in the bank when I am dead, for the future of my sons. And I must go to the church every Sunday—I must not forget—because all the things is God's. And I must find work. I will be glad . . . Any work, and *good* money; not twenty rands [for blacks] and the whites two thousand rands. And my house must look like the white houses"—she banged a finger on the table—"because *I work hard*. And they mustn't call us kaffirs." She added this last bit like an exclamation point, for "kaffir" is a racial insult as inciteful as is "nigger."

Bapsy looked up at her poster of Mandela, her accomplice in this dream, and when I asked what he meant to her, she hesitated not an instant. "He is our father," she answered softly. And she said it like a prayer. I would always remember that moment. In it, in Bapsy's unswerving faith in Mandela and all he stood for, lay much of the essence of the story I had come to write. I knew in my head that people viewed Mandela as the father of their nation. And I knew that this vast social movement known as "the struggle" was about dignity and justice and a better life. But in Bapsy's rendering, I now felt it in my gut: the simple rightness of it, the nobility of it. There at that little table streaked with sunlight from a tiny lace-covered window, the South African dream came alive. All else that I would see and learn in South Africa would flow from the visionary words that Bapsy gave me. They became the filter through which I would judge events in her country. And they became my own paradigm of liberation, as a journalist trying to pin down and explain the passion of South Africa's struggle.

Quite frankly, I shared that passion; it was in my blood, in a way. I was raised on the stories of my grandfathers—a postal worker and a carpenter— who fought whites who called them "nigger," of grandmothers who'd scraped by in jobs as domestic workers, of parents who'd struggled against racism to make it through college. During the 1950s and 1960s, when our own American quest for civil rights was at its most intense, events in both countries ran parallel for a time. The bombings, killings, and attacks on black schoolchildren in the American South weren't all that different from the bombings, killings, and attacks on black schoolchildren in South Africa. Watts, where my family lived in South-Central Los Angeles, blew up in race riots sparked by police brutality in 1965 a few months after we moved away. And I had seen "white flight" up close and personal in the city's Windsor Hills, a largely white middle-class neighborhood we helped integrate. I witnessed my white classmates disappear in the space of a couple of years. I knew what it meant to be called "kaffir," for white Americans back home had called me "nigger" on some occasions.

I knew the fissures of race all too well, and I knew what the absence of justice felt like. Struggling against racism was part of my being, as was the belief that the struggle itself was a cherished and noble act. The broad contours of South Africa's unfolding drama were all too familiar to me, which I suppose is why I found myself hooked: hooked on the story, on seeing it through, on being somewhere near the finish line when the race was won. I felt personally gratified to witness small victories, small steps forward. And it thrilled me, to be honest, when I could throw my two cents into the battle. Though it wasn't mine to fight, there were times when I became an accidental combatant. To be black and circulating back and forth across South Africa's color line, a certain amount of struggling was inevitable.

What joy it gave me to integrate a whites-only South African restaurant. It happened quite by accident that spring of 1990 in the Orange Free State town of Welkom, deep in the heart of the Afrikaner farming region where men wore pistols on their hips and had a reputation for brute force when it came to keeping "their blacks" in line. It happened in a shopping mall after a long day of running and gunning (journalistically speaking) through township wars. I walked into a restaurant with Michel duCille, then a photographer for the *Washington Post* and a Jamaican American. We were so famished and fatigued that we must have forgotten where we were, that we were black in one of the hostile regions of white South Africa. We just sauntered on in, fully expecting to be seated and served some of that great grilled Karoo lamb for which South Africa is famous.

But the white hostess quickly snapped us out of our fantasy. She looked at us like we were crazy. She stuttered and stammered and was finally able to say primly, by way of refusing to seat us, "But we are not multiracial!" as if we were bungling idiots for even thinking we could be served. Before I could even open my big mouth, Michel lit into the woman—diplomatically but firmly. "We are hungry American journalists about to spend a lot of money in your restaurant and you will serve us." Or something to that effect. We were not leaving. We decided to take a stand.

While the flustered hostess ran off to confer with her boss, all eyes were on us. White patrons seated in the main dining room seemed to have frozen in pure shock. At the bar closer to us, some thick-necked and very large Afrikaner men glared at us with obvious hostility. These are the last people you want to tangle with, I thought, as I kept an eye on them keeping an eye on us.

Finally, after a standoff of several minutes, the manager relented and we were seated. And here's the wonderful part: at the doorway to the kitchen, black workers kept poking their heads out, smiling at our little victory, giving the thumbs-up sign. The black woman who poured our water whispered to us ever so stealthily, with her head held low, that we were the first black people ever to be seated in that establishment. And that felt good. I was proud to break some new South African ground.

But you learn quickly, in tough places like South Africa, that it is unwise to let one's personal biases, one's own perspectives, get in the way of the reality. You can miss the truth; you can ask the wrong questions; you can make incorrect assumptions. That's what I had to guard against as I traveled from town to town, propelled by that Bapsy dream and the belief that Mandela was a kind of messiah who would lead his people to a promised land. In broad brush, that's what was happening. But the story was much more complex, much more nuanced, and much more rich for being less clear-cut than the feel-good paradigm I'd adopted.

The reality of South Africa required me to step out of my African American skin and understand that not all black South Africans agreed with the future Mandela envisioned or how he planned to get there. Not everyone was willing to let bygones be bygones. Despite the beautiful simplicity of the dream about to come true, of good on the verge of vanquishing evil, there was plenty of evil still afoot. Even as Mandela, de Klerk, and their negotiating teams got down to the business of hashing out South Africa's future, laws giving apartheid police extraordinary repressive powers were still on the books; a countrywide state of emergency was still in effect. Apartheid agents still were blowing up antiapartheid activists; still mounting cross-border raids to kill black opponents.

In a township called Botshabelo, not far from Welkom, I spent several days with the young "comrades" who organized the town's resistance. Rallies and boycotts still had to be organized, the people mobilized, for the final assault against apartheid. Change was unfolding too slowly for these young men, who, though in their late teens and early twenties, already had been in and out of jail for their activism. The comrades wanted to see a fight. They sang songs of the AK-47. They carved planks of wood in the shape of the weapon and carried them at protest rallies. They glorified MK, the armed wing of the ANC that Mandela founded before he went to jail.

Though they respected Mandela and his generation, the young comrades all over the country had become a pretty scary force in the eyes of older people. They disrupted schools. They intimidated township authorities and even their own parents. For people who did not tow the comrades' line, homes were firebombed, dissenters attacked. In the worst-case scenario that had stained the noble mantle of Mandela's movement, people suspected of being "sellouts" of the struggle or collaborators were set on fire with a flaming gasoline-filled tire around their heads. They called the method the necklace. The Botshabelo comrades weren't like that, at least not in my estimation. But they saw the need for violence to bring apartheid to an end.

"To tell you frankly," said Jack Matutle, the charismatic and dogmatic twenty-six-year-old leader of the comrades of Botshabelo, "the youth have a problem with negotiations." Some comrades were downright fed up and "believe in just putting fire to everything."

All over the country that spring of 1990, police buttressed by South African Defense Force (SADF) troops continued to mow down demonstrators: eighteen dead that March in Sebokeng; five schoolboys dead in Rammulotsi that April; thirteen dead in Thabong in May. I met Moses Tsoeu, a fifteen-year-old, in Thabong, just outside Welkom, on the day its street war flared. A small boy for his age, Moses had been running along the road, stoning police vehicles as they passed, when a police car chased him down and an officer inside "just pointed that rubber-bullet gun and shot it from the car," Moses told me. He took a rubber bullet above the eye and was holed up in the charred remains of a local house with a bandage around his head when I met him. But he would do it again, he said. He called it "helping my nation."

"If they come back, we will fight!" yelled a sweaty and bedraggled youth in Sebokeng, south of Johannesburg, as he shook a pint-sized bottle of gasoline, ready to burn something down that tear-gas-choked day of Sebokeng's terrible massacre. Just before police opened fire, people had marched down the street singing. "Don't be afraid of the gun. Mother, sister, brother, father: don't be afraid of the gun." The dead that day included a teacher, an electrician's helper, a coal and wood hawker, and a mentally retarded maker of handicrafts.

I went into Sebokeng that bloody day with the legendary Allister Sparks, a crusading South African journalist, as well as David Ottaway, then the resident correspondent for the *Washington Post*, and Chris Wren of the *New York Times*. We were a strange quartet: three tall white men and a short black woman—me, the newcomer to this mayhem. We'd stopped our car and gotten out near a home that had been set on fire by a petrol bomb. As the police descended upon us, our local guide, Richard "Bricks" Mokolo, a Catholic activist, wisely disappeared into thin air—wise for him, though not necessarily for us.

Surrounded by angry white security police with guns drawn, plus a few junior black cops known as constables, I stood petrified, faced for the first time with the fury of the apartheid state. Houses were burning all around us. Police combat vehicles were cruising, throwing off rounds of tear gas. Gunfire was popping on not-too-distant streets. But Allister hurled his righteous indignation at the cops and a few quotations from the lawbooks to talk us out of the confrontation.

"Welcome to South Africa," Allister said to me later, seeing I was still shaken as we drove back up to Jo'burg.

A few weeks later, once things had calmed, I returned to Sebokeng and bunked down with the generous hospitality of Lazarus Litau, a local Coca-Cola manager, and his wife, Leo. And I found Bricks again. We laughed about how he'd vanished that day of the massacre. But actually, he was quite worried. He was a wise young man, a student of the evils of apartheid like so many others. But unlike Bapsy, Bricks was not at all certain of what he saw when he looked toward the future.

"I am a bit worried about the new South Africa. What are they going to achieve after these negotiations?" he asked. "You cannot name a baby before it is born. Are we going to be able to reconcile Umkhonto we Sizwe with the SADF? As Christians, we have to ask: can you reconcile the devil and God and heaven and earth?"

Though the formal effort to begin reconciling South Africa's different groups was years away, I heard the seeds of it during my 1990 travels in the expressions of ordinary black people about their white countrymen. I fully expected there'd be a wholesale thirst for revenge. But there wasn't. Instead, there were varying degrees of acceptance of whites. Some blacks would welcome multiracial unity in the country because of a sense of African humanity called *ubuntu*, a word from the Nguni family of languages (Zulu, Xhosa, etc.) that translates, basically, as "people are people through other people." According to *ubuntu*, even the humanity of oppressive whites could be affirmed.

Less charitably, other blacks would accept whites as a bitter reality. After all, whites controlled the economy and the military, thus had skills and capital. Plus, the black view of whites was often sophisticated in its nuance. Blacks were skilled at distinguishing between whites who were oppressors and whites who were sympathizers with or participants in the liberation movements. What they despised, more than whites themselves, was the system of white supremacy.

In one of my many long interviews with the comrades of Botshabelo, Benny Kotsoane, a twenty-four-year-old, explained to me the evolution of his feelings toward whites, from a child who learned to hate them because they arrested his father and hurt his family, to an adult who came to understand that the system of apartheid was the real enemy.

"I felt that everything was to blame on the whites. I was told they took our country," said Kotsoane. "When I was at school at primary level, I used to be close to one teacher. He was an ANC member. He was a very old person. I liked history, and I liked to attack whites bluntly—you know, 'whites this and whites that'—and he used to take me to his place and talked to me. I learned gradually, gradually. As time goes on, I am able to distinguish that not all whites are bad. What is really bad is this apartheid system."

I'd heard similar sentiments expressed back in Zolani, the night that Bapsy took me to a friend's home to watch Mandela and de Klerk appear together on television. Zolani had no electricity, so the tiny black-and-white TV set at her friend's home was hooked to a car battery by jumper cables. Grainy dots obscured the picture, and a horizontal line kept rolling up and down. But Mandela's image was recognizable, his voice clear enough to satisfy the dozen or so people who gathered round in candlelight to hear him speak of South Africa's way forward. Negotiations to secure a new future, he was saying, were the realization of the nation's dream. He would conduct them, on behalf of South Africa's people, in the spirit of letting "bygones be bygones."

One of the people with us that evening, Gloria Mhlomo, a schoolteacher, was unfamiliar with that expression, letting bygones be bygones. Another teacher, Wenzi Nel, explained it as a combination of forgiving and forgetting. Gloria understood, but then spoke to the TV, as if speaking directly to Mandela.

"Yes, we can forgive them. But we can never forget what they have done to us."

* * *

I returned to Washington in May 1990. After I wrote a detailed series on South African life and covered the magical tour of Mandela in America, where he was greeted like a mix between a savior and a rock star, the South Africa story fell out of my hands for the next fours years while other correspondents rotated on the South Africa beat. But even as I returned to domestic reporting, I followed South Africa in detail and managed to meet Mandela in 1993 with a group of journalists conducting a roundtable interview. It was a sterile, lifeless meeting, I must say, in which Mandela formalistically explained the South African electoral process to come as well as the events unfolding in his country.

All hell was breaking loose even as the heavens seemed to open up and smile down on Mandela's people. The negotiations had evolved into constitutional talks over the shape of the South African government to come. South African exiles poured back into the country from their comfortable lives in New York, London, Lusaka, or from the wretched guerrilla bush camps of MK and other guerrilla groups. The Group Areas Act, one of the tallest pillars of apartheid, was repealed in 1991, even as apartheid security forces continued their covert killing at home and abroad. Strange attacks by masked men—later to be revealed to include white security force provocateurs—killed hundreds of black commuters aboard the trains that raced into the Jo'burg city center from Soweto and other outlying black townships.

In the midst of this chaos, South Africa tumbled perilously close to complete anarchy in April 1993 when white assassins gunned down Chris Hani, the beloved MK commander and Communist Party leader. Rioting broke out all over the country, only quelled when Mandela—not President de Klerk—went on national television to appeal for calm. Later that year, Mandela and de Klerk announced that South Africa, for the first time ever, would hold fully free elections in which all people could participate. The march toward reform became irreversible, and the two men, the architects of these momentous changes, received the 1993 Nobel Peace Prize for leading South

Africa out of apartheid. But even as he was feted as a visionary hero, de Klerk presided over a security establishment whose agents continued targeting and killing black activists as well as secretly training, funding, and arming the fighters of the Inkatha Freedom Party of Mangosuthu Buthelezi, the main rival of Mandela's ANC.

The Inkatha-versus-ANC battle was pure factionalism. The fighters on both sides were Zulu residents of the region known as KwaZulu, one of the ten partially self-governing "homelands" led by Buthelezi. Though many commentators and journalists seemed eager to call it tribalism, it was not. They also called it black-on-black violence, which it seemed to be at first blush. But time would prove that the violence was aided and abetted in a classic divide-and-rule maneuver by the white apartheid government.

The fight pitted Zulu traditionalists, who wanted to maintain their system of tribal patronage even with the help of arms and funding from the apartheid regime, against Zulu liberationists, who opposed any form of collaboration with the government. Their war began in the early 1980s in KwaZulu, and a decade later it had spread to the townships around Jo'burg. There it often took on a tribal cast as Inkatha Zulus concentrated in the region's gold-mining hostels fought against ANC members who were, in that region, often Xhosa and other tribes. They fought brutally, often in massacres carried out while police stood by or even withdrew from the scene.

Shortly after his release from prison, Mandela had appealed to the fighters to "take your guns, your knives, your pangas and throw them into the sea." But the cycle of attack and revenge was too deep, too entrenched. The killing not only continued, it increased. In their homes, people lived in expectation of attack. They filled buckets, pots, and tubs with water in anticipation of petrol-bomb attacks. They put sheets of metal over the windows and wood over the doors to stop the bullets or at least slow them. Snipers picked off people in taxi buses or walking up a hill. Families gathered up their bedding and clothing and fled their homes for safer ground. I waded into these battles on my return to South Africa in 1994 as part of our newspaper's five-person team to cover the elections, and even I, the eternal optimist about South Africa, had the very real fear that the fighting would subvert the entire march toward democracy.

By 1994, Mandela's ANC was politically ascendant. It was the largest of the many black resistance groups and had been a leader in the antiapartheid struggle for decades. Plus, news of Inkatha's collusion with the apartheid state, piecemeal though those early revelations were, had begun discrediting Inkatha in the eyes of its conservative backers in the United States and Great Britain, the ones with the money that had kept Inkatha well stocked. The fighting by Inkatha loyalists seemed, by 1994, the last attempt to at least smear the South Africa that Mandela's ANC would surely lead after the elections that April.

In a provocative move that police did not adequately control, Inkatha staged a huge march through central Jo'burg a month before the 1994 election. The march had been heavily advertised, and thousands of Inkatha supporters from the Jo'burg region arrived downtown by the busload. Many of them also carried the "traditional weapons" of rural KwaZulu—spears, clubs called knobkerries, and shields made of animal skins. Some reporters on the scene said they also spotted modern firepower hidden behind some of those shields, a familiar technique for Inkatha members.

Despite Mandela's appeals for de Klerk to cordon off Jo'burg to prevent violence, police actually withdrew as shooting broke out in the gardens of the city's main public library. At a high-rise building called Shell House a few blocks away, where Mandela's ANC had its main offices, guards claimed that armed Inkatha marchers tried to storm the entrance. The ANC guards opened fire, leaving eight Inkatha marchers dead. All told around the Jo'burg region, fifty-three people were killed that day in March 1994, in the worst bout of factional fighting the city had ever seen. The implications of the Shell House massacre would haunt Mandela for many months to come.

And at the same time, white right-wing extremists, propelled by a similar losers' revenge, were running riot. Extremist groups set off bomb blasts in downtown Jo'burg as well as at the international airport that killed a score of black people in those final days before the election. Crazed white extremists even started picking off black pedestrians on the roads, shooting them at random in what seemed a final explosion of white hatred.

But there was nothing whatsoever to stop Mandela. He would become South Africa's next president. He was the liberator. He was the symbol of all that South Africans had suffered. Even in KwaZulu, supposed turf of Buthelezi loyalists, Mandela was worshiped with a surging, crushing passion. And I choose those words deliberately, since one of my strangest moments in covering the 1994 election campaign came when I was almost crushed in a surging crowd of 250,000 people gathered to see Mandela at Kings Park stadium in the Indian Ocean city of Durban. As a group of correspondents wound its way through the throng, I fell behind and lost my footing in the crowd, which was heaving to and fro like an oceanic tide. I went down. People fell around me and on top of me, as I was on top of others. Luckily, Dudley Brooks, a photographer from my newspaper, heard me hollering and helped me get up from the pile and over a fence to safety. Though it shook me badly—I remain leery of large crowds to this day—I looked up quite happy to see Mandela onstage dancing that charming little two-step that had become the trademark jig of South Africa's venerable patriarch.

When April 27, 1994, dawned, the guns were silent. The bombs stopped flying. Miraculously, this most cherished day in the lives of millions of South Africans unfolded in near-absolute peace. Election day had arrived, and the people streamed out of their hovels, huts, shacks, cottages, mansions, and hostels in an awesome vote of confidence in South Africa's future. Young folk pushed the elderly in wheelbarrows. People walked for miles and miles to get to the polls. Photos taken from helicopters captured it best, those snaking lines of hopeful South Africans who waited five, six, seven hours to cast the first national vote they'd ever been afforded, to decide at last who would speak for them. This first-ever ritual of democracy was sacrosanct.

Administrative chaos stretched the balloting over four days. Ballot papers were lost or arrived late to polling places. The ballots themselves were confusing, with a long list of nineteen parties, including some so new or obscure that few people had ever heard of them. But voter turnout hit an amazing 86 percent of eligible voters. Overwhelmingly, they chose the ANC and Mandela.

He was called *tata* by some. It simply means "father" in Xhosa. Others called him "Madiba," his clan name from the royal court of the Tembu people, where he grew up in a fabulously beautiful region along the Indian Ocean, known as the Transkei. The great-grandson of a Tembu king, Mandela had been groomed for leadership from an early age. After the death of his father when he was a small boy, he was raised at the knee of a paramount chief and schooled in the courtly ways of the rural African aristocracy. His bearing, his magnanimity, still bore the imprint of those early days.

He assumed the reins of government on a sun-kissed day in May, with de Klerk also sworn in, this time as a deputy president along with Thabo Mbeki, a younger ANC leader and son of Govan Mbeki, one of Mandela's fellow Robben Island inmates. Dignitaries from around the globe, some four thousand in all, jammed the grounds of the old Afrikaner presidential head-quarters, the Union Buildings in Pretoria, for an occasion that was broadcast live around the world.

But I spent inauguration day with the people of Soweto, where the hopes of liberation ran deep. The day before, Soweto had been like a bride await-ing her groom. And on the day when Mandela took the oath of office, Soweto wed its freedom and burst into a full-throttled street party all over the sprawling community. *Braai* pits (barbecue grills) sizzled everywhere. Lord only knows how many cows were slaughtered that day in rituals of cel-ebration. Women who could afford it draped themselves in traditional African cloth, for this was a day to affirm all that apartheid tried to negate. Rough dirt roads were lined with the only decorations the poor could af-ford—brightly colored plastics from supermarket bags; strips of colorful newspaper. People sang and danced and drank themselves silly, including a band of unruly "comrades" I encountered who blocked the road to extort a "freedom tax" from passing motorists.

I spent that day traveling around Soweto with my friends Connie and Jerry Mabuza, she an actress, he an art dealer. At the moment of Mandela's swearing-in, we'd found a TV to watch the ceremony. In the Pretoria skies, South African air force jets roared in salute to the nation's new president in a stunning show of loyalty. And when a chorus broke into the new national anthem, Connie stood before the TV with her fist in the air and tears streaming down her face as she sang with all her heart, "Nkosi sikelel' iAfrika" (God bless Africa).

Mandela's ascension to power seemed a triumph of good versus evil, right over wrong. On that sparkling historic day, there seemed no other way to see it. South Africa's turn to democracy was the most exhilarating and promising turn of events in Africa in a long time. But of course, some analysts were already predicting that the pitfalls that faced other newly independent nations on the continent would soon trip up South Africa too.

Would Mandela rule as a true democrat or through the cult of personality already coalesced around him? Would the ANC, which won nearly 63 percent of the vote, really respect the new multiparty system? Would it seek to reconcile with the previous white rulers or merely to dominate them? Most of all, could a brand-new government inheriting the mess left by apartheid actually live up to the generous promises it made to uplift the black masses with houses, schools, jobs?

The urgency of the challenge that Mandela faced seemed to be underscored, for me, by events unfolding farther north in Africa. Up in tiny Rwanda, a slaughter of nightmarish proportions was under way even as South Africa was achieving its liberation. The Rwandan bloodshed, which I would write reams about much later but did not really understand at the time it unfolded, seemed a symbol of all that the pessimists on Africa feared and predicted—chaos, mayhem, and dysfunction. And Mandela's team was keenly aware that the Western world readily viewed Africa as one big mass of trouble, where events in Rwanda thousands of miles away were viewed as contagious.

Mandela, now president, would have to navigate all these pressures. He and his new cabinet would soon learn that governing would be a far more formidable endeavor than any among them had imagined. If their cause seemed noble to me during the struggle, now we'd all find out what Mandela's people were really made of. Several months later, when the chance came to cover Mandela's South Africa full-time as its resident correspondent, I knew there was no place in the world I'd rather be.

* * *

I moved to Jo'burg in 1995, ten years after those wacky days of graduate school in New York, when I'd wanted to be a foreign correspondent so badly that I pretentiously wore my trench coat with the collar turned up, in the fashion of those spies and globe-trotters in 1940s B movies. Being overseas as part of the "foreign service" of a major newspaper was the fulfillment of a dream.

Once ensconced in my new home in Jo'burg, I bought a giant wall map of Africa and began circling all the places I'd already been, like marking the turf in my new world. To tell the truth, that map intimidated me. There was so much to cover, so many places to travel, so many logistical nightmares lying in wait as I moved about the continent. But South Africa was the center of my universe, and the fact that I already knew the country relatively well gave me confidence.

I fully embraced the new and privileged perch on which I sat—the vaunted spot of the foreign correspondent able to explain distant lands to readers back home, though aware all the time that South Africa wasn't so very distant at all. So many Americans had been involved in the anti-apartheid battle, through campaigns for the economic sanctions the United States applied against the apartheid regime. African Americans especially had been arrested in protests against the old South African government and expended emotional capital on a country whose struggle mirrored America's in some key ways. Readers—perhaps more so than I originally fathomed—were hungry for news on how Mandela's new democracy was progressing. And policy makers and investors were keen to discern the extent to which South Africa would emerge as an African hope, an African success.

I developed an idea, pretty arrogant in retrospect, that Mandela and I had a symbiotic relationship: he as the leader destined to lead his nation out of racial bondage, and I as one of the key foreign correspondents on hand to report South Africa's progress for the world. Coming as I did from Washington, where journalists make waves all the time, I knew full well that what I wrote would have a lot to do with the formation of international opinions about Mandela's new government.

Mandela and his movement had set new goals for the country: equality under the law and in the economy; new opportunities in the workplace and in education; new amenities as basic as paved roads, clinics, schools, houses, plumbing, electricity, and telephones for the legions who'd gone without all those things for so long.

Mandela's agenda was Bapsy's dream. I, too, wanted to believe.

3

Mandela's Reality

The new multiracial Parliament stood in ovation as President Nelson Mandela entered the chamber. Shouts of "Viva President Nelson Mandela, vivaaaah!" roared through the stately, cavernous room, as his party faithful welcomed him in the style of the liberation struggle. Even his old enemies hailed him, the very ones who'd gathered in this same chamber during apartheid to maintain and refine their racial domination. For them, too, Mandela was South Africa's most treasured elder statesman, the father of this new venture into a democracy for all. Bad knees slowed Mandela that June of 1995, and his old-world formality made him appear stiff and grave. But as his face broke into that familiar broad smile and looked out over the sea of black, brown, yellow, and white people at last seated as governors together, he seemed a warrior well pleased.

I watched from high up in the packed public gallery, savoring one of those wonderful Mandela moments with which his presidency was replete. I felt the excitement, the energy, of this new country. I hoped, deep down, that the charged atmosphere of limitless new possibilities would be able to carry South Africa and Mandela through their next difficult passage.

Though the physical repression, legal framework, and daily psychological burden of apartheid had lifted, the legacies of the recent past—the economic inequality and the racial fissures—threatened constantly to pull apart the fragile sense of new nationhood. Even as the world celebrated South Africa's seeming new unity and welcomed it into the family of nations, the reality on the ground presented Mandela's new government with a huge and perhaps insurmountable task. He, as president, had to drive, juggle, and fend off the awesome forces of disunity in what amounted to a high-stakes experiment in the wholesale overhaul of South African society.

Mandela inherited a fractured and desperate citizenry, nearly as divided as they were under apartheid. Blacks were 78 percent of the population and represented a host of different indigenous language groups, with Zulu the largest, followed by Xhosa, then Sotho, Tswana, Shangaan, and Venda, among the best known. It became a point of pride and cultural unity for some coloreds and Indians to identify themselves as black as well, though they remained distinctive groups. Often called mixed race, the colored descendants of the Khoikhoi and San people as well as Malay slaves imported in the seventeenth century were 9 percent of the population. Indians, the products of migration early in the nineteenth century, were about 1 percent. And whites were 12 percent, though by no means monolithic. The Afrikaners, often called Boers, or farmers, were a majority among the whites and harbored a historic enmity toward their fellow whites of English descent. Before the Afrikaners rose to power, in the mid-twentieth century, the English had colonized the country and defeated the Afrikaners in the Anglo-Boer war that ended in 1902, during which the English impounded thousands of Afrikaners in concentration camps. A web of brittle mistrust crossing every conceivable ethnic divide formed the fabric of South African society.

All the more remarkable, then, that some people from all racial groups managed to overcome their narrow identities and grievances and work together for the heroic cause of the new South Africa. They crafted new laws together in Parliament. They joined forces in civic groups and think tanks. On new commissions established in fields ranging from housing to human rights to health, they toiled together to chart the way forward toward transforming the nation. Within their progressive, multiracial milieu, the "rainbow nation" seemed real.

But in the main, South Africa's people entered the democratic era in the same stations of life they'd occupied before, and the country's stark socioeconomic divides seemed an undertow threatening to drown the South African dream. Whites remained on top, running the economy and the state agencies and still holding most of the country's wealth. Despite that entrenched privilege, they were beset by insecurities over their minority status and by worries that their high standard of living would be eroded under black rule. Though black South Africa was expectant and full of itself, full of the new promise of democracy, blacks remained largely locked out of the economy except for the new and narrow class of business and political elites that rapidly rose to prominence as the thin edge of the wedge of black economic power.

There seemed little to bind South Africa's fractious people together. They competed for economic power. They exercised new rights that were often in competition. They shouted new demands, nursed old wounds, and staggered through the transition to democracy unsure whether to hate or to dream, to seek vengeance or rebuild. Like a shepherd trying to guide an unruly flock, Mandela had to soothe, cajole, even pander and placate to hold the dream together. As he had done while campaigning for peace and for the elections, he tailored his messages to the specific needs and fears of each group.

To blacks, Mandela emphasized that there would be opportunity and development, in a spirit of reconciliation and social transformation. To Indians and coloreds, many of whom felt betwixt and between as neither black nor white, Mandela declared that the new South Africa was as much for them as for anyone else. To whites, he offered assurances that they were welcome participants in the new society; that they held the skills and capital the country desperately needed and should not sit sulking beside their swimming pools in fear for their status.

In a deft move to neutralize the ongoing belligerence of the far-right-wing Afrikaners who tried to subvert the elections, he even agreed to consider their desperate bid for a territorial Afrikaner "homeland." Though no one in his right mind believed it would ever happen, Mandela justified his consideration of their proposal by saying, "If people have been turned around and are now cooperating, we as responsible leaders must sit down and see how we can meet them." Unsaid publicly, but very much of concern within the new government, was the fear that conservative, hostile whites in the armed forces had the power to undermine the new democracy militarily.

The interests of all these elements of the new society would be enshrined in a new legal canon. Parliamentarians down in Cape Town, the "mother city" and South Africa's oldest, were busily negotiating and writing a new and permanent constitution to replace the interim one that bridged the electoral transition. Cyril Ramaphosa, the secretary-general of the ANC, chaired the constitutional assembly, applying the sharp negotiating skills that kept the democratic transition on course when he towered over the pre-electoral talks. A former union leader, Ramaphosa was hugely popular within the liberation movement, and many within the ANC were disappointed that Mandela had not chosen him as his chief deputy president.

The Truth and Reconciliation Commission—the brainchild of the ANC—was in the planning stages as well, intended to ferret out the evils of the past and foster reconciliation between the races. "We can now deal with our past, establish the truth which was so long denied us, and lay the basis for genuine reconciliation," said Mandela that summer as he signed into law a bill creating the TRC. Ironically, it would be headquartered in Cape Town down the street from Parliament, on land that once sprouted the gardens of the Dutch East India Company, the shipping network of the seventeenth century that changed the course of history when it brought Europeans under the command of Jan van Riebeeck and a band of Dutch company employees to settle on Africa's southernmost cone for the first time.

Anglican Archbishop Desmond Tutu, that wonderfully churlish human rights crusader swathed in magenta robes, would lead the Truth Commission. He would try in every conceivable way—through Christian theology, through African traditionalism—to foster what he optimistically called the "rainbow nation of God." Tutu's stature as a humanitarian who'd joined the secular campaign against apartheid under the auspices of the church made him perfectly suited to lead this reconciliation effort. Most South Africans, regardless of their hue or faith, respected his spirituality and his moral grounding, though the truth-telling crusade belonged not to the church, but to the people.

The times were heady and enticing to anyone who understood South Africa's profound change or who merely felt the country's seductive pull. This was a new Africa in the making, the latest fresh start on a continent where so many beginnings had proved false, so many hopes a mirage. Academics and consultants from around the globe flooded in to assist with Mandela's exercise in "nation building." Foreign dignitaries and pop stars breezed through on red carpets. Everyone from Princess Diana of Britain to Whitney Houston of America beat a path to Mandela's door. And he never failed to oblige. (I also joined the ranks of people trying to get to him, though foreign journalists at that time were pretty low on Mandela's to-see list.)

To the world that had served as a midwife in South Africa's democratic birth, Mandela hung out the "open for business" sign. Come invest, come and help, he told the corporations and financiers of Washington, London, Paris, and Tokyo. Multinationals who'd pulled out of South Africa during the pariah years of apartheid sent delegation after delegation to test the waters of the new country. McDonald's prepared to erect its golden arches in South Africa. Coca-Cola snapped up a big bottling plant. But to a degree that would disappoint Mandela, many investors remained skittish about the security of their resources in the fragile new South Africa. With an ideology that seemed preserved in amber amid changing global times, Mandela's ANC espoused socialistic economic policies even as it rose to power. But in the post–Cold War era that seemed to prove the failures of socialism around the globe, investors were waiting to see how open the new South African government would actually be to the imperatives of the free-market policies that, for better or worse, dominated the world.

Mandela carried all of this on his shoulders. It was an awesome load. He had to assure his people and assure the world. He had to craft a sweeping vision for the nation and muster the resources and manpower to carry it through. He had to exercise a steel will against all kinds of pressures; to keep South Africa marching forward, away from the abyss that once threatened it. For this, he would use any means at his disposal, as had been necessary during the liberation struggle. His character had been forged, no one should forget, within a virtual war. In founding MK, the guerrilla movement, thirty years prior, and growing morally comfortable with the use of violence to combat extreme injustice and further a just cause, Mandela knew quite well the harsh and ugly decisions a leader must make for the sake of his vision.

Quickly that summer of 1995, I got a taste of just how complex Mandela's world actually was as I watched him shift from the shimmering panorama of South Africa's future horizons back to the hungry ghosts that haunted the country from its recent past. Mandela dropped a political bombshell. The controversy over the March 1994 Shell House massacre had not died, and Mandela had finally responded with a stunning revelation. It was he, he admitted, who gave the shoot-to-kill order to the ANC guards when Inkatha marchers descended on party headquarters during the pre-election mayhem.

Mandela, the great reconciler, the man of peace, had given an order that left people dead. Mandela's admission was politically explosive. Such outrage greeted his revelation that Parliament held a special session, which I attended, where the jubilation of his party faithful from the ANC was soon overtaken by the cries of outrage heaped on Mandela by opposition politicians out to skewer him.

He told Parliament that day that he had instructed the ANC guards to protect the headquarters "even if they have to kill people." In defense of his action, he explained that the violence was "not a bolt from the blue," but part of a widespread and orchestrated campaign to destabilize the pre-election period. Mandela told the chamber that he personally appealed to de Klerk to deploy more police that day, based on intelligence the ANC had gathered that Inkatha planned an attack. But de Klerk did not heed his call. And the police who were on hand for the violence beat a conspicuous retreat.

But Mandela had waited more than a year to reveal his role, which his opponents seized upon as virtually criminal. "Is this the manner in which justice is to be administered from now on?" demanded Clarence Makwetu, leader of the Pan-Africanist Congress (PAC), a much smaller party but one of the ANC's main black political rivals. Makwetu seemed puffed up with indignation, but his words rang hollow. Historically averse to multiracialism throughout the liberation struggle, the PAC once touted the rather violent slogan "One settler [Afrikaner], one bullet."

"We cannot have freedom and democracy grow in this country as long as we have an ANC and a president who think they should be above the law and above the constitution," yelled Ziba Jiyane, the secretary-general of Inkatha, who even demanded, quite predictably, that Mandela resign. Of course, that was ridiculous. The fact of the matter is that Inkatha, even then, was still fighting its political foes in the hills of KwaZulu, where blood continued to flow.

It was only a taste of the rabid political hectoring that would surround Mandela's presidency from the small opposition parties, black and white, who found little room to maneuver in the political space dominated by the ANC. But I should not make light of the faction fighting that continued to roil KwaZulu. Amid all the South African pageantry of freedom and promise, of progress and reconciliation, that political violence was the underside of the miracle. That's how complex Mandela's world was. Soaring hopes amid quicksands of conflict. Grand visions amid petty political battles. Liberated people still chained to their past. The country was a kaleidoscope of contradictions, which made it rich to write it, though often maddening to live it.

● ● ●

JOHANNESBURG

It took a while, in the early weeks after my arrival in 1995, to get accustomed to the way the new South Africa and the old coexisted. No matter how familiar I was with the country's history and politics, I was now living within its culture and had to learn to navigate it. Each time the buzzer at my front gate sounded, another lesson unfolded. The old South Africa would just slap me in the face. I'd trot out to sign for a package and forget until it was too late that even the simplest of encounters could be surreal. I was a magnet for cultural confusion. Deliverymen, meter readers, job seekers, and broom sellers were all taken aback by my presence. At the gates of large houses like the one rented by my newspaper, South Africans had been conditioned to expect to see a white woman, a madam. When they saw me instead, they figured I must be a maid.

"May I help you?" I'd say politely. Invariably, the visitor would ask, "Is the madam home?" And I'd fume.

I lived in a community called Waverley, in a house that had been a base for my newspaper's correspondents for several years. The rambling two-story house swallowed me up, with its four bedrooms and its huge yards, not to mention the tennis court and swimming pool. If I'd wanted, I could have found a smaller home upon my arrival. But I didn't want the hassle of moving and setting up the office anew. Plus, the house was great for entertaining and for putting up out-of-town guests. So I stayed, there in the northern suburbs of Jo'burg, a fifteen-minute drive from the city center, in a community that had never seen a resident the likes of me.

All of my predecessors had been white, which was a good thing in the bad old days of apartheid. Suburbs like Waverley were legally "whites only" under the old Group Areas Act. That law was a pillar of what was called grand apartheid, for it designated specific residential areas for specific racial groups. Though the law was repealed in 1991, de facto segregation lived on. Beneath the lovely lavender canopy of Waverley's jacaranda trees, the only other blacks I noticed in residence were the legions of ever-present maids and gardeners. Many of them wore the same royal-blue work ensembles for men and pink work dresses for women that were the apartheid-era uniform of domestic servitude.

Like other such suburbs, Waverley was the domain of "the madam," a breed of perfectly coiffed and heavily bejeweled white matron who presided over maids, cooks, nannies, gardeners, all of whom were black. A madam didn't have to be wealthy to have such domestic help; so plentiful was black labor under apartheid that most white households, regardless of affluence, had at least a maid. And the madams were such a staple of white South African life that a famed newspaper comic strip, *Madam and Eve*, bitingly chronicled the hilarious and somewhat sick relationship between the stereotypically arrogant madam and her crafty maid.

I was no "madam," obviously, but I had domestic staff too. They came with the house. Bernard Gumede was the groundskeeper, and Florah Moshabela was the domestic helper. With a roving job that would keep me on the road sometimes for weeks on end, I needed help. Even when I was home, the once-charming but now dysfunctional house required far more attention than I alone could give. Still, I never shook my moral discomfort about employing people who'd transitioned from apartheid to democracy in the same domestic jobs. I made one addition to the staff, hiring an office assistant named Phumzile Dlamini to help keep my one-person operation running smoothly. To assuage my guilt, I paid them all well above the average and doled out loans and monetary gifts as requested. And the requests were never-ending: a roof here, a doctor's bill there, school fees, a mortgage payment, funeral expenses, a new TV, a new fridge, you name it. Over time, I became a patsy. South Africans were poor, but I was not a bank.

My attempts to sympathize and be a caring employer introduced me to the realm of the supernatural too. Actually, it's called *muthi* (pronounced *muti*), or medicine. Practiced one way, it can be for good, for healing. But used another way, it can be for evil ends and casting spells. When things were amiss in life, many Africans—regardless of ethnic background—believed that forces not of this world were involved, often through the workings of *muthi*. When Florah found a couple of pennies in the toilet, she told me she feared someone was trying to cast a spell on her. (I confessed that it was I who accidentally dropped those pennies in the commode and forgot to fish them out.) On another occasion, Bernard told me that someone had stolen hairs from his hairbrush, obviously to use in some *muthi* potion, he claimed. It all became too much. I told them I respected their beliefs, but I did not want to be distracted with their worries of *muthi* conspiracies. When I went to South Africa, I had no clue that I'd be mediating so many issues of economics and the supernatural. Sometimes I'd laugh at myself in the mirror and think: Oh my God! Have I become a madam?

Meanwhile, back at my front gate, I had to get through the strange confusion I sparked for the visitors who looked at me and thought I was a maid. It really troubled me, at first, to find South Africans still so locked in the old ways. But I turned the ritual—the ritual of being a confusing black American—into a kind of game. When it was a black deliveryman who mistook me for a maid, I'd politely explain that I was the head of the house. His face would register fleeting confusion. Then he'd get it. He'd heard my accent on TV. An American, that's what she is. He'd break into a whole fanfare. So happy to meet an American! I love your accent. You are my sister. How do you like our country? I'd make small talk on these very large issues and we'd laugh a bit.

To a white deliveryman, I'd speak equally politely, but also mysteriously, just to confuse him, to drive home the point that the old South Africa was gone. "There is no madam here," I'd say flatly, and let the words hang with no explanation. That ought to teach him! Or I'd simply say that I was the head of the house, but never the madam. But then, of course, the white man, no matter what I said, would pick up my American accent and that delightful fanfare would erupt anew.

Most South Africans I encountered had an unquenchable curiosity about Americans in general and African Americans in particular. Michael Jackson, Bill Cosby, and Michael Jordan—those were the black Americans they'd come to know from television. So meeting me, an African American in the flesh, opened a window onto a world they had only imagined. I met one young man who cast a suspicious eye on me when I told him that, no, I had never met Michael Jackson. With that, he seemed to question my bona fides as a real black American.

But the tickled fascination could be deceiving. This was, after all, South Africa, meaning racism often lurked beneath every sentence. Sometimes the white chitchat would degenerate, and it wouldn't take long for them to inform me, unsolicited, that black Americans weren't like "our blacks," meaning the Africans in South Africa. I knew the litany of stereotypes that would come next; I'd heard them all before. But I'd goad the white folk nonetheless, and the stereotypes would pour out: Africans weren't as well educated, not as driven and capable as black Americans. One time I told a white man that the black South Africans I knew were very intelligent and more than capable. But he played the foreigner card and told me I couldn't really know them because I wasn't one of them. Partly right, partly wrong. But no point in arguing. I found some whites to be quite cemented in their views.

The fact is I had a unique window onto their racialized world precisely because, at first glance, I looked like many other black South Africans. As I circulated through their divided society, whites served up an array of intentional indignities: passed over at shop counters, ignored by bellhops at some swank hotel. In my bank, I walked up to the customer service counter just as a white male customer was yelling at a black bank employee he accused of bungling. I guess he assumed I was also one of the alleged black bunglers, because he started yelling at me too. (I yelled right back.) Another time, in a supermarket, I dawdled while the checkout line moved forward and an impatient, elderly white woman upbraided me gruffly. "You people must pay attention!" I knew that tone well. Some whites seemed always to be trying to teach blacks how to behave. And even in the new South Africa of black rule, these whites had the nerve to just keep on being condescending and abusive. It burned me up, but I held my tongue and ignored the crotchety old lady out of respect for her age.

These weird racial tiffs happened so often that I commiserated with one of my close friends, another African American woman, Phyllis Crocket, who at that time was reporting for National Public Radio. She, too, was having these annoying racial encounters. We wondered if our traditional black American chip on the shoulder was the problem, or were some white South Africans still so thickheadedly racist despite all the changes around them? We decided it was a combination of both.

My next-door neighbors were a lovely older couple who'd pleasantly surprised me shortly after my arrival in the neighborhood by sending over a cake via their maid. Actually, I should say they sent the cake with their "girl," as they called her. And they persisted in referring to Mr. Gumede, the roughly sixty-year-old gardener at my house, as a "boy." Life would run smoothly at the house, they assured me, because "your boy is very reliable." It didn't even occur to them that I might find this terminology offensive. Matter-of-factly, I told them, "He isn't a boy. His name is Mr. Gumede." The other side of the coin, though, is that "boys" and "girls" treated that way all their lives sometimes become the part. In watching Bernard, I witnessed how some old habits of subservience hang tough too.

Rambling around that big house alone except when guests were on hand, I stayed vigilant about security. I'd inherited a cool hound named Brutus, a giant Rhodesian Ridgeback, and I added a ferocious shepherd I called Gabby when I realized Brutus had no security consciousness. (Later, after both Brutus and Gabby passed away, there'd be Shaka and Bobi, two seriously hyper but lovable shepherds.) And I urged Bernard to be more careful about visitors at the front gate. I didn't want people coming onto the property if they didn't first ring the front-gate buzzer and talk to me on the intercom. I wanted to know in advance who was coming into the yard.

Lo and behold, someone knocked right on the front door one day. I opened it, thinking it must be Bernard, only to find a complete stranger, a tall white man, standing there claiming to be a roofer (though his truck bore no such markings) and looking for an address that did not exist. Bernard had opened the gate and let this man drive right into the yard. At least the dogs were on their worst behavior that day and jumped around the man like they were out of control.

When I asked Bernard why he had opened the gate, he told me the man had been "cross" with him. There it was, the old power equation: a rude and pushy white man intimidating a black man. So to bust through that old pattern, I revised my policy. I urged Bernard not to let anyone on the property unannounced, *especially* if it was an angry white man. Nothing could have been more uncomfortable: a younger woman instructing an older man, a prideful Zulu no less, on how to behave. But it was a two-way street. I was a relative innocent in the ways of South African life, and sometimes it was my lax attitude that really annoyed Bernard. He chastised me on several occasions, demanding that I be more aware of security; that I be more careful as a woman alone. One day he really put on a show, trying to demonstrate how I should grab the dogs by the collar and struggle to hold them back so that visitors would think they were ferocious beasts.

He'd been around long enough to know who was who and what was what in the neighborhood. He was my eyes and ears, really, my pipeline into the neighborhood grapevine. He'd tell me who'd been burgled, hijacked, or shot. Before the terrifying episode when someone took a heavy tool to the security bars and tried to break into my house twice in one night, Bernard had warned me of a strange man watching the house. I should have paid more attention to him. But that night, shaking from fright as I pressed the "panic" button on my house alarm, I wasn't sure who was more ominous: the burglars who might still be lurking outside or the heavily armed whites of the police "flying squad" who scaled the six-foot fence, then prowled combat-style through the yards with their submachine guns.

South Africa was a violent place. If the onslaught of bizarre crime news wasn't enough to drive home the point, then surely the gunfire in my neighborhood made it clear. Some of my neighbors were armed and had itchy trigger fingers. Periodically, deep in the night, I'd roll out of bed and onto the floor at the sound of gunfire just a little too close for comfort. I'd scan the newspapers in ensuing days for reports that would explain the shooting. But finding no clues just added to the mystery of what was happening outside the security of my high gates late into the night. I felt relatively protected, especially after we found a man's shoe in the yard and figured some unlucky interloper had tried to come over the fence and stepped into the jaws of the hounds. Dogs weren't surefire protection, though, with stories rampant of criminal gangs poisoning dogs so they could gain access to people's homes. (When Brutus died a terrible and sudden death, I had the vet perform an autopsy to see if he'd been poisoned. He had not.) My anxiety rose with each report of a friend or acquaintance getting carjacked, kidnapped, held hostage at home, raped, shot, you name it.

I'd started my Jo'burg life as a great apologist for crime. The surge in such activity had given white critics of Mandela's new government an easy sore point to use for political ends. The 1995 decision by the nation's Constitutional Court, the new high court and a pillar of the new democracy, to outlaw the death penalty just added fuel to the fire in the crime debate. To his white critics, Mandela and his government were soft on crime. The fear of crime reached near hysteria, for some, and I countered it in dinner party conversation by explaining it away like a sociologist, as a "transitory by-product of the volatility in postapartheid society." I had a whole "don't let security concerns overwhelm you" rap ready for American visitors who'd call me seeking advice on South Africa travel.

But wasn't I the biggest hypocrite! I lived behind high walls, always with two big dogs, in a house rigged with an armed-response alarm system. And before I went to bed each night, I clamped a big padlock on the so-called rape gate built into the walls at the top of the stairs, in case anyone broke in down below.

I stopped explaining away crime after I witnessed a murder in my rearview mirror. It happened in Alexandra township, ten minutes from my home, in a working-class but also severely impoverished community chockablock with shacks, foraging cows, garbage heaps, open sewers, and more than its share of thugs and illegal immigrants with no jobs. So many Mozambican immigrants crowded into Alexandra that people called their section of the township Maputo, after the Mozambican capital. Inching up the London Road in traffic crawling along Alex's outskirts one day, I spotted two men running out of the shanties and onto the street. Then they opened fire at the spot I'd just passed. They pumped several bullets into a motorist two cars behind me. They yanked the dead man's body out of the car, then jumped in and hooked a screeching U-turn in their newly hijacked vehicle. It happened so fast. And so close.

But I learned to live with it. As a foreign correspondent in a politically stable but socially volatile country, I had no choice but to become more vigilant about security than I'd ever been in cities where I'd worked and lived: Los Angeles, Washington, New York, and Miami. Jo'burg beat them all.

It was a Wild West kind of place—raucous, aggressive, and vibrant—and it had always been that way, ever since its founding back in the nineteenth century at the height of the South African gold rush. Zulus called it Egoli, "City of Gold." And they meant it literally. Jo'burg sat atop the Rand, the Witwatersrand, a "ridge of white waters" that was a geological marvel. About sixty-two miles long and twenty-three miles wide, the Rand contained some of the richest rock in the world, filled with seams of gold. The discovery of gold in the 1880s sparked the founding of the town, named for the two officials (Johan Rissik and Johannes Joubert) sent out to survey the land. Jo'burg attracted all manner of men seeking fame and fortune—Africans, Afrikaners, and British as well as Europeans, North Americans, and Australians.

Financed by the astonishing South African diamond deposits already discovered in the town of Kimberley and modeled on the racially rigid labor hierarchy in place there, Jo'burg saw its rise as a global gold-mining giant take off in earnest with the intervention of British colonial capitalists like Barney Barnato and Cecil Rhodes. These men lorded over the South African gold and diamond rush on which South Africa's industrial economy was built. Their mining houses were among the first buildings to go up in what became the Jo'burg city center, which evolved into a towering financial district of gleaming skyscrapers, banks, stock exchange, hotels, theaters, museums, art galleries, restaurants, shopping malls, courts, and public libraries. Before the ethnic cleansing of the apartheid laws took effect in the early 1950s, Nelson Mandela and Oliver Tambo opened their law practice—the first-ever African practice—in center city Jo'burg, not far from the offices of the famed Anglo American mining conglomerate. Thereafter, though, blacks were not allowed to own businesses in downtown, though they remained a presence in the city as workers for white firms.

Downtown became progressively more African as apartheid laws loosened in the 1980s and 1990s. Amid the skyscrapers, curbside hawkers of fruits and vegetables clogged the sidewalks. More and more minibus taxis careered through the choked streets, ferrying blacks from the outlying townships to their jobs or to the shopping malls, movie theaters, and downtown government buildings. The human rights groups and law firms that supported the antiapartheid cause maintained offices downtown too, as did the nation's large newspapers and some foreign consuls.

Jo'burg was as schizophrenic a city as you'll find. The city felt bold and brassy, and yet also desperate. People, whether black or white, seemed to always be rushing, scheming, planning, racing, scrambling, as if they weren't sure what to expect or what would happen next. I think that's what drove people to such madness on the roadways, where everyone was a speed demon. If you weren't racing fast enough, people would drive right up on your bumper and flash their high beams at you, even honk their horns. Though South Africa had the world's highest murder rate—at 61 murders per 100,000 people, higher even than Colombia—I feared death on the highways much, much more.

Jo'burg was hip and modern, yet terribly brittle. White South Africa and black South Africa converged on its streets and its places of work, then retreated at day's end to their separate communities, their separate ends of the socioeconomic spectrum. Its whites had been among South Africa's most liberal and progressive during apartheid, but emerged in democracy as among the most disgruntled. Its blacks were filled with a new and showy pride in their culture, yet their xenophobia against immigrants from other African countries was startling. With the advent of democracy, immigrants (legal and otherwise) from all over Africa began surging into South Africa in search of jobs. And South Africans didn't like it one bit. They unfairly blamed Zaireans and Nigerians for bringing crime and drugs into the country. Some did, but not all. Immigrant Africans—be they Ghanaians, Zimbabweans, whatever—who hawked fruit on the street faced periodic attacks from angry local blacks who felt their own opportunities were being squeezed by the newcomers. Black police conducting sweeps of illegal immigrants would sometimes arrest a very dark-skinned South African on the assumption that he or she was an illegal immigrant from blacker Africa to the north.

In fostering a tolerant nationalism, Mandela had his work cut out for him, and in that summer of 1995 came a gem of an opportunity to rally the nation around a symbol of unity.

• • •

PORT ELIZABETH

Rugby fever hit South Africa. The Springboks, the national team, stood a real chance of winning the 1995 Rugby World Cup. South Africa hosted the series for the first time ever, after years of banishment from international sport because of its racist apartheid policies. South Africans of all kinds surged with pride at this coup of a comeback for South African sport. All anyone talked about was the Springboks, named for the antelope-like animal, or the Amabokoboko, as the Africanized vernacular dubbed the team. Rugby fever went so wild that good taste went out the window. A Springbok billboard campaign showed the animal mounted on the rump of another beast, having its way.

The Amabokoboko, despite that African name, were all white. Only when a colored player was added to the roster midway through the series did the Amabokoboko show a modicum of integration. Like so much else in those early years after apartheid, the team very much symbolized the old South Africa and rugby itself symbolized Afrikanerdom. Its organization, its development, its sponsorship by the old government, made it part and parcel of the old Afrikaner state.

Nonetheless, Mandela co-opted rugby as a vehicle for the unity he so desperately wanted to foster. He pushed the "One Team, One Nation" slogan. He urged blacks to support the team, even though soccer was the true black sporting passion. Mandela painted the gloss of "rainbow nationhood" over the largely white event and succeeded, at least for a time, in convincing whites that their sport, their passion, was very much a part of the new black-led South Africa. Many blacks, especially in the Cape region, had nurtured a passion for rugby for many years, though they'd been prohibited from playing in the major leagues. The rugby crusade filled South Africans of all kinds with a swelling nationalistic pride.

That June, a traditional Zulu work song, "Shosholoza," became an unofficial national anthem. Its lyrics are pretty banal in their English translation: "Work, work, working in the sun, we will work as one" and so on. But sung in deep basso Zulu voices, it was infectious. The national TV network played the song over and over as the theme for South Africa's struggle to win the Rugby World Cup. At all the rugby matches, even the Afrikaners sang it. Everyone sang it. It was all over the airwaves, a rallying cry for the nation. And when the Springboks beat the Australians in one of the early matches, whites and blacks poured onto the streets of Jo'burg, dancing, hugging, and celebrating together. It was heartwarming. It was the kind of South Africa all its well-wishers wanted to see. But was it real? I was skeptical. I found it hard to believe that these bursts of national pride would have a lasting effect in a country so fresh from bitter racial division and virtual warfare. I wanted a different take on the story—the story under the radar, so to speak.

I arranged to meet a group of black kids who were part of a development program sponsored by the South African Rugby Football Union. These kids, in years to come, would integrate the sport. They were from Zwide, a black township outside Port Elizabeth, on the Indian Ocean coast. They were part of the legions of boys from poor black townships who played rugby shoeless, on unmarked fields, without goalposts or proper balls. The Zwide boys were scheduled to put on a rugby exhibition as part of the pregame warm-up for South Africa versus Canada. Afterward, I'd attend the match with them and see what it felt like from where they sat.

Port Elizabeth is a major industrial city, with auto assembly plants and an important Indian Ocean seaport. It is in a region, the Eastern Cape, where antiapartheid activism was perhaps most staunch and where state repression was perhaps most brutal. Mandela and many of his top cabinet ministers hailed from this region. Stephen Biko, the popular Black Consciousness leader who was beaten to death by police in the 1970s, was from there too.

So with some apprehension, I pulled my rental car into the edges of the dirt parking lot outside Boet Erasmus Stadium. It was named for an old Afrikaner rugby official and mayor of the city, known to his people as Brother Erasmus. I felt edgy venturing into the deep Afrikaner scene, though I also kind of liked the idea of penetrating their closed world. A heavy cloud of smoke hung overhead. The parking lot was a vast nightscape of tailgate parties. Afrikaners stood over their *braai*—that's Afrikaans for "barbecue"— and drank much Castle lager, the most popular beer. Everywhere I looked were big-drinking, big-eating Afrikaners, *die volk* (the people). Often called Boers, or farmers, since they'd traditionally lived off the land, the Afrikaners are an earthy, emotive people whose imposing physical stature gave rise to their stereotype as a thick-necked, thickheaded people. As I walked through the parking lot toward the gate, I saw nary another black face and I just hoped none of these Afrikaners would give me any guff. Inside the stadium, there were many more blacks already seated, but they were few and far between in the huge Afrikaner crowd.

I found my Zwide kids and their coach, Alfred Mzizi, who seized the opportunity to tell me all about the travails of township rugby. Money was desperately needed, despite the rugby union's alleged commitment to upgrade the sport for poor boys. Mzizi's statements suggested that rugby "development" might be a sham. It seemed difficult to attract funds, Mzizi said. "There are people who think that rugby was made for people who have the other pigmentation."

The boys finished their exhibition down on the field and ran to the locker room to change into their burgundy school blazers, ties, and gray slacks. I found their formality charming. It was a big contrast to the throngs of spectators in T-shirts and blue jeans. Siyabulela Koza, a fifteen-year-old among Mzizi's group, told me they wore their uniforms out of honor for the big rugby event. As we talked, four smaller boys were busy pooling their coins to go buy one hot dog that they would all share. But Koza was transfixed on the field, waiting eagerly for the match to begin. He loved rugby. He played it at school. His favorite Springbok was James Dalton, known to his fans as Bullet. Koza did not name Chester Williams, the only nonwhite Springbok player, and that surprised me. But Koza, a wise young man, said it did not matter to him that the team he had come to cheer was all white.

"That's okay," he said, "because it's the team of my country."

There it was again: that Mandelian reach across the racial chasm, by a boy of only fifteen. These whites did not know how lucky they were to live in a nation where retribution for all they'd done was not in evidence. The absence of white humility or contrition never ceased to amaze me. And the prevalence of white arrogance was galling. There at Boet Erasmus, some Afrikaner die-hards held aloft three huge flags of the old South Africa—the white-, orange-, and blue-striped flag that symbolized the apartheid era. Sure, the new flag of democratic South Africa flapped prominently around the stadium, and some of the spectators had painted their faces in the new flag's "rainbow nation" colors of blue, green, gold, red, black, and white. But those tricolors of the old era were so big and so prominent that they seemed an insult to the new country.

The apartheid flags weren't the only evidence of Afrikaner resistance. There was an embarrassing moment during the playing of the new national anthem, which combines abbreviated versions of a Zulu-language anthem and the original Afrikaans anthem of apartheid—another of the ANC's many gestures of unity. When the band struck up the tune of the anthem, there was a vast silence from the gathered Afrikaners. Only a few brave black voices sang, "Nkosi sikelel' iAfrika" (God bless Africa). But when the Afrikaans section of the anthem came up, the stadium burst into full-throated song: "Die stem van Suid-Afrika" (the call of South Africa). True to form, Koza and his pals sang every word of every section in both languages, with their hands held over their hearts. They'd been schooled in good manners and schooled as well in their nation's new hopes.

So, no, I did not buy the rugby-fever hype of unity, rainbow nationhood, the crossing of racial divides. It was a goal, and a laudable one, but would take years to materialize, if ever. Still, Mandela worked it. He pushed for reconciliation, for the new nationalism. Back in Jo'burg, the World Cup finals pitted the Springboks against New Zealand in the jam-packed Ellis Park Stadium. And South Africa won. While the city erupted with joy, Mandela strode out onto the field wearing the green and gold no. 6 jersey of the team captain, the much-loved François Pienaar, and the dramatic scene sparked several astonishing minutes when scores of thousands of whites chanted, "Nelson! Nelson!" to hail their country's president. It was among the most exceptional early episodes of his presidency, a sparkling moment that told the world what South Africa could be: black and white, together, behind a new national pride.

Mandela spent the rest of that summer piling on more gestures like this. He sought to disarm the Afrikaners, to charm the Afrikaners, to use his embrace to neutralize whatever threat they still posed to his new democracy. Truth be told, the Afrikaner state was alive and well. Mandela inherited a government machinery populated by the same men and women who had once been sworn to repress any and all signs of black power. Except for parliamentarians, cabinet ministers, and a few national department heads, Afrikaner loyalists of the old National Party of apartheid still dominated the whole of the governing apparatus of South Africa. That meant the courts, the armed forces, the police, the civil service, and state-run concerns like the phone company and the electric utility. More troubling—and more threatening for Mandela's government—was the white right wing, which had its roots in the military. While the world feted Mandela and his victory, his government faced the very real threat of chaos, even of coups, during its first year.

The harsh South African reality was that Mandela's ANC did not defeat its Afrikaner foes, not in any military sense. In fact, Mandela had spent the final months before the 1994 election cajoling and bargaining with right-wing Afrikaner leaders whose followers had tried to derail the election with bomb blasts all over the country, even a pathetic coup attempt in one of the black "homelands." For the sake of stability, Mandela's ANC had little choice but to leave the Afrikaner machinery of state in place. In a controversial sunset clause that would dog Mandela's government, the ANC agreed not to chuck out Afrikaner bureaucrats when blacks took over the government. The apartheid-era civil servants could keep their jobs till they reached retirement age.

Mandela and his team knew that South Africa needed its whites. Apartheid had worked so thoroughly for so many generations that blacks did not have the expertise or experience to go it alone. Those who'd managed, either at home or more probably abroad, to receive higher education and specialist degrees weren't great enough in number to fill all the necessary posts. So out of a realpolitik urgency, whites, including the Afrikaners who'd actively upheld apartheid and the British descendants who'd passively benefited from it, had to be embraced in the new dispensation. These whites slid into democracy facing few consequences for the past. No payback, no retribution, no prosecution, for South Africa could not afford revenge. And Mandela did everything he could to keep his whites happy.

He trekked to the white separatist stronghold of Orania, deep in the desert of the Northern Cape, to take tea with Betsy Verwoerd. She was the ninety-four-year-old widow of Hendrik Verwoerd, the reviled apartheid president whose government sent Mandela to prison. The prosecutor in that case was Percy Yutar, and these many years later, in the spirit of reconciliation, Mandela even threw a lunch in Yutar's honor. For a time, Mandela's many gestures succeeded in putting whites at ease, especially the Afrikaners. He had pressed all the right buttons, touted all the right symbols that lent them a sense of security. I was surprised even to hear a leader of the sinister old Broederbond, the once-secret society of Afrikaner business and political leaders who now called themselves the Afrikanerbond, praise Mandela's efforts.

"As the man who has to shape the reconciliation base, Mandela is succeeding remarkably well," Tom de Beer, the Afrikanerbond chairman, told me when I went to meet him at his Jo'burg office. "I would not be surprised if more than half the whites support him."

But Mandela's reconciliation agenda, focused so heavily on whites, had started to grate on the nerves of some blacks. Black demands and aspirations were being fulfilled ever so slowly in that first year, and millions were still awaiting democracy's promise: the houses, the electricity, telephone service, and indoor plumbing; the clinics, schools, and job opportunities. Though most blacks were still deeply wedded to Mandela as the father of their liberation from apartheid, I began to hear blacks grumbling "enough already" each time their leader performed one of his acts of ritual outreach to whites.

"He is bending over backwards at the expense of the black masses to appease whites," wrote Jon Qwelane, a local black columnist. And those whites, he continued bitterly, "are the same people who once labeled Mandela a 'terrorist' and 'communist' until they realized he had no intention to change their traditional South African way of life."

The one-sidedness of the reconciliation drive would become glaringly apparent later, as it became clear that Mandela was reaching out to people who rarely reached back.

4

In Need of Armor

lying into Angola in the summer of 1995 felt like traveling back in time. I left Jo'burg, a city of the new Africa, and landed in Luanda, a city mired in the backwash of old Africa and the dirty Cold War of the 1970s and 1980s. By the mid-1990s, Angola was the last outpost of southern African mayhem, the last bloodstain on a region that was shaking off the past and cleaning itself up. Zimbabwe was churning along nicely, back then, as a moderate-sized semi-industrial economy. After a two-decade war, Mozambique set about rebuilding its agricultural economy, even its ruined roads. Zambians and Namibians were consolidating their new turns to democracy. But most important of all, South Africa's liberation from apartheid set the region on a new course. Once the bane of its neighbors in the days when the South African military used to bomb them into submission and even invaded and fought a war in Angola, South Africa under Mandela emerged as an engine for peace and development in a region that seemed all too ready for both—except in Angola.

The Angolan war had raged for three decades, even before the country's independence from Portuguese colonialism in 1975. The antagonists since then were the government of President José Eduardo dos Santos and the infamous guerrilla movement led by Jonas Savimbi, one of Africa's most intractable rebel leaders. I'd studied this conflict in broad brush as an undergraduate at Columbia University and followed its story in the 1980s news accounts when Angola was at the height of international intrigue. Angola's wasn't just some small bush war over power and resources; it was big-time geopolitics. The Soviet Union and the United States tried to checkmate each other's strategic moves in Africa, and Washington escalated the competition by waging a secret war in Angola through the CIA, European mercenaries, and the apartheid regime in South Africa. During the war years, Agostinho Neto, the first Angolan president, then dos Santos, who assumed power after Neto's death in 1979, ran Marxist governments allied with the Soviets and their Cuban allies.

But by 1995, a long-shot attempt at peace was under way, and I'd arrived to report on its shaky prospects. The country remained on a knife's edge, and sporadic fighting continued to break out in the hinterlands. Angola remained a fraught and complex place, which is why I'd sought background briefings from Angolan diplomats in Washington, as well as from officials at the U.S. State Department, before leaving the United States. In South Africa, I'd picked the brains of some of the local Angola experts and steeped myself in background reading on the country's recent history. Deplaning at Luanda's Aeroporto Internacional 4 de Fevereiro, I felt the adrenaline rush of entering an arena of major African conflict, a place where my bona fides as a tough foreign correspondent could be established.

It was my first trip abroad—meaning outside of South Africa—and I'd prepared obsessively. I knew that the relative comforts of electricity, plumbing, telephone service, paved streets, and hygienic food would be absent in Angola. I knew that the war had caused human suffering on a massive scale, with the capital, Luanda, awash with war refugees. I'd have to become adept at navigating difficult circumstances if I were to survive and thrive on the continent. In addition to my visa and my letter of invitation from the state-controlled press center, as required of all journalists, I had plenty of ready cash in small denominations, as well as cash for the full trip hidden in a secret belt compartment. I had my smoky coils to repel malarial mosquitoes, and candles and flashlight for any power outages. Energy bars were stuffed deep in my bag, for those times when and if the local food turned my stomach. Most important, I had all the cables and equipment I'd need to connect my laptop modem through the local phone wires and file my stories back to Washington.

Ed Cody's warning echoed in my head. A former foreign correspondent who'd had his share of gonzo journalistic adventures on the road, Cody was one of my foreign desk editors. Jokingly, but in what I took to be all seriousness, he'd warned that I should never, ever be unable to file my stories. No matter what technical or logistical difficulties I faced wherever I might go, I had better be able to transmit my stories. He put the fear of God in me, so to speak, and I worried that I'd be considered an utter, total failure if my work got tripped up by technical difficulties. I suspected that some of the men on the foreign desk thought women correspondents were soft, and I planned to prove to Ed and the rest that I could do this.

So there I stood, waiting my turn in the immigration line, turning nervous thoughts over and over in my head, when I realized with a shock that my travels were about to be derailed. Up ahead, I spotted a man in a white tunic who turned out to be an airport health examiner, and he was checking the international vaccination cards of each and every person on line. He clasped his hands behind his back professor-like, suggesting he took his task very seriously indeed. All the travelers—businessmen, aid workers, oilmen, diamond miners, and maybe even a mercenary or two—seemed to know the routine. They held up the health card for inspection, no conversation required. The examiner nodded with satisfaction each time he saw the proper documentation proving that a new arrival had been vaccinated against some dreaded disease.

Yellow fever? Cholera? I'd been vaccinated against everything, and I could prove it—if only my international vaccination card were in my hand instead of sitting on my desk back in Jo'burg. In all my preparations, I'd forgotten this most important little document, and I had no idea what would happen when the man discovered I'd arrived without it. When the health examiner stood before me, I stared at him innocently and just said, "Bom dia" (good day).

"Cartão internacional da saúde?" He asked for my vaccination card.

I explained in my rudimentary Portuguese that I was an American journalist. I hoped this would somehow exempt me from the rules. He was unimpressed and asked again for the card. All I could say was "Nao, senhor." My traveler's Portuguese, mixed with a smattering of Spanish, broke down on me. I forgot how to say "forgot," as in "I forgot my yellow card, but I am clean, disease free, just believe me." The man tut-tutted and shook his head from side to side. He signaled with his index finger for me to follow. I did. I had no choice. Plucked from the line like a fugitive, I trailed the health examiner across the worn linoleum floor and down a short corridor into a small medical office.

Really, it was just a spare room filled with vaguely medicinal supplies, including a foul-looking examining table, a rickety little desk and chair, and a rusted metal shelving unit listing against the wall. And on those shelves, I saw a battered old shoe box. And in that shoe box, I saw a pile of syringes. Some were wrapped. Most were unwrapped. They were dirty, previously used, and just lying there collecting grit and grime and God knows what kind of bacteria in Angola's tropical air. The examiner rifled through the needles, as if he actually thought I would allow him to inoculate me right there on the spot. All I could think of was AIDS. Quickly, I shifted to plan B.

I suspect he knew it would come to this. The rifling through the dirty syringes was probably just an act, a prelude to the deal. I would see many variations on this theme, many bribe seekers going through a weird Kabuki in lieu of being so crass as to come right out and ask for cash. Fearing deportation at best, inoculation at worst, I knew that cash would be the most effective solution to this tricky problem. I dug into my pocket and pulled out two twenties, shrugging my shoulders as if to ask, "Will this do?" He responded with a smile. In return for my payment, the health examiner handed me a smudged but stamped, dated, and signed health certificate to slip into my passport, then sent me on my way.

It was the first payoff I'd ever made. I knew it would happen sooner or later, based on all I'd read and heard about getting things done in some of Africa's unstable and chaotic countries. Still, I felt guilty. In the blink of an eye, I'd become complicit in a practice that was eating away at African society. Sure, it's not a purely African phenomenon. Any society in transition can become prey to the venal or desperate greed that fuels shadowy deals. Think Russia and its Mafia.

But I was in Africa, where many nations were far more fragile than elsewhere in the world and could scarcely afford the degenerative effects of corruption. Angola was part of a long list of African countries where extortion had become systemic or was on the road to becoming so. Nigeria, Zaire, Kenya, Congo Republic, and Cameroon: war, economic collapse, and patriarchal patronage all conspired to make extortion a way of life in those countries. And it wasn't a ground-up phenomenon devised by small men trying to make ends meet. No. It was a top-down dynamic, in which economic mismanagement and corruption among a country's leadership filtered down to the common man, along with the sense of impunity that let corruption flourish. In some cases, corruption and mismanagement had eaten away at society so deeply that most commerce took place in off-the-books or black market transactions.

I was at least glad that my brush with bribery hadn't been any more threatening. As a woman traveling alone, I stayed vigilant for any sign that a confrontation would take a turn toward gender. In fact, I tamped down my usual feminine trappings, especially on the road. I wore modest shirts, khaki slacks, minimal makeup, and generally kept a remote attitude when in public. After that strange airport encounter, I vowed to travel with even more cash in the future, even with some of it stashed in my socks and my panties. (And as soon as I returned to Jo'burg, I would buy my own personal syringe and never leave home without it.)

• • •

As I left the airport with a hired car and driver after my brush with the health examiner, I sat back to take in the sights of the sadly crumbled city. There were shanty settlements on the city's outskirts, where people lived amid huge mounds of garbage. There were crumbling, ancient Portuguese colonial buildings in a rainbow of faded pastels. High-rise apartment blocks that spoke of the 1960s ambitions of the colonialists had been blackened by mold and rot. Nearly a third of the national population of 11 million had been displaced in the war, either by fighting or in forced marches to clear their villages. A city built for 500,000 people, Luanda saw its population swell to about 3 million, awash with war refugees. Luanda seemed a museum of European colonial cruelty, Cold War machinations, and African revolutionary failures. With its deep-sea oil and its plentiful deposits of diamonds, Angola under peaceful, less corrupt circumstances could have been a major economy in the region. Instead, its natural resources were fueling the conflict, not rebuilding or developing the nation.

The closer my taxi edged to the city center, the slower traffic crawled. And then I saw the war's most tender victims, the street children. They were everywhere, barefoot and brazen. They darted in and out of traffic—boys in torn, dirty T-shirts that hung off frail shoulders, girls in overlarge hand-me-down dresses that flapped around their hungry little bodies like broken wings. Bands of these wretched pixies swarmed around the cars and stood at windows rubbing their tummies. They cupped their hands to plead for money. Some shouted insults when their begging failed.

Others hobbled about on crutches, like the platoons of limbless soldiers in tattered army uniforms who also begged on the city's streets. They were the *mutilados*, the mutilated ones—adults and children left limbless by land mines. Angola emerged from war with at least 100,000 such land-mine amputees, the highest proportion in the world. More land mines were sown in its soil than in that of any other nation, rendering its fertile highlands untillable, many of its roads impassable. In some villages, people could barely walk much farther than their huts, for fear their footfalls would set off an explosion that would take a leg, an arm, or a life.

Motherless and maimed in more ways than physical, the street children mortified me. There were so many. And they seemed so young. Some looked six or seven years old. Then again, their growth may have been stunted. Some of them had heads of reddish hair that offered a telltale sign of the chronic protein-deficient malnutrition called kwashiorkor. I found no relief even after checking into my hotel. Up in my fourth-floor room at the Hotel Tivoli, I went to the window to take in the sights along the broad but crowded boulevard, the Rua da Missão. And there I saw a sight that became, to me, a freeze-frame of a nation's debasement. Atop a vehicle-sized mound of garbage across the street, children scavenged in the refuse, where dogs also rooted around for food.

By night, the children slept on the streets. I would not have noticed them on my own. My traveler's eye was unskilled, my vision not yet focused enough to spot the less obvious horrors of a country at war. I cruised the streets one night with a UNICEF doctor, Djibril Beye of Mali. He operated a mobile clinic in a van converted to an ambulance, and had treated nearly three thousand children over the nine months of its operation. In a tour of Luanda's dark streets, Beye pointed out to me the many ways that the children laid themselves down to rest. Beneath a sheet of dirty plastic tarp, you could see them, or under piles of crumpled newspaper. They found their rest huddled up against darkened storefronts downtown or nestled in clumps beneath trees out on the beautiful beaches on the Isle of Luanda, called the Ilha (pronounced *eelyah*), a long spit of land arching elegantly out into the Luanda bay. With its quaint seaside cafés, the Ilha provided rich pickings for the little scavengers.

They were, by and large, children whose families had been killed in fighting in the interior, or children who'd become separated from their loved ones while fleeing villages and towns under siege. They came from places with lovely names—Huambo, Luena, N'dalatando, Malanje—that had become hell. I met some of them that night traveling with Dr. Beye. The headlights of Beye's minivan beckoned and the children came rushing out of the darkness as Beye parked in a bleak section of town, below the hilltop diplomatic quarter of Miramar where the U.S. Embassy compound sat behind high, well-guarded walls. The children clamored at Beye's open van doors, eager to present their malarial fevers, parasites, septic wounds, and oozing sores. I sat inside the van, squeezed into a corner, taking photographs and scribbling notes as Beye and his nurse ministered to these miseries.

A little girl arrived, a sad and listless little girl. She wore a flouncy red skirt with a tidy white blouse tucked in beneath a blue and white sweatervest. Cecilia was her name and she was ten. Her older brother hoisted her up, for her leg hurt too much and she couldn't climb into the van on her own. A thick bandage turned brown with dried blood wrapped her right calf. With her brother holding her arms, Cecilia jerked in agony as the nurse unwrapped the wound and applied antiseptic. What started as a gash in her shin had become a gaping hole eaten away by infection so thoroughly that it nearly exposed the bone. Looking at it, even the doctor winced. Beye warned her, as he had before, that his treatments were not enough. She must go to the hospital for proper attention or risk losing the leg, he told her. Her brother nodded with concern, but said they had not had time to go. Beye gave Cecilia penicillin and admonished her again to take care. Cecilia shimmied down from the bright van and hobbled back with her brother into the pitch-black night of a society that had no capacity to cope with her needs.

As we cruised the streets, Luanda's darkness coughed up many other children like Cecilia. It seemed a whole generation of young Angolans was lost, and for what? Greed? Superpower rivalry? The logic of war had made great sense to its practitioners. But it presented most Angolans with a life of desperation and suffering. The injustice of it tore at me. I returned to the Tivoli late that night feeling depressed. In my room, I cried. I don't mind admitting it. I'd have never done it in public, and certainly never around a male colleague. When I needed to be tough, I was tough. But letting some tears flow was my private release, and I found in that first trip to Angola that I needed this release more than I'd have expected. In my journal, I wrote of Cecilia that night and concluded, "This tour of duty will break my heart over and over, even when it can't seem to break anymore."

People who work amid brutal conflict and vast human suffering build up a protective emotional armor. So much of what you see out in the field in places like Angola or Congo or Rwanda is so devastating, so shocking, that absorbing all the pain can leave you immobilized. Without that armor, you could go mad. I hadn't yet learned to wall off my heart. And each new episode on that trip to Angola hit me like a body blow. My senses, my mind, my emotions, were tossed and flipped and spun around daily. Angola rattled me in ways I'd never anticipated. I had vertigo, in a sense, from traveling this new reality.

The assaults on my senses came from all directions. I became sick from bad water or food, compounded by the nauseating smell of the smoky mosquito-repelling coils I burned as protection against malaria. I spent a lot of time in my hotel bathroom, where one evening something strange caught my eye. I don't know how I'd missed it before, for it was right there, high in a corner of the bathroom above the sink: a thick vine protruding about a foot out of the wall. It unnerved me. It felt menacing. My imagination ran wild. If this vine could be growing way up through a fourth-floor wall, then the bowels of the building must be crawling with tropical vines—the electrical wiring, the plumbing, everything. Sick with the bends, I was in one such state of bewilderment one night when the lights went out. The whole hotel went dark. The street outside went dark. A blackout: not a time you want to be caught with your pants down. I lit a candle and a cigarette and stood at the window overlooking the garbage heap, feeling sorry for myself, for Cecilia, for Angola.

* * *

Angola's degraded state had its origins in a time even before the war, when nearly five hundred years of domination by the Portuguese set the stage on which the nation's history would be written. From the time in the late fifteenth century when Portuguese explorers first made contact with a king known as the ManiKongo, seated in a region known as MbanzaKongo in what is now northern Angola, the region witnessed a relentless and brutal shift in African history. The Kongo kingdom, a loose federation of villages and clans, had existed for a century before the Europeans arrived with their dazzling new products to trade (namely, guns) and their mystifying religious beliefs (namely, Christianity) seeking converts. The localized slaving the ManiKongo practiced became an international enterprise with the Portuguese. The European appetite for human chattel ultimately far outpaced the ManiKongo's willingness to provide. Slavery depopulated much of the region around the Congo River estuary that was the center of the old Kongo kingdom. The Portuguese moved down the coast, to what is now called Luanda, and applied a similar program of conquest to its contacts with the kingdom of the Mbundu people, whose king was called the Ngola, from which Angola's name derives. Angola, from then on, by and large became a slaving enterprise for the Portuguese, who shipped millions of people to Brazil, to the islands of the Caribbean, and to the colonies of North America.

The struggle for Angola's independence was, as in other African nations, rooted in that long tradition of subjugation. But Angola's independence, though sought by three liberation armies, would come far later than in most of Africa. Not until 1975, following a coup in Portugal, did the colonizers finally relinquish control, grant independence, and depart Angola with a rapacious vindictiveness that became legendary. The Portuguese took anything they could, even plumbing fixtures and lightbulbs.

After a struggle between three rival liberation movements, the Popular Movement for the Liberation of Angola (MPLA) assumed power. Not willing to accept independence under a rival black movement, the MPLA's main postindependence rival, the National Union for the Total Independence of Angola, known by the acronym UNITA, took up arms against it. UNITA's leader, Jonas Savimbi, would be one of the continent's most infamous rebel fighters for decades to come.

The war had strains of class and ethnic rivalries: a Portuguese-assimilated coastal elite of Mbundu people versus the largely Ovimbundu peasants led by Savimbi in the interior highlands. Influenced by the Cold War, ideology drove the conflict as well. The MPLA took up a Marxist line, while UNITA touted itself as an opponent of Marxism (never mind that Savimbi had once been a Maoist). With the Cold War shaping global affairs, it was only a matter of time before the competition between the United States and the Soviet Union started shaping Angolan affairs as well. Because he espoused an anticommunist line, Savimbi became a favorite Cold War proxy of Presidents Jimmy Carter, Ronald Reagan, and George Bush the elder.

And so Angola and its people became pawns in a wider war run by powers that cared not a whit about development and prosperity. The superpower rivalry that descended on Angola through the 1970s and 1980s was all about checkmate, each power trying to thwart the perceived expansionism of the other in one of Africa's most resource-rich prizes. The Cubans sent thousands of troops into Angola to support the MPLA, while apartheid-era South Africa sent its army in to support UNITA. The Soviets stood with the Cubans, and the United States stood with the racist pariah government down in Pretoria. Even when the U.S. Congress prohibited it, the United States sent secret aid to UNITA, largely in the form of arms shipments flown in via neighboring Zaire. Zairean President Mobutu Sese Seko, another of Washington's favorite anticommunist strongmen, received millions of dollars in cash from the CIA for aiding the covert arms supply line. The United States even built an airstrip at the southern Zaire town of Kamina, near the Angolan border, from which it could fly in heavy weaponry for shipment across the border to Savimbi. The pro-Savimbi aid program would total about $250 million through the early 1990s.

But by then, the Angolan war—in the context of superpower rivalry—had been rendered obsolete. The fall of the Berlin Wall and the end of the U.S.-Soviet rivalry in Africa stripped Angola's war of its previous importance. The United States dropped Savimbi. Angolan President dos Santos dropped Marxism too. The two sides agreed to a peace deal that led, in 1992, to U.N.-supervised presidential elections that were flawed, for sure, but declared free and fair enough to be credible. Savimbi fell short of victory and faced a runoff with dos Santos. But rather than let the process take its course, Savimbi rejected the results, and his movement renewed its war in what would be the most brutal round of fighting yet. The return to the battlefield stripped Savimbi of most of his remaining credibility in the West.

A weekend of brutal urban warfare broke out in Luanda but was quickly quelled by government forces. Fighting raged virtually all over the country, but worst of all in the highlands cities of Huambo and Kuito, which were virtually destroyed. UNITA forces pushed hard into Angolan government-controlled territories in the Kwango Valley in the north, as well as the two Lunda provinces of the northeast, and seized a region rich in the resource that would buy its arms, feed its troops, bribe its allies, and line its pockets for years to come. Angolan diamond mines, renowned for their high gem-quality stones, fell into UNITA's hands, allowing the guerrilla movement to become as much a war machine as a diamond-smuggling syndicate. It sent men to be trained in South Africa as diamond divers, evaluators, and sorters. It mined in partnerships of convenience with foreign firms already operating in the regions UNITA now controlled. And it established its own centralized diamond-selling center deep in the African bush at a town called

Luzamba, connected to the world via satellite telephone. Estimates by both human rights groups and industry experts placed UNITA's diamond revenue from 1992 to 1998 at nearly $3 billion.

With states of the former Soviet Union flooding the international arms market, UNITA procured massive amounts of heavy weaponry with its diamond proceeds. It beefed up its transport infrastructure in rebel territory with airstrips for heavy supply planes. A United Nations arms embargo imposed on UNITA in 1993 only forced UNITA supply networks to become more expensive to operate and more stealthy. Nations friendly with UNITA, such as Zaire, Congo Republic, and Zambia, became way stations in Africa's most lucrative and busy covert arms and supply pipeline. Very much a creation of the West, UNITA would prove to be a destabilizing force not only for the Angolan government but also for the middle African region.

While UNITA fueled its fight with diamonds, the government could rely on oil. Angola had at its disposal so much oil, pumped through partnerships with firms like Chevron and Gulf, that the government could secure loans against expected oil revenues in a strange practice that truly mortgaged the country's future. And the United States was Angola's main oil customer. By the 1990s, most Angolan crude was shipped to the United States, comprising seven percent of all U.S. oil imports. Where once the CIA had been at the forefront of United States policy in Angola, now the United States oil companies held that distinction—for the sake of commerce, mind you, not spying. And U.S. firms weren't alone. Oil companies from around the globe competed for leases on the deep-sea Atlantic oil fields off Angola's shores. Angola was on course toward eclipsing Nigeria as sub-Saharan Africa's prime oil producer. Oil financed the government's massive arms buildup during the post-1992 war. And while South Africa was in the throes of its own difficult transition, Angola hired some of its white apartheid-era soldiers and covert operatives as mercenaries to help beef up the Angola military for a final push on UNITA. By 1994, the government pounded UNITA into submission in withering attacks on rebel strongholds that put much of the highlands region under siege. And

UNITA finally acquiesced to a second peace accord, named the Lusaka Protocol after the Zambian city where it was signed.

• • •

During my trip to Angola in 1995, I flew to Lobito, a southern port city and site of the U.N. peacekeeping troop headquarters, aboard a cockroach-infested World Food Program (WFP) supply plane. Because of the war, there was no in-country commercial air traffic, and the WFP flight coordinator, David Schad, obliged my request for a seat, as he did with many other journalists. Far more than in Luanda, I could see in Lobito and its sister city, Benguela, the total devastation of the long war. Once Angola's most significant port, Lobito had been the continental exit point for a mother lode of mineral exports from the Central African copper belt. The mines of northern Zambia and southern Zaire shipped their copper to Lobito via the Benguela rail line. But Savimbi's UNITA rebels years ago had blown the rail line to bits, and the Lobito-Benguela region had been devastated by fighting that left its buildings pocked by artillery fire and mortar blasts.

Refugees were everywhere. They squatted in the abandoned, shot-up buildings of the Lobito business district and in the empty old oceanfront villas on a stretch of glorious beach called Restinga. They languished in camps on the outskirts of the town, where I met several people who told me their stories. Mariano José's was a typical case. Because of fighting, he'd walked a hundred miles from his town, Chongoroi, two years before. He settled along with ten thousand others in a camp for displaced people set up by a German relief organization. For two years, the thirty-two-year-old had been hoping to get back home, but those were years like all the years before in which generations of Angolans had been stalked by war and taunted by peace that failed to materialize. The United Nations had tried to nurture peace before in Angola, only to have its efforts shut down by fighting. And even as U.N. troops gathered at Lobito for deployment throughout the country, hit-and-run raids, mine blasts, and other violence continued to underline the country's deep insecurity. A peace accord was one thing. But would it hold?

"Every day we are thinking of going back," Mariano José said. "As soon as the peace will be effective through security for the people, we are ready to return."

"People are trusting in this peace," Joaquim Leiria told me plaintively. A twenty-nine-year-old former shipping clerk, Leiria served as my guide and translator in Lobito and Benguela. But, he added, no one could really say if peace would hold. Even the U.N. commanders charged with making the peace work weren't sure if it would.

On this and numerous other trips to Angola, the vagaries of the "peace process" would occupy my reporting. UNITA fighters were supposed to assemble at demobilization camps, hand in their weapons, receive money to get them home and resettled or, for those who wanted it, sign up for integration into the national army. On paper, sure, it made sense. On paper, sure, UNITA's Savimbi agreed to this process, and his representatives dutifully attended the weekly meetings in Luanda of a joint commission set up to monitor the peace process. The commission was comprised of the MPLA government, UNITA's civilian representatives, the United Nations, and the troika of powers—the United States, Portugal, and Russia—most intimately involved in Angola's modern history. Much to my dismay, I had to rely on these foreign diplomats for more than I'd have liked, because the very cloistered government of dos Santos had been so unaccustomed to outside scrutiny for so long that you could go crazy trying to get an interview with even a junior government spokesman. On one of my many trips to the country, I finally decided to go right to their offices, to stake them out until someone, anyone, would talk to me. To no avail. I had to develop other, nonofficial Angolan sources, but in the climate of war and fear they rarely spoke on the record.

As if they were duty-bound to report that their efforts were not in vain, the "troika" diplomats hailed small signs of progress, even minuscule steps forward, and tried to downplay the routine bouts of fighting, seizure of territory, and other evidence of backsliding on peace by both sides. Once the American, Russian, and Portuguese diplomats bought into the logic of the peace process, I suppose they had no choice but to portray the peace as real.

The problem was that the logic of the peace process was actually illogical. It presumed that Savimbi could be taken at his word, though nothing in his history suggested as much. At each and every stage of the process, UNITA found a reason to procrastinate and prevaricate. The troops he was demobilizing weren't really troops at all, at least not the hard-core body of fighters that diplomats believed he was holding in reserve. The weapons he was turning in weren't the heavy artillery and other serious firepower that UNITA clearly had.

But in Angola in 1995, 1996, and 1997, I was hard-pressed to find any diplomat who would interpret these developments as signs of the peace process falling apart. After its failures in the Somalia debacle of 1993, when a peace mission degenerated into combat that left eighteen U.S. servicemen dead, and after its failure to intervene to stop the 1994 genocide in Rwanda, the United Nations was hungry for an Africa success. I found that the U.S. diplomats operated similarly. At the U.S. Embassy in the affluent Miramar neighborhood overlooking the bay, my briefings with U.S. Ambassador Donald Steinberg were long recitations of the incremental progress being made, with fighting and other problems given a back burner as if not important. Steinberg, a chatty diplomat who'd originally trained as a journalist, was committed to the logic that if you kept UNITA even minimally attached to the peace timetable, then peace would finally take hold. At least that's what he'd say on the record.

But war had defined Angola for decades, and it did not seem about to change. The Angolan reality was cold and sinister. From its origins in the quest for liberation to its capture by Cold War interests, the war had become Savimbi's power game. The plain truth is that the rebel leader wanted to rule Angola. And he would fight as long as it took to achieve that goal. I heard more than a few diplomats and aid workers declare, off the record, of course, that the war would not end as long as Savimbi was alive. But the old guerrilla fought on and on—and while the fighting proceeded, there was, alas, money to be made. In the diamond mining regions especially, war made it possible for commanders to make a killing. Even as the antagonists paid lip service to this thing called peace, both sides of the conflict were profiting from the chaos. It seemed to me that stability really wasn't in their interest.

On the diamond front, there was a free-for-all. Some government MPLA generals had private deals with UNITA commanders, or so I was told on a trip to Lunda Norte Province in 1996. There U.N. peacekeeping officials told me that UNITA controlled the west bank of the Chicapa River, while the MPLA army controlled the east bank. And each side had armies of illicit diamond miners, known in Portuguese as *garampieros*, who worked for these military-units-turned-diamond-syndicates. The workers included children forced into service. This form of mining was relatively easy, because the diamonds lay close to the surface, in the silt, or alluvium, of the riverbanks and tributaries. Angola's northeast was literally awash with diamonds.

"A lot of people have come to my house to offer me diamonds—children, men, anybody," said Colonel Roque Gallego, one of the regional U.N. commanders based in the Lunda Sul town of Saurimo. I got a small taste of this diamond glut when I landed in Saurimo on a cargo flight with two male colleagues. One of them ventured behind the plane's wheel well to take a leak, and a man had approached him and stuck his tongue out to show off a diamond for sale.

The diamonds that fueled UNITA were voraciously soaked up by global diamond concerns like the South African–based De Beers mining syndicate, at a time when the stigma of "conflict diamonds," or stones illegally mined in war zones, had not yet emerged as a human rights issue. And while the U.S. government and international creditors pushed dos Santos's government to actually account for all the huge oil revenue that could not be found in the country's budget, U.S. oil companies pumped hundreds of thousands of barrels in Angolan partnerships that abetted, perhaps unwittingly, the systemic corruption and mismanagement. The war provided a smoke screen behind which the government could shield its shadow economy.

As the strange stalemate between war and peace dragged on in Angola, I always remembered what another American diplomat said to me back in 1995. He was Edmund DeJarnette, the first U.S. ambassador posted to Angola after the dos Santos government committed itself to democratic change. DeJarnette told me adamantly that he believed the warring parties realized they had to make this peace accord work. And he offered up a line that seemed to me absurd. Angola, he said, was "one of the great opportunities of

Africa." I should have asked: For whom? But I already knew the answer. Angola was a great opportunity for the international oil and diamond concerns, among which Americans were prominent. Increasingly, American foreign policy in Angola, as elsewhere in Africa, was all about commerce. U.S. policy makers talked about goals like peace, democracy, and development in Africa, but if money could be made for U.S. companies in the midst of Angola's chaos, so be it. The country's body count rose. And the oil kept flowing. Not that the Americans—or the British, French, Italian, and other nationals doing business in Angola—were responsible for the country's sorry mess. But decades of United States engagement with Angola, whether strategically or commercially, had produced much for America and little for Angola.

I believe that Angola would have had a chance at normalcy if the superpowers had not transformed its conflict into something larger and more lethal than it probably would have been. Perhaps UNITA, without outside help, would have petered out into nothing. And without the enemy breathing down its neck, perhaps Angola's young government wouldn't have gone so harshly Marxist and would have made a stronger push for postcolonial development. But we'll never know. And that always struck me as the real tragedy—not only for Angola but also for other countries where superpower manipulation drastically changed the course of history. It's like the impact of the slave trade. We'll just simply never know what many African countries could have been if their contacts with the outside world had not been so brutal, so destructive.

5

Smoke and Mirrors

arrived at Kinshasa's N'Djili International Airport in January 1996, armed with attitude and ready for anything. The dangers and obstacles not only of traveling in Zaire but of just arriving there were infamous among foreign correspondents. Navigating the airport was a form of combat. Though I'd become much more savvy on the road, having already visited Angola, Zimbabwe, and Zambia, nothing could have prepared me for Zaire. For a capital city of 5 million people, the airport looked incredibly small-time. There was but one old terminal building, a few hangars, and several ancient aircraft parked on the tarmac's fringes. All arrivals deplaned down movable stairways, and even before I stepped onto the tarmac I knew that the stories I'd heard about the terror of a Kinshasa arrival had been understated.

A frenetic crowd of men surged toward the deplaning passengers. They descended on us in a strange siege, surrounding each of us in a swarm of flailing arms and grabbing hands, trying to snatch a bag, a passport, or anything that could be ransomed back for a bribe. I had no intention of letting go of anything. I swung my small bag in front of me, slamming the knees of whoever was in my way. I shoved through the crowd, shouting, *"S'il vous plaît. Laissez-moi tranquille!"* (Please. Leave me alone.) But my protestations had no impact. I was a foreigner, which meant I had money, and the men on the tar-mac were hell-bent on getting it. That was the Kinshasa game.

In the garish Kinshasa fashion statement of deeply pleated pants and bil-lowy synthetic shirts of gaudy golds, purples, and greens, the men on the tarmac were an institution unto themselves. *Le protocole*, they were called. Protocol men. They were minions in the airport bureaucracy, men on the take like so many others at all levels of the regime of President Mobutu Sese Seko. I'd arrived at the nadir of the infamous Mobutu era that for three decades had picked Zaire clean. So thoroughly had corruption taken root that political scientists dubbed Zaire a kleptocracy. Mobutu and his cronies perfected the art with their routine siphoning from the national budget, and the system had filtered down to the common man. In the absence of pay from the looted national budget, a vast system of extortion took root. People called it *débrouillez-vous* (fend for yourself). Business, politics, education, and government—everything in Zaire was a free-for-all.

Clerks who stamped official documents demanded a bribe, what they called a fee. Police threw up roadblocks willy-nilly in the city, demanding payment from whomever they chose to stop. Unpaid teachers demanded "fees" from their students. Prisoners in jail had to rely on their families to bring them meals, and their families had to pay a "fee" to enter. Hospitals re-fused to release patients unless their families paid the bill. So routinely were medical supplies stolen that it behooved patients to check in with their own thread for suturing, their own needle for injections. Mama Yemo, the city's largest hospital, named for Mobutu's mother, was so unhygienic that it may as well have been a petri dish for growing disease. An attaché at the U.S. Embassy would later tell me, only half in jest, that if I fell ill or was injured, I should just get to the airport and take any flight out of the country rather than be taken to Mama Yemo. But even then, I'd have to be ready to pay an airport protocol man at each step of the way: for carrying my bags, handing my passport over to the immigration officials, and navigating the security in-spections. You could end up paying your protocol and three or four other people before escaping from the airport's grip. Charmingly, as was the Zairean way, some bribe grabbers called it a "little gift," *le petit cadeau*.

Struggling that morning through the siege on the tarmac, holding on tight to my suitcase, computer bag, and backpack, I could see a man holding up a sign from my hotel, the Intercontinental, scrawled with the name "Madame Duke." I headed toward it, waving my hand at the sign bearer near the arrivals' hall. I thought I was almost free of the surging crowd when suddenly a protocol man blocked my path. *"Passeport! Passeport!"* He didn't say it, he snarled it. I caved in and gave him my passport. My escort from the Intercontinental arrived at my side seconds later, thank goodness, and negotiated with the protocol man to smooth my passage through the airport. The escort was named Effi, and, of course, his services, too, required a fee.

I would learn later that the affable and accommodating Mr. Effi was a sergeant in Mobutu's army who moonlighted at the Intercon. In a national armed force in name only, where training was almost unheard-of and where enterprising officers made a hefty personal profit by selling off the weapons, soldiers were paid so irregularly and so poorly that many took extra jobs. But that day, I didn't know or really care just who Effi was. He had a sign and it bore my name, like a life preserver in the N'Djili arrivals madness. Effi had trouble pronouncing "Duke," so he divided it into two syllables and applied his Congolese-accented French. In Kinshasa, I would be called "Madame Duqué."

I had flown in that January of 1996 to cover breaking news. Two days before, a plane had crashed on takeoff at another airport in Kinshasa and reportedly killed as many as 350 people in a sprawling hawkers' market. That death toll, though it turned out to be inflated, would have represented the world's highest on-the-ground casualty count from a plane crash. My editors back in Washington expected me to arrive in Kinshasa and file a dispatch that very day. I had to hustle. Effi led me out of the airport to a chauffeured car from the Intercontinental, where he sat up front and I sat in the back and shocked the driver when I told him to forget about the hotel and head straight to the scene of the crash.

It had happened at Ndolo Airport, a secondary Kinshasa airfield that served mostly small private craft and large cargo planes. But unlike N'Djili, which was on Kinshasa's outskirts, Ndolo was right in the middle of a city of 5 million people, near a stadium and a rail line. If that wasn't dangerous enough, Ndolo's main runway ended just across the street from a huge out-door hawkers' market, called Somba Sikida, popular for its dirt-cheap goods.

As we arrived at the crash site, the roads were clogged with a stream of people pushing away wooden handcarts they'd piled high with sheets of metal and other aircraft debris. The area of the crash itself swarmed with people, with no sign of any police or soldiers attempting to secure the scene. Whatever investigation would take place, it certainly wouldn't hinge on forensics. Surrounded by the smashed, charred remnants of hundreds of wooden hawkers' stalls, the crashed Russian-made Antonov-32 cargo plane lay cracked in half and heavily burned. Miraculously, the two pilots survived. The hundreds who were injured and killed—the figure was later put at per-haps three hundred—were victims both of the plane's impact and explosion and of its propellers. The Antonov's rotor blades sliced people up as the plane skidded through the market. As I got out of the car, a crowd of people in silent shock stood in a circle nearby, peering down at a severed head.

The plane's fuselage literally crawled with people. Men who'd scaled the wings and body were hacking and banging away with saws and machetes, then handing the scraps down to their fellows in a kind of scavenger's as-sembly line. What had once been an aircraft was now a mere scrap heap. On the ground, people scooped up wooden planks from the market wreckage. The enterprising Kinois, as the city's residents are known, could collect and resell virtually anything, could somehow make it through the worst social degradations. Despite the bad press they persistently received, the Kinois could not be surpassed in their desperate resourcefulness. Men routinely hot-wired their cars when the ignitions gave out and there was no money for spare parts. Housewives harvested crops by the sides of roads, on traffic me-dian strips, on any available piece of land. Family members ate in shifts, every other day if need be, to stretch their meager food supplies. Children sold empty cans and dirty rags; somebody could use them for something. Low-cost markets like the local Somba Sikida were filled with used, discarded merchandise.

Not only did each and every individual have to fend for himself, but all semblance of Zaire's bureaucratic order and regulation had broken down years ago. Though a country as vast as the United States east of the Mississippi, and endowed with fabulous natural wealth in forestry, hydroelectric power, uranium, cobalt, copper, diamonds, and gold, Zaire was flat broke. The country's public coffers had become the petty-cash kitties of Mobutu and his cronies. Robbed of resources, state institutions were left to wither. The state mining conglomerate, Gecamines, was on the ropes. The national airline, Air Zaire, was bankrupt. The national telephone system died from corruption; cell phones, for those who could afford them, were the only means of communication. Regideso, the national water utility, was just a bad and sickly joke. Amoebas swam Kinshasa's untreated water, leaving a large part of the population sick much of the time, especially its children.

Even the military, every dictator's last resort, had been allowed to degenerate. Only Mobutu's elite troops, the Special Presidential Division, were routinely paid. As for the army regulars, they had to fend for themselves. And they did, quite brutally. Twice, the troops' anger exploded in riots known as le pillage, in 1991 and 1993. The looting, with civilians joining in, was nationwide and wreaked destruction on the economy. In Kinshasa, the looters emptied markets and storehouses. They smashed businesses and stripped schools, clinics, and hospitals of all supplies. Le pillage shoved Zaire beyond the point of no return. Nothing was regulated. Life was a free-for-all, and the crash at Somba Sikida was a direct result.

The land where the market stood had once been an Ndolo Airport runway extension, used for training and emergency landings. Ndolo was the main airfield during the days of Belgian colonialism, when Kinshasa was called Léopoldville. But over time, when N'Djili became the primary airfield, Ndolo apparently no longer needed such a long runway. Road construction cut it in two. Then the hawkers converged and Somba Sikida was born, with no official care given to the possibility of an air-to-ground disaster. Zoning? Forget it. There was no such thing.

"We asked the government and the authorities of Kinshasa to take away the market," lamented Lessendjina Ikwame lpu'Ozia, the earnest-sounding chairman of Régie des Voies Aériennes, the airways control authority. He just shrugged his shoulders when I asked him who was responsible for that failure to act. "The inquiry will tell," he said.

The plane was licensed and managed by Scibe Zaire, a firm owned at that time by one of Zaire's richest and most ostentatious men, Bemba Saolona. He was a portly métis, or person of African and European parentage, who occupied a treasured spot in the orbit of mega-rich Zaireans who swirled around Mobutu. He managed a nationwide empire in telecommunications, aviation, and trade from his home in the relatively plush Gombe district of Kinshasa, not far from the Intercon, on a property I'd visit later and see its private discotheque and its man-made brook. As was often the practice in the murky world of African air charter companies, Scibe may have leased the plane to another company or to an individual. But the fact that the paper trail of the ill-fated Antonov led back to Scibe provided a rare glimpse at the links between the wealthy Mobutuists and the region's smuggling networks. Neither Bemba nor any other Zairean was held accountable for the crash, which was not at all surprising.

Instead, the Russian pilots took the fall. They were part of a wave of aviators from the former Soviet Union who'd washed into Africa in the early 1990s in search of work. They found willing takers in the region's rebel movements and among their illicit suppliers. The pilots admitted during their trial a few months after the crash that they were attempting to fly to northern Angola to resupply troops of the rebel movement UNITA, as they'd done many times before, despite U.N. sanctions against such flights. But just who hired them—and precisely what the Antonov carried—remained a mystery. It was just one in a long series of episodes that confirmed Zaire's status as a major conduit for arms and supplies to the rebels in Angola, its neighbor to the southwest.

• • •

In the days following the plane crash at Somba Sikida, the details of the tragedy were suffocated in the Kinshasa miasma of rumor, conspiracy, and portents of supernatural powers. The "sidewalk radio," *radio trottoir*—what Americans call the grapevine—hummed with a speculation verging on certainty. The series of strange "accidents" that had befallen the capital in rapid succession—a deadly truck crash, a deadly bus crash, and now a hugely deadly plane crash—could only be the work of powerful men, crafty men,

men with pull beyond this world. And of all such men, of whom there were many, none was as transcendently powerful as Mobutu Sese Seko, the nation's all-powerful "guide," as his propaganda machine claimed. So, no. That plane did not just crash. In the popular imagination of the markets and the street-corner gossips, Mobutu's hidden hand, his supernatural hand, plucked that plane from the sky. Some market women told me this conspiratorially, as if letting me in on the inside story.

"People are being sacrificed," said Sophie Kanku, a seller of shoes at the Gran Marché, the city's main outdoor market. "It's as if the leaders are sacrificing them for the elections." One of Sophie's customers, Prisca Nta, a student, said that Mobutu and others in power had caused the series of recent crash deaths "to strengthen their power."

I understood that people believe in higher or lower powers and other realms of being. In the spiritual hierarchy of African life, there exists between God and man a host of divinities and ancestral spirits to whom people turn in navigating and understanding ordinary life. But this idea that Big Men like Mobutu could make planes fall from the sky seemed beyond the pale. I'd often wondered why ordinary Zaireans did not rise up against Mobutu and his cronies, for they knew how deeply such men had ruined their country. There in the Gran Marché, I got a glimpse of an answer. If you believe a Big Man can pluck a plane from the sky, then you believe yourself utterly powerless to do anything against him. Of course, Mobutu's power and the people's attendant fatalism were aided and abetted by the thuggishly deadly army of spies and soldiers that Mobutu had set loose on society. Opponents were snatched from their homes and tortured in secret cells. Political murders were common. And ordinary people lived at the complete whim of troops who could stop a civilian at any time and demand all of his money.

But ancient and traditional perceptions of power and spirituality worked to Mobutu's benefit. In Congo's many traditional cultures, the most powerful men—kings and chiefs—are believed to be guides of daily life through their spiritual powers to mediate between the temporal and supernatural worlds; between man and the ancestors. In this way, leaders served as high priests, in effect, to whom their subjects looked for guidance or toward whom their subjects showed all deference. Mobutu's trademark leopard-skin hat was no mere fashion statement; in traditional culture, only the ruler could wear the leopard skin and appropriate the animal's symbolism as king of the realm.

Mobutu built on this traditional cosmology and succeeded sinisterly in crafting his own mythology. His rule, beginning in the early 1960s, ultimately became messianic. For thirty years, Mobutu fashioned himself an all-seeing leader, sometimes known as the Guide, at other times the Helmsman. He maintained "permanent" contact with his people, or so his propaganda machine said, and he was everywhere. His portrait beamed down from public installations all over the country and moved ubiquitously through daily life on the brightly colored cloth from which people made skirts and shirts. State television broadcasts were replete with Mobutu's image floating down from the clouds.

A soldier trained in the waning days of Belgian colonialism, Joseph-Désiré Mobutu was named chief of staff of the armed forces of the independent Congo that came into being in 1960. Ostensibly, he was loyal to the country's first prime minister, the charismatic idealist Patrice Lumumba. Lumumba assumed the country's leadership in May 1960, at a time when it would have been impossible for anyone to manage the rapid decolonization of a country that had been as brutally repressed as Congo had been under the Belgians.

The Belgian Congo, as it was often known, had been a colony of extreme terror and racist paternalism. Belgian King Leopold II staked a claim to this territory spanning middle Africa even before the infamous European "scramble for Africa" in the 1880s. European explorers, some operating in the king's employ, penetrated the African interior and journeyed through the maze of rain forests and rivers of the Congo. Of them all, though, it was Joseph Conrad's odyssey in the 1890s that produced the template of Africa in the Western mind. Congo, in Conrad's hands, was a place of primordial savagery that produced the profound debasement of those Europeans who sought its plunder, as if its "heart of darkness," as Conrad called it in his infamous novella of that name, was infectious.

Little reason, then, to think of African life as anything more than labor, and Leopold's Congo Free State, as it was called, became nothing but a place of brutal colonial slavery. As the automotive age took off in Europe and America at the turn of the twentieth century, the rubber that made the world's tires was harvested largely in Congo. Huge rubber vines snaked through the rain forest that covers half of Congo. People called it the wood that weeps. Soon the people were weeping too. Millions of Congolese died or were mutilated in the era of the "rubber terror." Belgian colonial agents chopped off the hands of workers who didn't fulfill their production quotas, or they held the wives of male workers hostage until the ransom of the rubber quota was paid.

In the cities, meanwhile, Congolese who achieved a modicum of "westernized" education and could speak French were deemed evolved enough to be treated with a tad bit more respect than others, but only a tad. Like their white counterparts down in South Africa during apartheid, the Belgians believed that Congolese were destined for servitude and had no use for higher education. In a vast country of some 15 million people at the time of independence, there were but seventeen university-educated Congolese.

A missionary-educated postal worker, union organizer, and beer marketing manager, Lumumba formed the first national political party in the country, the National Congolese Movement. He drew his ideological lineage, in part, from the pan-Africanist liberation movements fast sweeping through Africa under the guidance of Kwame Nkrumah, first president of Ghana, which in 1957 became one of the earliest African nations to achieve independence from colonialism. A fierce resolve for African sovereignty informed Lumumba's staunch anticolonial politics, which made him wildly popular in Congo as the preeminent symbol of freedom. But Western powers concerned about the direction of this nation, filled as it was with a mother lode of coveted mineral wealth, viewed Lumumba as a wild card at best, a potential Soviet pawn at worst. Washington, especially, liked its African friends to sound politically moderate, even racially neutered. Even as Lumumba was sworn in as the duly elected prime minister in 1960, the cold warriors of President Dwight Elsenhower's administration flagged him as a leader who bore watching and began conspiring against him.

Congo began fracturing along tribal and regional lines almost immediately after independence, eclipsing the Congolese liberation aspirations that

Lumumba embodied. Black troops mutinied against their Belgian commanders. Belgian troops still in the country despite independence seized
some towns, especially in the southern region of Katanga, where Congolese
secessionists clearly backed by the Belgians declared a separate state. Katanga
held most of Congo's vast deposits of copper and cobalt. Most important,
uranium from Katanga had fueled the American nuclear industry. Lumumba
requested American military assistance to deal with the Katanga secession,
but Washington turned him down. Lumumba locked horns repeatedly with
the United Nations over the international body's reluctance to help break the
Katanga secession. And yet another secession broke out, this one in the Ka-
sai region just north of Katanga.

With the country spiraling into chaos in its first weeks of independence,
Lumumba and his president, Joseph Kasavubu, each ousted the other in
back-to-back national radio addresses. Their dispute created a leadership
void that opened the way for the ambitious army chief of staff, Mobutu, to
step in. Once an aide to Lumumba, Mobutu turned on his old ally and over-
threw him with a military coup in September 1960. Mobutu had already
been identified in Washington as a key U.S. asset in Congo. He appeared far
friendlier to Western interests than did Lumumba. The United States supported Mobutu's takeover and the establishment of an interim government,
and the CIA joined the growing ranks of the anti-Lumumbists plotting the
ousted prime minister's demise. It is well documented that the CIA dispatched an agent to Kinshasa carrying a poison with which to assassinate
Lumumba. Published declassified cable traffic between the U.S. Embassy in
Kinshasa and the White House has made it clear that President Eisenhower's administration believed Lumumba was becoming a Soviet client and
wanted the new leader removed. But before the U.S. poison plot was carried
out, Lumumba met his end. Mobutu had him arrested and shipped off to
Katanga, where the secessionist army murdered him in January 1961.

Mobutu tightened his grip, like a backstage Oz pulling the strings while
a civilian government put up the pretense of running the state. But in 1965,
with full-fledged rebellions having torn the country apart for four years—
requiring intervention by the United Nations, Belgium, and the United
States—Mobutu cracked down again. He mounted yet another coup and

declared himself president, with his first order of business to crush all remnants of rebellion. Within just a few years, Mobutu centralized all national
power and created a one-party state. Though he'd plotted against Lumumba
in earlier times, Mobutu's party, the Popular Movement of the Revolution,
co-opted Lumumba's popular brand of nationalism. Then in the early 1970s,
Mobutu hit on the idea of *authenticité* to restore Congo's Africanness. People
were forced to replace their Christian names with African ones, to stop wearing Western dress. Léopoldville became Kinshasa. The country called Congo
became Zaire, as did the mighty river running through it.

And the man known as Joseph-Désiré Mobutu took on a name in 1971
that told an epic of omnipotence. Mobutu Sese Seko Kuku Ngbendu wa za
Banga, he called himself. Translated from his native Ngbandi, it means "the
all-powerful warrior who, because of his endurance and inflexible will to win,
will go from conquest to conquest leaving fire in his wake." Mobutu and the
state became increasingly inseparable, and he finally decreed "Mobutuism" a
constitutional principle. The mythology of his very being became the basis
for a governing creed: basically, Mobutuism was the worship of the leader as
the national savior, with his brand of iron-fisted paternalistic leadership the
law of the land, even taught in the schools. He was a classic African "big
man," an autocrat, some would say a megalomaniac, but definitely a grandiose
figure who, like Louis XIV, the Sun King, believed "L'état, c'est moi" (I am
the state).

As lavishly absurd as his rule became, Mobutu is credited even by his
critics for creating a sense of national pride and verve. And after decades of
the extreme brutalities of Belgian colonialists, Zaire desperately needed to
reclaim its African soul. The bold new sense of Zaireanization helped hold
the young nation together despite its vast size—Africa's third largest state
territory—and its many language groups, said to be around 250.

But all that rhetoric of nationhood turned out to be Mobutu's own prelude to the deal. Skimming off revenue from all moneymaking state enterprises, he amassed wealth that analysts tallied in the region of $4 billion.
Much of it, though, he doled out over the years in the patronage that kept his
family, entourage, close generals, and other political allies in line. His real es-
tate holdings spanned Africa and Europe. There was the palace, known as

the Versailles in the jungle, in northern Zaire near the Ubangi River in his home region of Gbadolite. It was equipped with a hotel for his guests and a runway long enough to accommodate the Concorde. He owned a castle in Spain, a palace in Switzerland, and residences in Paris and on the French Riviera, as well as in Belgium, Ivory Coast, Portugal, and, through proxies, in Cape Town too.

When in Kinshasa, he lived in a vast Marble Palace or at a presidential villa inside a military compound. By the early 1990s, though, he spent much of his Kinshasa time aboard his yacht, the Kamanyola, drifting out on the Congo River a safe distance from the swirling conspiracies of a capital city in turmoil.

But wherever he was, Mobutu symbolized raw power. Even as the cancerous corruption of his rule had metastasized so thoroughly that state coffers were empty and most Zaireans were forced to live like feudal serfs, Mobutu loomed within the national consciousness and constantly stirred the political pot.

He committed himself to democratic reform and an end to his one-party state in 1990. But this proved a sham. So many of the new parties that sprang up were mere fronts for his ruling group that cynics began to call multipartyism "multi-Mobutuism." The Sovereign National Conference, a group of delegates that were to lead the transition to electoral democracy, became a political tug-of-war, with Mobutu suspending the conference over and over. He rejected the prime minister that the conference elected, and appointed one of his own choosing. His government was a revolving door. He made prime ministerial appointments nine times in just five years, including two figures hired, fired, and appointed again and again. One of his prime ministers lasted a laughable seven days. Even his opponents had at one time or another been in his government. In his early years, Mobutu had his foes killed. As he matured, he simply jailed them, released them, co-opted them, dirtied their hands, and thereby stripped them of any credibility as potential opponents.

Social scientists called Zaire a "collapsed state." When it came to government and the bureaucracies of nationhood, that assessment certainly did seem true. Take the Ministry of Information, for instance. A once-beautiful skyscraper built after independence, its murals of ceramic tile and mirrored glass shimmered along walls of windows and futuristic cement walkways and plazas. But the place was a virtually empty ruin by the time I visited in 1996—except for the offices of the ministry, located ridiculously on the top floor.

On my first visit to the ministry, I did what anyone would do in a high-rise building. I walked over to the bank of six elevators in the lobby and pressed the button. My guide and translator that day, Mbongo Mamanisini, told me that only one elevator was working, and only manually. To call for it, you had to bang as hard as you could on the elevator door with the palm of your hand. That way, the man who operated the elevator car would hear you from on high. I did as instructed and banged on the door, understanding just what the term "collapsed state" meant.

• • •

Whose fault was this mess? It seemed too simple just to blame Mobutu. Surely, one man couldn't create such chaos alone. It was easy to demonize Mobutu, but the fact remained that a host of others benefited from the corrupt system he initiated. In Zaire, the point of politics wasn't power. It was wealth. And the entire political class around Mobutu had grown filthy rich.

There was no way I would get an interview with Mobutu himself, I was told, for he'd grown leery of the bad press that seemed to trail his every move. So I went to see his "Terminator." His real name is Honoré Ngbanda Nzambo Ko Atumba, a special counselor to Mobutu and a former head of the National Protection and Intelligence Service, known appropriately by its French acronym, SNIP. Because SNIP was known to terminate people, its head came to be known as the Terminator. Of course, I did not call him this in person, for I was pretty certain he would not appreciate it. He was also a Christian and led televised Bible studies. And like so many others wrapped up in Mobutuism, the Terminator was a sycophant through and through.

His office was wood-paneled, dark, and rich. Like all Zairean officials and businessmen, he was impeccably and expensively dressed. And his manner was understated, calibrated, controlled, as he held his hands atop his desk, palms together. This interview was my introduction to the maddening

Zairean doublespeak and insouciance that obscured the truth in just about all official encounters, especially when the subject on the table was corruption and mismanagement.

"We are concerned by this situation. We are all concerned by this situation," the Terminator said of the country's economic crisis. "There are different aspects. There are internal factors and external ones. As far as internal factors, there was a general misgovernment in the country. The outside point of view about misgovernment—only the president who is accused for that, whereas we know here in Zaire that it was everybody. President Mobutu did not manage Gecamines. He did not manage Air Zaire . . . So if those enterprises are no longer working, it means they were mismanaged by their leaders . . . What I deplore in our country is the impunity. Those who are committing mismanagement are not punished."

Ah, yes, the impunity. That was the problem. They all let each other get away with it, and they spoke of the problem as if it were beyond anyone's control. Léon Lubitsch Kengo wa Dondo was on his third go-round as prime minister, so if anyone knew "the system," he surely did. He was a dreaded and loathed figure in Kinshasa, in part because of his acerbic political style, in part because he was of mixed parentage (Polish and Zairean or, some believed, Rwandan). But the United States latched onto him as a skilled technocrat who'd already instituted some impressive reforms. Despite the fact that he'd held senior posts in a regime that made a mess of Zaire, Kengo was seen in Washington as a man who could help Zaire find a way out.

He was a punctilious character who managed his office down to the fine details. His chief of staff even warned that I should dress properly for the interview, not like some sloppy journalist. That's exactly why I always traveled with one nice suit. Appropriately decked out, I arrived at the riverside office of the prime ministry for a strange interview that left me feeling paranoid. As Kengo peered at me over his gold-rimmed glasses, I got the distinct impression he wanted to shout at me or cuss me out. He clearly was not fond of journalists. But he spoke rather softly, quite diplomatically, as he touted the reforms he'd put in place.

Zaire's economic growth had been a negative 15 percent when he took office in 1994 and was now at 0.6 percent. Inflation had been 9,780 percent and a year later was a mere 380 percent. Kengo also reined in the Bank of Zaire, the central bank, which was overflowing with counterfeit currency. At one time, two-thirds of the currency in circulation was counterfeit. And he'd slimmed down the civil service too. Like everyone else in the political class that had revolved around Mobutu, he expressed deep, grave concern about the moral fiber of a group that seemed to prosper despite the deepening crisis. Kengo and the Terminator seemed to be reading from the same playbook.

"All Zaireans have their part of responsibility—I, as many other Zaireans—first of all because none of us was courageous to denounce the situation and each of us wanted to adapt to that environment so that we could go on working. And also, the system: there was impunity in the system, and that led to loss of moral values."

I had to ask him flat out if he'd pocketed money through corrupt practices. Well, I didn't *have* to ask him, but I wanted to.

"I didn't come to enrich myself. I came to serve," he replied.

But what about his *maison blanc?* I could not resist that little jab. Kengo had begun construction of his very own White House, so called because its large front columns bore a resemblance to its namesake in Washington. It was high on a hill in the Binza section, haunt of the villas and mansions of the city's fat cats and location of Mobutu's Marble Palace. When people in Kinshasa spoke of Kengo, they ridiculed his gall, his nerve, to be building a huge villa while children all over the country went hungry. After all, a sumptuous prime minister's residence already existed along the river.

"People have talked so much of that house that I stopped building," said Kengo, with no hint of contrition in his voice. Criticism of his mansion was the problem, you see, not the mansion itself. The White House was never finished.

My favorite line on the subject of corruption came from a former prime minister, Mabi Mulumba, who at the time I met him was the head of the Zairean equivalent of the General Accounting Office. He could cite chapter and verse on the country's out-of-control debt, its steep decline in copper production, its rampant mismanagement. As we sat out at the Intercon's poolside café, my interview with him was perhaps the most factually informative and credible one I would ever have in Zaire. Until we got to the issue of corruption. Charmingly, as if gently scolding me for sounding naive, as if trying to help me avoid an embarrassing intellectual error, he said benevolently, "When you talk about corruption, this is journalist's language." But of course, that was not true. It wasn't just a linguistic creation of the press; it was a reality of ordinary Zairian life.

I went out one night, with Mbongo as an escort, to a nightclub in the Matonge section of La Cité. Mbongo had admonished that you couldn't really know Kinshasa without going to Matonge, where the famed figures of Zairian high-life and soukous music once were based. After roving streets that thumped with music, we ended up at the Club Mathé, where a trio of young men became instantly intrigued at having an American afoot in their haunt. Joining our small table beneath red and purple lights, they introduced themselves as Faust, Honoré, and Andre. More than their names, though, they wanted me to know that they were "new Zairian intellectuals" and they ticked off their educational credentials in psychology and architecture.

"Not because we want to boast of ourselves," Faust explained in English, shouting over the music, "but because intellectuals have a bad reputation outside Zaire."

"Moral prostitution for the sake of money," said Honoré, describing Zaire's elite.

These guys said they were different, younger, wiser than the political fat cats ruining their country. Their intellectualism wasn't about class, said Faust, for "Everybody understands that what is wrong with this country is Mobutu. Everybody lives the same reality."

"An intellectual is someone who struggles for life and tries to adapt himself," said Honoré.

No, Faust objected. "An intellectual is someone with an objective point of view. Even animals struggle for life."

And amongst themselves, they debated the difference between animal and man and the Mobutuist politics that had blurred the distinction.

6

Comrades and Capitalists

ORANGE FARM, SOUTH AFRICA, MARCH 1996

shack was a place called home for 8 million of South Africa's 40 million people. Two-by-fours, sheets of metal, plastic tarp to keep out rain, rocks to anchor the roof: that was a place called home. A toilet was a bucket in an outhouse, or maybe just a hole in the ground. In the two or three tiny rooms, electricity arrived as a novelty for some, but candlelight, for others, remained a staple.

By the spring of 1996, when I began writing regularly about the challenge this desperate poverty presented to Mandela's new government, the blight of apartheid's legacy continued to spread. The shacks sprawled across the salt flats outside Cape Town, out of sight from the picturesque Atlantic port city that tourists loved so much. Over on the Indian Ocean coast, the shacks climbed the lush hills above Durban that undulated with tropical greenery and dire poverty. On the arid high veld, or plain, around Jo'burg, shacks sprouted among the tall grass and brilliant wildflowers where homeless people staked their claim to a better life. And when dusk fell on the bleakness of all these shanties, a smoky haze hung beneath the purple sky as the poor lit their kerosene stoves and stoked their fires of coal in shack after shack after shack.

Each time I drove the Golden Highway south from Jo'burg and saw the many miles of shanties spread out before me, the new South Africa confounded me. What on earth was Mandela's government doing? The two years since apartheid's end wasn't very much time in which to replace all these shacks with proper housing, but surely the government ought to have been attacking the problem more urgently. Those shacks struck me as foreboding. I'd signed on to cover South Africa in the belief that Mandela's country would be different from any other in Africa, and to a large extent it was. But I'd seen enough of the continent by 1996 to know that South Africa's level of impoverishment—though not as deep as elsewhere—fit a continental pattern. I'd learned enough of postindependence Africa to realize that the promises of Mandela's new government were the same kinds of promises once made—and broken—by a host of other leaders in newly liberated African nations. And I'd seen elsewhere in Africa how the unifying vision of liberation struggles often splintered once liberation was achieved, with the agenda of the ruling elite not necessarily the same agenda as the ordinary people they claimed to represent.

I hoped South Africa would be different. But the shanties stood as the most glaring threat to the kind of South Africa Mandela hoped to create. I saw them as South Africa's crucible, the places that would truly test Mandela's African National Congress and its commitment to uplift the nation's poverty-stricken masses. Once upon a time, I believed that commitment was unwavering. But by 1996, with no dramatic movement forward, I was no longer certain.

I found myself tooling down a dirt road in a shack settlement called Orange Farm, about twenty-five miles down the Golden Highway, when I happened upon a small plot where a woman stood amid a pile of building materials. At the time, I was writing a piece about the government's struggle to provide housing, and as I pulled over to introduce myself, I imagined the wonderful little dispatch I would write about a happy South African family erecting its brand-new home. That's how badly I wanted to report proof of South Africa's promise. But the good news I thought I'd find on Sarah Makhubu's tiny plot turned out to be nothing of the sort. Instead, it was a story of the wind and the rain and the shack that came tumbling down while Sarah Makhubu waited for the day when her dream of a real house would come true. That's what it was like in Orange Farm. Just about everyone who settled there did so with the dream of a better life.

I'd been intrigued by Orange Farm's story since I first happened upon the place in 1990, when an anti-apartheid activist took me to the abandoned orange grove from which the town's eventual name would come. Back then, Orange Farm's settlers numbered a couple thousand, at most. They'd squatted on the farmland in the late 1980s, with the agreement of the old farm owner. Those early residents had been apartheid-era labor tenants on large white farms in the region, where their families had lived and worked in many cases for two or three generations in feudal-style servitude to their white bosses. But they'd been set adrift by a wave of farm evictions in apartheid's waning years. Such evictions were pervasive and ugly, often sparked by a white farmer's decision that elderly members of a particular black labor-tenant family were a drag on the productivity of the farm.

Those early Orange Farm settlers lived in tents. They gathered water from a stream and devised schoolrooms from the abandoned chicken coops and horse stables. With no basic infrastructure—no roads or water or anything—Orange Farm seemed but a transit point for people set adrift as the flotsam of apartheid. When I first saw the settlement, I assumed it would just fade away. But as apartheid reforms took hold in the 1990s, such as the repeal of the Group Areas Act and the Land Act that forbade black landownership in most areas, a torrent of new settlers converged on Orange Farm. They were escapees from the black "homelands," or they were rural workers in search of a city life, or families from the wretchedly crowded backyard shacks of Soweto, all in search of a plot of their own. Those early residents were squatters, basically, and so many people converged at the old farm that the apartheid government relented and put in some pit latrines, communal water taps, even a rudimentary grid of paved roads. The exploding population astonished me when I returned in 1996. It seemed unbelievable that in far less than a decade a settlement could mushroom to 250,000 people, which is what demographers conservatively estimated Orange Farm's population to be. And new people were arriving daily.

Officially, Orange Farm was called an informal settlement, meaning it had not been formally proclaimed a town. Except for a few gasoline stations and small roadside markets, there had been no commercial development. The place was so caught between the urban and the rural that it wasn't unusual to see minibus taxis vying with mule-drawn wagons along the town's secondary dirt roads. Old ways and new ways blended together as well: people visited the settlement's public health clinics, but they also frequented the diviners and herbalists they believed could cure their ills.

As in other desperately poor communities, there was plenty of crime in Orange Farm—robberies, faction fighting, murders—and a high incidence of child molestation and rape that mortified mothers and vexed sociologists. I knew one Orange Farm woman, desperately poor like most others, who told me with tears in her eyes that she was so afraid her daughters would be attacked that she'd scraped together money for target practice and planned to buy a gun. I tried to argue against the idea, but I knew my advice was hollow, considering that I was an outsider. And I knew the intensity of the crime threat firsthand, after a bout of frantic, evasive driving one day in Orange Farm to get away from a carload of guys chasing me through the dirt roads.

All those problems were troubling, which is why the many bright spots I encountered seemed so meaningful, so courageous. Small things caught my attention, like the tiny patches of immaculately tended lawn and short beds of blooming flowers that fronted many of the shacks. One woman landscaped her small yard with cacti and rocks and painted her metal shack a fashionable ocher. Self-help community upkeep projects had sprouted around the area, along with a campaign to change the community's name to Palestine, because the Orange Farm struggle had been bitter.

Orange Farm, despite its poverty, struck me as a place of heroes. People swam the tide of rising expectations, though some among them were drowning in disappointment. The settlement voted overwhelmingly for Mandela's ANC in the 1994 election, and its loyalties remained intact. A surprising number of people told me that their patience was generous. Mandela has only had a few years, they would say. Give him time. In their own small ways, in their own corner of the new South Africa, they tried to make their lives better the best way they knew how, against crushing odds.

In a nation where nearly half the black population lived below the poverty line and nearly 40 percent of working-age blacks were unemployed,

Orange Farm's straits were even worse. Some 60 percent of its people had no formal jobs. But the officially unemployed were busy working nonetheless in the informal, off-the-books economy. Sizakele Manabela, a handicapped woman, sewed dresses on order for the local women, since there were no clothing shops in Orange Farm. There was no butcher, either, so Princess Zililo, a mother of two boys, bought meat in Jo'burg and stored it in her freezer for resale in Orange Farm. Lucky Nokwe, a quiet but industrious mother of five, ran a day-care center in her backyard in an old, donated shipping container. Petrus Kodisang, a warm, funny man who lived with his wife and three children in a two-room shack, worked as a builder, though work for pay was hard to find. People made ends meet whichever way they could. One shack displayed lengths of toilet paper for sale.

"If ever there was money, Orange Farm can be all right," Kodisang said when I visited his shack one day. "We would be living in a small heaven." He mockingly called his home a "pigsty," but that certainly wasn't true. His tiny yard was green and well tended; his shack was tight for five, but spotless. Kodisang provided a cheerful warning as I probed him for details on how life was changing. In Orange Farm, he told me laughingly, "there are no oranges."

I thought of his witticism some weeks later as I listened to Sarah Makhubu, the woman at the building site, explain that she sure did wish she had a new house. Instead, she had the remnants of her old worn-out shack, scattered on the ground. The high winds that roared across the Orange Farm region had blown off her roof the night before and knocked down the rest of the structure. Makhubu and her three children had no shelter. A few friends were helping her to rebuild.

Makhubu, thirty-three, was one of the rare people I met in Orange Farm who had a formal job. She worked as a painter in a shipyard near Vanderbijlpark, an industrial town on the Vaal River to the south. But her monthly wage of about $156 wasn't enough to afford a proper house, so shack living was her only recourse. Like so many others in Orange Farm and elsewhere, Makhubu was of the impression that the houses Mandela promised were supposed to just materialize. Someone would build them, or bring them, or something. Housing was, after all, described in the new constitution as a basic human right. In Orange Farm, Makhubu pursued her dream by placing her name on a list of Orange Farm people in need of proper housing in the event of new construction in the area.

As we spoke in her yard under a sky still threatening rain, she told me excitedly, "I have a copy of my plan." Amid the waterlogged furniture, clothes, and pots and pans on the ground around her, she rummaged through a battered old trunk and pulled out a neatly folded piece of paper, wrapped in plastic. It was the floor plan of her dream home: two bedrooms, a kitchen, dining room, indoor toilet, even a garage for the car she did not yet have but believed she someday would.

While Makhubu daydreamed of her future, one of her friends, Selina Khanyile, planted herself firmly in the disappointment of the present. She took a break from hammering and heavy lifting, stretched her arms out wide, and said with heavy sarcasm, "We've seen no houses. Where are the houses?"

. . .

The people of Orange Farm weren't privy to the fractious economic debates raging within Mandela's ruling party. They could not know that a battle for the ideological soul of the new South Africa was brewing behind closed doors, pitting the interests of the country's white capitalists against the imperatives of the new black government, and the interests of the global free market against the needs of South Africa's poor. The compromises and contradictions of governing had muffled the ANC's once-soaring rhetoric of revolutionary change. The 1 million new houses that Mandela promised seemed nowhere on the horizon.

Thabo Mbeki, Mandela's deputy president, told me in an interview at his Pretoria office in 1995 that the pace of material "transformation" in South Africa was being slowed by the behind-the-scenes rewriting of policies that affected how the new government would roll out its vision. And white resistance to change also posed obstacles to the rewriting of laws and bureaucratic mandates. Despite the hay then being made in the press—meaning, at that time, the white press—about the snail's pace of change, Mbeki took the long view and predicted that the people would be patient.

"You are not going to get any mass rebellion on the part of the people on the issue of delivery," he predicted as he puffed on his trademark pipe. "What the people are expecting is movement forward." When they see houses being built, even if not in their own communities, "it then says to the people: this progress that has started will reach me next year."

But even as he spoke, people in search of the right to housing were growing restive. Thousands of people around the country had begun taking things into their own hands by invading land. They staked illegal claim to freshly demarcated plots in planned housing subdivisions, or they paid bribes to criminals running protection rackets to secure plots of land. I began to seriously wonder how long people would be patient with a government that, for whatever reason, backpedaled on its promises to the very people who put it in power.

"Transformation" proved tricky. The concept was fundamental to the government's broad postapartheid agenda, as described in the policy document that became its 1994 election platform, the Reconstruction and Development Program. Called the RDP, that document laid out a blueprint for a "fundamental restructuring to create a strong, dynamic and balanced economy that will eliminate the poverty created by apartheid" while at the same time committing the state to sound monetary policies and macroeconomic prudence. The RDP said Mandela's government would build a million houses in five years and extend electricity, health care, and schools to areas living without them. That transformation was needed was beyond debate, and Mandela, Mbeki, and a host of others bandied the term about all the time.

But who, precisely, would be transformed? That was the central question. Every sector of South Africa society made legitimate and aggressive demands on the new country, all of them in competition. The black masses, like the people of Orange Farm, demanded the houses and jobs the government had promised. The country's huge black labor federation, the Congress of South African Trade Unions, an ally of the government, demanded protections for the jobs of those already employed and ever-higher wages. Big business, which at that time meant white big business, wanted to break the hold of big labor on the economy and minimize the new black government's reach into the private sector. The International Monetary Fund (IMF), and the free-market consensus it represented, pressed Mandela to privatize state companies, shed jobs through downsizing, relax trade policies, and hold down government spending. Such moves became the preconditions sought by foreign investors as well, and South Africa sorely needed foreign investment. But some economists within the ANC pressed the government to spend its way out of the unemployment problem in the kind of New Deal recovery and reform program that U.S. President Franklin D. Roosevelt used to help quash the Great Depression.

In broad brush, the choices were these: Should the new economy attempt to grow or attempt to deliver? Should it place the global free market first or South Africa's own needs first? Yet even before tackling these choices, Mandela, Mbeki, and their team had to come to grips with the ugly fact of their inheritance: blacks held political power in South Africa, but the economy wasn't theirs at all.

The white minority of 12 percent owned 86 percent of the land and more than 90 percent of the wealth. Though blessed with vast reserves of gold, diamonds, and platinum as well as a relatively high level of industrialization and a sophisticated financial infrastructure, the South African economy that once served a white minority could in no way serve all of its people. Democracy made no sense with the vast majority of South Africans locked out of the economic game. It made no sense when half the black population lived in poverty and nearly half were unable to find formal work. And for those who did work, especially in the mines, factories, and commercial farms, their positions were often at the lowest levels of the economy and reminiscent of the labor exploitation under apartheid.

This was the apartheid legacy, and tackling it is where South Africa's next miracle would be needed. But how? It was a question that ANC members had asked themselves and debated for many years, and their ideas raced the length and breadth of the ideological spectrum even as the party prepared, in the early 1990s, to assume power. At times, key ANC spokesmen touted the kind of socialistic nationalization of big business that the movement had espoused for many years, despite its failures in other African countries. At other times, its key officials espoused the free-market capitalism pushed by

Washington and the World Bank. Historically, the ANC had always been all over the map with an eclectic mix of economic tendencies in what it called its "broad church" of different ideological strains. There were capitalists, African nationalists, socialists, and communists who'd nurtured their views while in jail, in exile, or in bush camps. They were men and women, comrades all, who'd been steeped in lofty, highly theoretical debates and dogmatisms about how best to uproot the legacy of apartheid and the white economic monopoly it created.

Mandela emerged from prison in 1990 still carrying the nationalization banner, if not waving it. A speech he delivered in 1990 in Jo'burg to South African business executives was the first of many by Mandela and other senior ANC leaders that sent scattershot mixed signals about their economic policies.

"We still believe that there must be further discussion of the issue of nationalization of assets that might at the moment be privately owned . . . It should not be ruled out of the court of discussion simply because of previous bad experience or because of a theological commitment to the principle of private property."

Such language set off alarm bells, both in South Africa and abroad, for Mandela seemed so out of step with the times. The Berlin Wall had fallen. States of the former Soviet bloc were hobbled. The Soviet-style socialism that third-world liberation movements once worshiped had proved a failure. Each time Mandela raised the issue of nationalization or "vigorous state intervention," stock prices tumbled on the Jo'burg Stock Exchange. South Africa's business leaders would in no way support a new government intent on seizing their assets or penetrating deeply into the economy with the might of the state. The battle was joined to sway the economic heart of the ANC.

Mandela's growing circle of corporate friends—including Harry Oppenheimer of the Anglo American mining conglomerate—began lobbying him and the ANC in the early 1990s to wake up to the realities of the new world they would inherit. The free market reigned far and wide, the capitalists argued, and to become a player in the global economic game it was necessary to bow to its dictates. Along with South Africa's own capitalists, the IMF, the World Bank, the U.S. government, and others put the hard press on the ANC not to marginalize itself with economic policies no longer suited to a changed world.

South Africa needed only look a wee bit north to see the results of post-colonial nationalization. Zambia under Kenneth Kaunda, another old man of Africa, entered independence back in 1964 by nationalizing copper mines with disastrous effect. Mismanagement, a plunge in the global copper price, and the wartime closure of the Benguela rail outlet to the Angolan port of Lobito had conspired to hobble the industry. By the 1990s, Kaunda's successor, a union leader and reformer named Fredrick Chiluba, was briskly attempting to sell off Zambia's crown jewels, the copper mines, to private owners who, he hoped, could return them to profitability.

Much of the continent began to view less state intervention, more fiscal discipline, and aggressive privatization as the way forward. To be frank, most of the continent was forced to see it that way. As their economies failed under the weight of the old state-driven and socialist model, many African nations sought IMF loans to keep their economies afloat. In return, the IMF demanded "structural adjustments" in African economies: spending cuts, lowered wages, reductions in civil service jobs, and privatization of state companies. Africa's plight was quite the contrast to the roaring economies of the high-growth "Asian tiger" countries, whose successes seemed to prove the genius of the global free market, for a time. Within the so-called Washington Consensus, as the free-market orthodoxy has been called, the quid pro quo facing South Africa seemed to be: open the economy, relax trade and monetary policy, cut government spending, and the global economy and investors will rush in to reward you. It was too good to be true, of course. But what choice did Mandela have? South Africa could not isolate itself from the global economy.

By 1991, Mandela's change of heart was audible. In a speech at the University of Pittsburgh, he turned 180 degrees from his words of a year earlier. "We are convinced that the private sector must and will play the central and decisive role in the struggle to achieve many of these objectives," he said. "Let me further make the point that the ANC has no ideological commitment to nationalization. This provision appears in policy documents of the ANC adopted more than thirty-five years ago, at a time when the word 'privatization' was not in anybody's dictionary."

The ANC's turn from left to right was astonishing. Once a champion of the masses, the ANC, in the space of a few years, became a champion of the market. Even a think tank established within the party became a casualty of the ideological shift. Established in the early 1990s, the Macro Economic Research Group (MERG) had crafted a broad economic policy framework heavy on state spending and intervention to expand the economy and fulfill the popular mandate for change. But at the same time, the RDP—crafted around the same time—pushed the ANC toward the ideological center with its calls for fiscal discipline and macroeconomic balance. And much to the chagrin of the increasingly marginalized left, the ANC even agreed, voluntarily, to the IMF's structural adjustment principles. As part of the multiparty transitional group that governed South Africa through its last year before the election, the ANC in 1993 signed on to the principles of fiscal discipline and free markets in exchange for an IMF loan to South Africa. To be fair, the ANC learned of some harsh economic realities in 1993 that no doubt were sobering. As a ruling party, the ANC would inherit budget deficits so high and state revenue so squeezed after four years of recession that it would be hard-pressed to do anything dramatic, like "transform" South African life.

After the 1994 election, a "democracy dividend" seemed to buoy the economy for a while. In 1995, South Africa registered its highest economic growth in a decade, a modest 3.5 percent. It created the welcome impression that Mandela's country was on an upward trajectory. Manufacturers were producing at a healthy clip. Foreign investment started flowing in. Ever so slowly, the government began its development program of home construction and electrification. At the other end of the black socioeconomic spectrum, a new class of "comrade capitalists" emerged as the government pushed to integrate the commanding heights of the economy and break up the huge monopolies that had fed on one another during the cloistered years of South Africa's bunker state.

Cyril Ramaphosa was the most prominent of the new capitalists who led the way toward "black empowerment," another of those promising slogans that disguised their true complexity. Ramaphosa was the former leader of the National Union of Mineworkers who became secretary-general of the ANC in the early 1990s, then president of the constitutional assembly after the democratic transition. In 1996, the ANC redeployed him to the private sector. He became a principal in New Africa Investments Ltd. (NAIL), one of two black empowerment consortia that combined to become shareholding partners with the Anglo American Corporation in controlling one of Anglo's holding companies, the Johnnies Industrial Corporation, with interests in the automotive, beverage, tourism, and publishing industries. The deal represented a significant first step forward for black ownership in the economic big leagues. But with so many of the black participants coming to the table with little capital of their own, these empowerment deals were often so highly leveraged that it would take years before the debts were paid off and financial benefits started to flow. But empowerment had to happen. The new government had to break up the exclusive white control of the economy and foster integration. These empowerment deals, said Ramaphosa, were just a start.

"This deal must be seen as a deal that enables people to have a springboard," Ramaphosa told me when we spoke in 1996. "Empowerment was never thought to be an event. It is a process."

Suddenly, with the likes of Ramaphosa now situated in the economic big leagues and a rush of new comrades-turned-capitalists negotiating similar deals, commentators both black and white criticized black empowerment as a vehicle for enriching the few while creating few benefits for the many. The criticism was unfair, though underpinned with a kernel of truth. Black control of huge corporations did not automatically create jobs or raise wages. To the contrary. South Africa's corporations, whether run by blacks or whites, had to downsize and restructure to remain profitable. The issue was green, not black or white. At a breakfast meeting he held with foreign correspondents in 1996 in Jo'burg, another key figure in the Johnnies deal, Nthato Motlana, the head of NAIL and Mandela's former physician, said black empowerment means "affluence will at least become multiracial. This does not mean poverty will disappear."

So while the thin ranks of the new black capitalists began to grow with

much media and political acclaim, the other, less fortunate South Africa remained stuck. In fact, joblessness actually continued to grow. The market
could not absorb the young adults reaching working age. And the economy,
by 1996, began to slow. At the same time, the gold price fell to its lowest level
ever, hitting a sector of the economy that accounted for about a third of export revenue. Emerging market woes around the world were also hitting
South Africa, whose currency, the rand, lost 20 percent of its value in 1996
alone. The domestic private sector wasn't rushing to invest, for it remained
skeptical about the ANC's ideological bent and its administrative acumen,
not to mention the ongoing currents of racial conflict between the white-
minority interests represented in the industrial economy and the black-
majority interests of the new government.

Perhaps the harshest reality check of all, for the ANC, was that direct
foreign investment did not pour in as the ANC had expected and as its foreign partners once seemed to pledge. The investment that did stream in,
while substantial compared to the apartheid years, tended not to create jobs.
Multinationals who'd divested to protest apartheid rushed to relink with
their old South African subsidiaries, or they invested in new machines and
equipment, not labor-intensive enterprises. The strength of organized labor
gave them pause, for South Africa continued to be a land of strikes and high
wage demands.

So new and so full of promise, South Africa's democracy had landed in a
vicious cycle. Without new jobs, there could be no social and economic stability. Without stability, there could be no investor confidence, domestic or
foreign. And if investors saw no reason to pour money into the economy,
South Africa would witness the unraveling of what could have been a fabulous African development story.

By early 1996, Mandela stated the obvious. Considering what it had to
work with inside the country and the obstacles that would bear down on it
from the global economy, the new government discovered it had punched
above its weight with its program to overhaul social and economic life in
South Africa. Ever the cheerleader for South Africa's progress, even Mandela
felt compelled to warn Parliament that things weren't working.

"The potential for economic growth and development is better than in many decades," Mandela told the nation's legislators. "But let us be brutally frank. Despite the welcome rate of growth, very few jobs have been created. In fact, against the backdrop of new entrants into the job market, there has been a shrinkage in opportunities. We need a national vision to lift us out of this quagmire."

MERG had been cast aside. The RDP also bit the dust, effectively, when Mandela abolished the cabinet ministry devoted to reconstruction and development. In its place, Mbeki, the deputy president, ushered in a new government policy called GEAR, or Growth, Employment and Redistribution. GEAR signaled a seeming end to all economic ambiguity. This would be the ANC's policy, Mbeki said in no uncertain terms. The market would rule, under GEAR. Fiscal discipline and deficit reduction would become more stringent, with less government intervention in the economy. Privatization would unfold faster. The labor market would become more flexible, meaning wages would have to fall. Trade barriers would be reduced, making it easier for foreigners to do business with South Africa. And all of this would greatly please the global market, so the theory said. Investment would pour in and the economy would expand rapidly, with redistribution of wealth a natural outcome. Or so the theory said.

"We do not subscribe to the notion that growth on its own can rectify the backlogs of apartheid in a mysterious trickle-down fashion," Mandela had said in that February parliamentary speech. But with GEAR, the trickle-down seemed to me to be all that South Africa's poor would see, for a while. The comrades had effectively become the capitalists! And as could be expected, GEAR outraged the leftist labor wing of the ANC, once so powerful in the movement. Privatization and labor market flexibility were direct assaults on the power of organized labor, which had already flexed its postapartheid muscle with a series of relatively small strikes. But even capitalists raised their eyebrows. GEAR seemed a policy more suited for a normalized economy, not an economy as skewed, unhealthy, and imbalanced as South Africa's. In relying on market forces to solve South Africa's problems, the ANC ran the risk of locking in its country's inequalities. Like the old adage says: money goes where money is. And very little seemed destined for development of the poor. Whether intentionally or not, the ANC's new economic orthodoxy seemed to betray its grand promises.

* * *

Ismael Mkhabela of the National Housing Board could have been describing the whole governing enterprise when he said, about housing, "It's one thing to form a vision. But to translate it into projects and outcomes, it's another." That was an elegant way of saying, in effect, that the housing revolution had fizzled. After two years of false starts, of scandals in housing contracting procedures, of homeless people squatting on land in ever-greater numbers, even Mandela admitted that housing policy was "bedeviled," as he put it to Parliament: "It is a matter of common knowledge, painfully common to those without housing, that many constraints have bedeviled the proper implementation of this program."

Budgets were too tight in the provinces. Inexperienced new bureaucrats were feeling their way through to a brand-new policy. On the ground, the problems were even uglier. When land was cleared for new projects, squatters descended on the sites, illegally claiming plots. Police had to use force to run them off, causing ugly scenes reminiscent of the old apartheid forced removals. Planners, builders, banks, had to be brought on board with new housing policies, but all were loath to carry undue financial burdens in the unprofitable low-end housing market. The "new patriotism" that Mandela tried to foster did not extend to changing business as usual, as far as some were concerned.

"If it's in the bill of rights that housing is a basic right, that's the government's responsibility," Lance Edmonds of the Council of Southern African Bankers told me. "Banks cannot lend to people who cannot afford to pay." In one of its many moves to get the housing program restarted, the government set up indemnity funds to lure banks into low-end finance by protecting them against potential losses.

The promised flood of new housing became a drip—steady, but a drip nonetheless. Officials stopped talking about building 1 million houses in five years. Instead, they talked of creating "housing opportunities." And ever so slowly and steadily, they did. Over time, driving the Golden Highway, I could see new developments of small starter homes. The government granted subsidies to help individual families build these homes, or to upgrade existing homes, or to help them purchase a home in housing developments. But the basic new-home subsidy was so low that it barely covered the cost of a plot on which to build a shack. Two-by-fours, sheets of metal, tarp to protect against rain, and rocks to anchor the roof against the wind: that, still, was a place called home, a democratic shack in the new South Africa.

Truth and Chains

he curtains hung deep red, as red as fresh, flowing blood. I cannot think back to that day inside a Victorian-era chamber in the coastal town of East London without seeing that color. A bloody sepia tone washes over my memory. There were many widows present that day. They were dignified in their humility. They clutched tissues to dab their eyes. They held the hands of their relatives. There were grannies in head wraps and shawls, yellows and blues, bent but not bowed by what had been done to their families. There were fatherless children, orphans of murder; and broken men, victims of torture. There were counselors to console the mournful. There were translators arrayed in soundproof booths to broadcast the testimony into South Africa's many languages. And banks of television cameras focused in tight on the faces of the forlorn, recording the grimaces and the tears.

A banner hung across the stage of the cavernous East London town hall that April day of 1996. It read, "Healing Our Past," as if this public spectacle, unprecedented in the entire world, could be reduced to a slogan. Beneath that banner stood Desmond Tutu, the retired Anglican archbishop, wearing his familiar vestments of flowing magenta. He lit a candle in honor of the many, many dead. And then he prayed that day in East London. He prayed that the Truth and Reconciliation Commission (TRC) he now led would achieve its distant goals.

"O God of justice, mercy, and peace. We long to put behind us all the pain and division of apartheid together with all the violence which ravaged our communities in its name . . . We pray that all those people who have been injured in either body or spirit may receive healing through the work of the commission . . . We pray, too, for those who may be found to have committed these crimes against their fellow human beings, that they may come to repentance and confess their guilt to almighty God and that they, too, might become recipients of your divine mercy and forgiveness."

With that simple prayer, for survivors and killers alike, Tutu opened the first series of public hearings in what would be a long and traumatic national journey toward a new truth. It would become such a routine part of daily life—its broadcasts, its shocking revelations—that it rose as a national touchstone. But in what would become the disturbing pattern in this national exercise in catharsis, few whites were in attendance that day in East London, as if apartheid happened to somebody else and had little to do with them. That's the kind of psychic distance that white South Africans seemed to put between themselves and the horrors committed in their name: I didn't do it; I didn't even know it was happening. South Africa was so haunted, so divided, so brittle, that the gathering inside the town hall felt like an exorcism. That vast chamber, with its tall windows, soft light, and somber dark wood, filled up quickly with terrifying descriptions of hacked bodies, tortured genitals, burned flesh; mothers with dead sons, daughters with disappeared fathers, and the broken hearts of widows forever unable to heal.

The chamber fell silent. The widows leaned in toward their microphones. What courage it took for them to do this, to publicly take themselves back to that terrible time a decade ago, in June of 1985, when their husbands disappeared from the face of the earth. Their words speak for themselves, now part of South Africa's new history.

Nombuyiselo Mhlauli, a teacher, a mother of two: *"So I kept waiting for him, expecting him and he never turned up on Thursday. And then on Friday I saw a newspaper. I read this article; that these people were actually missing. But I thought to myself that they must be detained."*

Detention had happened so often. Her husband, Sicelo Mhlauli, and Matthew Goniwe, Fort Calata, and Sparrow Mkhonto were antiapartheid organizers from the town of Cradock. Apartheid police routinely hounded them and hauled them off to jail. The wives had come to expect it. So in the belief that the men had been detained yet again, Mrs. Mhlauli focused on taking her husband some comfort.

Mrs. Mhlauli: "*Yes, I thought that they are definitely in jail. So what I needed to do now was go and get him a warm tracksuit and a pair of training shoes and warm shirts, too. So I dashed into town immediately to get those things.*"

Nomonde Calata, a hospital worker, a mother of three: "*I was awake, suffering from insomnia. When I looked out, there was a Casspir [police combat vehicle] and vans. Not a single car moved around as they usually did. This was also an indication that something was wrong. I had this premonition. And I was very expectant [pregnant] at the time . . . We were really in the dark. We slept uneasily on Friday as we did not know what happened to our husbands. Usually the Herald [newspaper] was delivered at home . . . During the time that it was delivered, I looked at the [Saturday] headlines and one of the children said that he could see that his father's car was shown in the paper as being burned. At that moment, I was trembling, because I was afraid what might have happened to my husband, because I wondered: if his car is burned like this, what might have happened to him? . . . After a few hours, some friends came in and took me and said I must go to Nyami [Nyameka Goniwe, widow of one of the disappeared], who was always supportive. I was still twenty at the time and I could not handle this. When we got to Nyami's place, Nyami was crying terribly.*"

Mrs. Calata's voice fell silent. Her words died, strangled by her sobs. Her body suddenly wrenched backward. A piercing wail rose from her mouth, the sound of purest pain. It seemed to rise and hover. It filled the chamber like a presence. Heads could only bow. Hands could only wipe eyes. Sobs gurgled up and were muffled. Tutu had said the pain would be cleansing. And here it was. I almost gagged. I could barely hold back the huge lump in my throat. A foreigner who had not ever known such pain, I felt overcome by just witnessing it. I took quiet deep breaths and stared straight ahead. I looked away from Mrs. Calata. I stared at those curtains, the color of blood.

Counselors embraced Mrs. Calata and consoled her. During the pause, the audience softly sang in Xhosa. It was a mournful song of the struggle. "Senzenina? Senzenina?" "What have we done? What have we done? Our only sin is the color of our skin."

Mrs. Mhlauli: *"When I got back home, I found many people there. When there is a reverend and people who pray, you know immediately that something terrible has happened. So I fainted. And when I came to, I was given the bad tidings that they have not come back, but also that their bodies have been found."*

A fisherman discovered the men from the town of Cradock, known in death as the Cradock 4. The police assassins who murdered them also mutilated and burned them, then dumped their remains along the sand dunes of the eastern Cape's Indian Ocean coast, yet another batch of corpses shrouded by lies as thick as fog from the sea.

"Go well, peacemakers," Victoria Mxenge, a human rights lawyer, said at the heroes' funeral of the Cradock 4 several days after their death. "Tell your great-grandfathers we are coming." Two weeks later, assassins suspected to be police murdered Victoria Mxenge, too, just as they would murder her husband, Griffiths Mxenge, also a "struggle" lawyer, in 1991. The great-grandfathers received much company.

Mrs. Mhlauli: *"I read the postmortem documents. Reading them, I was really worried, because it has to explain in detail what happened. I read through and came to understand that he had many wounds. In the upper abdomen were five wounds. These wounds indicated that different weapons were used to stab him, or a group of people stabbed him. In the lower part, he also had wounds. But the wounds in total were forty-three. One other thing that we understood: they poured acid on his face. After that, they chopped off his right hand, just below the wrist. I do not know what they did with that hand."*

Unfortunate visitors to police torture chambers believed they saw the hand there. Members of the police "security branch" based in Port Elizabeth kept a human hand in a jar filled with liquid and showed it to targets of interrogation, a torture victim told the TRC. These police were feared throughout the eastern Cape region. They were specially trained to crush black dissent. Some came from the dreaded Koevoet (Crowbar) police counterinsurgency unit that killed and plundered in neighboring Namibia under South African occupation in the 1970s and '80s. To apartheid's leaders, the security branch police were loyal, effective combatants against the black "terrorist" threat. To blacks, they were just cold-blooded killers. In the mid-1980s, they worked at full throttle, as the confessions they submitted to the TRC would reveal. In May 1985, before they killed the Cradock 4, some of the same police hacked and burned another group of activists: Sipho Hashe, Qaqawuli Godolozi, and Champion Galela, known in death as the Pebco 3.

Some of the most brutal of these police were based down the coast from East London, at the industrial city of Port Elizabeth. Their offices, the places where they tortured, weren't hidden away, but sat right there in the heart of downtown, inside the high-rise Sanlam Centre owned by a large Afrikaner insurance firm of that name. The police took high-priority activists to room 619, the "room of truth." Steve Biko was its most famous visitor. The powerful Black Consciousness Movement leader died from a severe pounding of the head he received in that room in 1977. The security police had hosepipes for beatings, broomsticks for torture, shackles for control, and that hand floating inside a jar.

Mrs. Mhlauli heard of this hand. She became convinced it belonged to her husband. She told the TRC she wanted truth, she wanted justice, and to make her husband whole.

Mrs. Mhlauli: "*I would gladly love to know the murderers of my husband, and they should also come to the fore and tell their story and the reason why they committed such brutal actions. And I think in order to be able to achieve what we are all hoping for, justice should prevail. The law should take its course . . .*

"*Even if I say those people should be given amnesty, it won't return my husband. But that hand. We still want it. We know we have buried him but, really, to have that hand which is said to be in a bottle in Port Elizabeth. We would like to get the hand.*"

● ● ●

Nearly three hundred activists were assassinated during the last three decades of apartheid, according to South Africa's Human Rights Committee. That number does not include the thousands of people mowed down during protest marches, ambushed, abducted at roadblocks, blown to smithereens in bombings, or simply found in the tall grass of a hushed field of wildflowers with a bullet in the back of the head. At least seventy people died in police detention during that terrible three-decade period when more than eighty thousand men, women, children, even the elderly, were packed into jails and held without trial. Thousands of them were tortured. With electrodes, they were shocked. With wet bags, they were suffocated. With fists and pipes, they were beaten. Or with a more passive evil, they were driven to distraction, like the women held in solitary confinement and denied any hygiene, not even when bugs crawled on them, not even when they menstruated. There were also the rapes.

The people who did these terrible things by and large walked free. Not jailed, not even accused, perhaps sometimes tortured in their own souls, they blended into the woodwork of the new South Africa. Some were in the new police force and the newly reconstituted military. Some were in civilian clothes and retired. Their secrets, and the trail of pain that haunted the nation, constituted a menace to the new democracy.

Perhaps the clerk at the bank was a former soldier who blew up bases of the exiled activists. Or maybe the man in line in front of you at the hypermarket was a former cop who'd opened fire on unarmed civilian protesters at Sharpeville or Sebokeng or Soweto. Or maybe a seemingly normal business had once been a front company for old covert programs, like the state-sanctioned chemical and biological weapons project whose scientists experimented with killing agents that were sometimes deployed in the war against black liberation: anthrax-tainted chocolates, botulism-laced candies, whiskey spiked with toxic herbicide. The research into compounds for making black women infertile did not succeed.

After the World War II defeat of Nazi Germany, thousands of Nazi torturers and murderers who killed millions of Jews were tried as war criminals at Nuremberg. After the defeat of the *génocidaires* who slaughtered hundreds of thousands of Tutsis in Rwanda, many of the suspected killers were rounded up and imprisoned to face justice for the genocide. But after apartheid, no such "victor's justice" would be applied. There was no outright victor.

Rather, the conflict of the apartheid years produced a stalemate that led to a negotiated but fragile peace based on compromises from both sides. And one of the key accommodations that Mandela wisely made—and that he was forced to make—was that witch-hunts and show trials would not be held in South Africa. Instead, the ANC began in the early 1990s to cobble together a middle road between the extremes of pure retribution and pure forgetting. Though many in the ANC and other black groups wanted to see their apartheid tormentors in the dock or in jail, such was the array of forces at apartheid's end that judicial retribution by the black majority would have unleashed the wrath of the white-minority troops and completely derailed the negotiated end to apartheid.

Odd how it all turned out. Justice had been one of the main goals of the campaign against apartheid. And yet justice turned out to be almost impossible to apply to those who deserved it most. To pursue a kind of victor's justice in South Africa, Tutu told me, would have left South Africa with "justice and ashes." Still, someone would have to account for the past, at the least to undo the lies and uncover what had been covered up. Perpetrators of injustice would have to somehow be revealed so that the nation could find its truth and, theoretically, be made free. Too many people needed to know what really happened to their loved ones. Though black South Africans had lived with tragedy for some years, even become all too familiar with trauma, many still did not have the answers that would bring closure to their grieving.

Said Tutu: "They are aware that basically it was the members of the security forces. But who did what? Why? And the nation wants to know. You can't just sweep it under the carpet, because it will fester . . . Most of the people are saying what they do want is to know who did what and why."

So a new formula had to be found, a new way to reconcile South Africa's victims with their victimizers and build a bridge between past and present. The idea for the Truth and Reconciliation Commission, enshrined in South African law in 1995, emerged from the negotiations in the early 1990s between Mandela's ANC and de Klerk's government. Numerous international human rights experts offered their assistance to the endeavor, and South Africa also drew from the experiences of other commissions around the world, of which there have been many. But none were so muscular as South Africa's.

The TRC's proceedings were held in public, not shrouded in secrecy. Though it was not a judicial body, its official investigations were backed by the power to subpoena. It did not offer blanket amnesties, as had been the South American model. Instead, TRC amnesties came with strings attached: individual perpetrators had to make full disclosure of their crimes and convince the commission that deeds were done for the political ends that defined the antagonists during the apartheid years.

And human rights abuses committed on all sides of the apartheid-era conflict would be examined. That the United Nations General Assembly once called apartheid a "crime against humanity" did not mean the anti-apartheid liberation movements would escape the scrutiny of the TRC. Abuses committed by Mandela's ANC and other liberation groups were also probed, much to the dismay of many party leaders. The TRC itself could not prosecute; that was left to the criminal justice system, which operated on a separate track. But the fact that several prosecutorial probes of apartheid-era hit men were under way when the TRC was launched certainly helped to compel perpetrators to confess to the TRC and seek amnesty.

The ultimate message that the TRC intended to send to South Africans was this: The apartheid battles happened. They were horrible. We have revealed as much as could possibly be found about who committed atrocities and who suffered. The victims of those atrocities have been recognized and repaired to the extent possible by a government that now represents them. The perpetrators have confessed their brutality; some have been granted amnesty from prosecution in exchange for their truth. Others not granted amnesty or who did not even seek it may be referred for potential prosecution, as the evidence merits. Now let us write a new history of our nation's truth and then go forward as one people, reconciled and made whole.

It was an ambitious appeal to South Africa's better nature, to prompt people to rise above their base instincts, to put aside factional interests. The composition of the TRC itself attempted to put forward an example of reconciliation. It was multiethnic, and included lawyers as well as members of the clergy, like Tutu, the former Anglican archbishop. Though Tutu's spiritualism infused the TRC proceedings with a certain degree of religiosity, the commission was strictly a secular effort charged with a gargantuan task: to attempt to foster a sense of the importance of reconciliation between South Africa's divided peoples. Such a new national ethos would help the country move forward with a common sense of purpose.

But the theory of the TRC assumed that South Africans wanted to unite behind a national vision, which they did not. It assumed they shared an understanding of the importance of reconciliation, which they did not. And it assumed that they believed that telling the truth was important for the task of healing, even that healing itself was necessary. Perhaps I was too cynical, but my experiences in South Africa told me that its citizens shared few of these goals, especially across color lines. Perhaps the TRC could ultimately foster all these values and truly be an instrument for national unity. But it would be a long time coming. Quite frankly, I was a skeptic. It seemed to me that at least some of the most senior apartheid-era political and security leaders ought to be held legally accountable. The idea of a TRC was laudable, but it also happened to betray the quest for justice for which so many people had fought. It seemed a slap at the memories of those who had died.

I caught up with Tutu before the launch of the April 1996 hearings. I needed to interview him for a TRC preview I was writing, but I also needed to come to grips with the process personally. How were the victims of apartheid-era violence supposed to accept their abusers' freedom, if that came to pass? It seemed a surefire method for injecting more bitterness into a brittle society. Tutu's schedule was packed, so we ended up conducting the interview while riding in his chauffeur-driven car, between engagements.

I very much believed Tutu was almost destined to lead the truth-telling effort. Even more than Mandela, Tutu was the kind of figure who appealed to all people on a human level. He was a humanist, really, who believed that even the most wayward souls, the most evil people, were capable of redemption and could not be cast aside. That was *ubuntu*, the humanistic African view of life I'd encountered in my travels and discussions with ordinary people about their ability to move forward in life without harboring hate against those who had done them wrong. *Ubuntu* defines the essence of African communalism. One's humanity, according to *ubuntu*, resides in one's engagement with others. For many Africans, it informs the fundamental connectedness of community life. Seen through the lens of *ubuntu*, reconciliation and forgiveness seemed totally possible. Fused with his Anglican faith, *ubuntu* led Tutu to believe in ever-new beginnings.

Something about Tutu was utterly convincing. Maybe I perceived him this way because I envied the intensity of his faith. But his personal aspect, too, seemed enchanting, with his long magenta robes, his singsong cadence and cheerful chortle, always accompanied by grand gestures with those knobby hands. He's a small man, and yet he towered above so many. During the campaign against apartheid, he wore his moral righteousness like a shield and used his faith as his only weapon.

Rising through the ranks of the Anglican Church in South Africa, in which he'd ultimately become its archbishop and official leader, Tutu rallied the church in defense of human rights throughout the last decades of apartheid. He campaigned against state violence and on occasion, during protest marches, braved tear gas and arrest. Abroad, he crusaded for international sanctions to punish the apartheid state, which he called "evil and unChristian." In 1984, he won the Nobel Peace Prize. Like no other figure (especially since Mandela was silenced and in prison at the time), Tutu riled the Afrikaners who supported apartheid. He could claim a true morality, not the false righteousness of those apartheid supporters who claimed divine justification for their actions.

His belief in nonviolence set him apart from the ANC, which sanctioned violence in the liberation struggle, through MK and other groups. Tutu even faced down the dreaded necklace, the form of death in which a tire is placed around the victim's neck and set afire. For a time in the 1980s, it was the preferred method that street fighters in the antiapartheid campaign used to kill suspected sellouts or spies. Following the funeral of a fallen antiapartheid activist in the 1980s, Tutu stepped in, literally, to stop a bloodthirsty crowd about to commit a necklacing.

But leading the TRC would prove to be a challenge of a far different level of difficulty and delicacy. The risks were great, the stakes quite high. And Tutu knew this better than anyone. It could turn out, he told me, that few perpetrators would come forward to reveal their truth and seek amnesty. It could turn out that Afrikaners would feel stigmatized and alienated because of the revelations that would emerge about their old state. It could turn out that blacks would walk away from the process and decide reconciliation could not be achieved. But the risks had to be taken.

"It's not to say this is a foolproof scheme. It could go wrong. But on the basis of *ubuntu*, you have to forgive," he told me that day in his car.

Tutu truly hoped to see some of the apartheid killers emerge as men of remorse and contrition. And some would. But many, if not most, would not. They would merely tell whom they killed, how they killed, and why they killed and hope the revelations were enough to secure amnesty. They did not have to show any remorse. They did not have to say they were sorry. This, to me, was among the fatal flaws of the reconciliation process. Even if perpetrators didn't feel sorry, couldn't they have been compelled to articulate precisely what they felt about their crime as part of their bid for amnesty? But they didn't. And without contrition by perpetrators, reconciliation would become a one-way street: of victims forgiving their abusers, while those abusers didn't even see a need to receive forgiveness. But the TRC wasn't about religious concepts of confession and forgiveness. It was about the politics and practicalities of the times in which it was born. Even Tutu admitted that this was a hard thing to bear once he realized that the TRC made no provision for remorse.

"When you apply for amnesty, there is no requirement for you to say I am sorry. It hit all of us kind of in the solar plexus," he said of the commission's realization that regret was not required. "But that's the cost. That is part of the price that had to be paid for the [negotiated] settlement."

Tutu knew quite well that within black South Africa there was a need for justice in the broad sense, of seeing perpetrators held accountable in some way. By forcing perpetrators to confess their crimes publicly in exchange for amnesty, Tutu said, society would be extracting a price for their deeds, at least in a moral way. The perpetrators would be shamed. "Suppose your family didn't know you were a perpetrator and suddenly your child, your wife know that you are a murderer?"

I suppose that would be traumatic. But that's not quite justice.

• • •

JOHANNESBURG

As we entered a small café at Jo'burg International Airport, heads turned. I felt honored to be walking with her. A few patrons whispered their recognition. "It's Mrs. Biko," I could hear them say softly as they watched Nontsikelelo Biko, the late Steve Biko's widow, move through the room.

We had never met. I'd seen her only on television and read of her in papers and books. I had long admired her slain husband and his Black Consciousness Movement of the 1970s, and I admired the quiet, steely dignity of this widow who'd had to endure the pain of Biko's death and the cover-up that followed. I met many women whose husbands or sons had been martyred, and they often carried themselves with a restrained defiance, as if telling the world that even the most violent storms could neither break them nor drive them insane. Mrs. Biko, a nurse in the small city of King William's Town on the Eastern Cape Province coast, struck me that way too.

But she was different from many widows, in that she did not intend to sit before the world and plead for help in finding the truth of her husband's death. The Biko family already knew the truth. They knew the group of men who beat Biko. They knew where it happened. To an extent, they knew how. And they could not accept that no one would be held accountable for the crime. The Bikos wanted what so many South Africans wanted but were told they could not have. They wanted justice.

Biko's 1977 murder remained one of the most bitterly contested cases in the country, followed closely abroad as well. Biko had been a charismatic man, struck with the genius of racial insight and a charismatic power. He wasn't specifically antiwhite; in fact, he made good friends with at least one white journalist of the day, the crusading writer Donald Woods, who would play a pivotal role in uncovering the truth of events to come. Biko was, rather, completely pro-black. He espoused physical and psychological liberation. The black man, he believed, had to remove white supremacy from his mind as well as from his land. His philosophies fired a generation of antiapartheid fighters, such as those who marched and died in Soweto in 1976. (And twenty years after his death, black consciousness remained a main current in South African politics and society.)

But his following was too great, his philosophy too strong. The apartheid regime decided to break him. The security forces tailed him. They threw up a roadblock to stop him one night near Port Elizabeth in August 1977 and detained both him and a colleague, Peter Jones. They shoved Biko into jail, took his clothing, and held him for two weeks, naked. Then they transferred him to Sanlam, to the "room of truth."

Precisely what happened inside that room—who specifically hit him and with what—remains a mystery to this day. There were five white security branch cops against one black man they believed to be arrogant and aggressive and in need of a lesson. They would testify later to the TRC about the chain of events that led to the melee that left Biko a virtual vegetable: When Biko sat, they ordered him to stand. One of the cops yanked him up by his shirt. And then the beating began. Biko ended up dazed, virtually unconscious, and unable to speak. They chained him to a metal door grille, in the crucifix position, and left him there for several hours. They denied him medical care even when the signs of incapacitation were clear. He blabbered and foamed at the mouth. He wet himself and could not walk. Finally, days later, they loaded him into the back of a Land Rover for a six-hundred-mile drive up to Pretoria. There he died, on the cold floor of a prison cell, from neurological damage from a massive blow that caused his brain to shunt from side to side in his skull and come loose.

Woods, Biko's friend and admirer, hounded the police and kept the killing in the news. In the schizophrenic old South African way, the same society known for its systematic violence also made quite an efficient show of investigating itself. The Afrikaner legal establishment loved "commissions of inquiry" and "inquests" that seemed never to uncover any truth. And so it was with Biko's death. Three inquests were held, and each was a whitewash. The officers involved in Biko's "interrogation" said it was all an accident. The inquests, predictably, found no one to blame. Now, twenty years later, the killers were confessing and taking responsibility. They wanted amnesty from the TRC, for assault and culpable homicide. Should they win, it would mean they could never be charged criminally or civilly for Biko's death. Not ever.

And so Nontsikelelo Biko launched a quiet crusade to stop them. She went head-to-head with the TRC and placed herself fully in opposition to the kind of reconciliation being pushed by Mandela and Tutu. Along with the family of Victoria and Griffiths Mxenge, the slain lawyers, the Biko family took its case to South Africa's Constitutional Court, the nation's highest judicial body. They asked the court to declare the TRC's amnesty provisions unconstitutional because they foreclosed their right to pursue civil or criminal justice against the killers.

When I met Mrs. Biko that day at Jo'burg International, Mhleli Mxenge, brother of Griffiths, was with her. They'd flown in for a television appearance. Their challenge to the TRC was big news. The Mxenge and Biko families, like countless others, were traumatized people, but also clear-thinking. For them, the courts were the proper venue for handling the crimes done to their families, not the hearings of healing offered by the TRC. Crowded around a small table at the airport café, we leaned in close to hear each other over the din. In an odd way, I felt like a coconspirator. I sympathized with their position. Justice is what black people in South Africa had been denied for centuries. It seemed only natural that people should want it now. And Mrs. Biko felt she was speaking up for a silent segment of society that, like her, was not satisfied with the free pass that killers were being offered.

"There are so many others who are in my position. Some of us know the truth. Some of us have been through inquest proceedings," she said quietly, calmly. "They say we must reconcile. But I don't see any reconciliation without justice." She wanted a trial. She wanted the killers prosecuted. "I want it to be reopened in court. I'm not prepared to go and sit with the [truth] commission and listen to lies."

Mxenge brought it all into focus. The TRC had become an escape hatch for killers, a way to evade justice. "What we hate about it is it's being used by criminals who were supposed to be prosecuted long ago," he said.

The Bikos and Mxenges felt betrayed. Mxenge recounted what Tutu had said those many years ago at Griffiths Mxenge's funeral. It was a promise, the promise of freedom, and the thing for which so many had fought.

"He preached about justice," Mxenge said sadly, "reassuring us that when the government of the people took over, justice will be done."

• • •

NEW BRIGHTON

George Bizos: Did you or did you not assault the late Mr. Biko?
Harold Snyman: I did not assault him, Your Honor.

South Africa's most famous human rights lawyer, Bizos rarely looked directly at Snyman, a retired police major. That was not Bizos's style. Instead, Bizos glared out over the audience from the stage of a community hall in New Brighton during the September 1997 hearings into Biko's death while he hammered away in a voice familiar to all South Africans. Syrupy thick with sarcasm, that voice sounded to me like the voice of justice bearing down on the men who wanted amnesty for killing Biko. Along with Snyman, they were Daniel Siebert, Gideon Nieuwoudt, Johannes Beneke, and Rubin Marx.

The Bikos had lost their court bid to squash amnesty. They'd ended up here inside a community hall in New Brighton, a town just outside Port Elizabeth, fighting against the amnesties that Biko's killers were seeking. The five former police security branch members had confessed for Biko's death and asked the TRC for amnesty. These hearings would decide if they'd get it. It was a far cry from a court of law, but at least the Bikos had Bizos on their side.

The old apartheid security apparatus detested Bizos. A squat, jowly, white-haired Greek–South African human rights lawyer, Bizos's withering cross-examinations and righteous indignation elevated him to a heroic status. He'd argued on behalf of the Biko family in the earlier inquests, the whitewashes, and he'd been involved in just about every major human rights case in South Africa for the past thirty-five years, including the 1963–64 trial of Mandela and his comrades. Bizos knew chapter and verse of the apartheid regime's draconian evil. And the hundreds of people packed into the community hall that bright Eastern Cape day seemed to hang on his every word.

Snyman, the man on the hot seat, was no match for Bizos. The faded old cop was sixty-nine, a pensioner and suffering from cancer. He was thin-lipped and gaunt, sipping lots of water. Seated beneath a banner touting "truth" and "reconciliation" and other concepts foreign to the hard-core Afrikaner mind-set, Snyman seemed like an old man lost. Even his polyester-and-pomade style seemed sad to me. I almost felt sorry for him. But he was from the Sanlam building. He was the police major who presided over the deadly Biko interrogation those many years ago. And Snyman lived a bloody life indeed. He was seeking amnesty not only for Biko's death but also for the deaths of seven others: the Cradock 4 and the Pebco 3. Snyman had been central to the Eastern Cape terror, as had the other security branch men who killed Biko.

That day at New Brighton, Snyman was on the stand, so to speak, trying to deny the assault for which he himself had confessed and sought amnesty. Either he was confused in his old age or he was suffering from a case of denial deeper than anyone could imagine. To receive amnesty, one had to admit a crime had occurred. But the whole point of Snyman's testimony that day was a denial that a crime had been committed. Should he persist, he would effectively disqualify himself for amnesty. That's precisely what Bizos wanted. He led the old major into the trap.

> Bizos: *Did you associate yourself in any way with any assault that may have been committed on him?*
>
> Snyman: *As I've said in my testimony, there was no assault on him other than to bring him under control.*
>
> Bizos: *But that was justified, that was not an assault, if your evidence was correct.*
>
> Snyman: *That is correct, Your Honor.*

Bizos: You never witnessed any assault, if I understood your evidence?

Snyman: That is correct, Your Honor.

Bizos: If there had been no assault, why then have you taken the oath and made the claim that there had in fact been an assault? You see: you, in your own words, say that there was an assault during the interrogation. Please tell us what form the assault took.

Snyman: In the course of the scuffle with Mr. Biko, there were punches thrown by the members who attempted to restrain him.

Bizos: On your version, the security policemen did nothing wrong. They acted in self-defense, all four of them, against an attack from Mr. Biko? That is what your story is?

Snyman: That is correct, Your Honor.

At one point, Snyman sought a recess. "Your Honor, I just want to ask you. I am very tired," he said. The crowd laughed at him, seemed to revel in his misery. There was no room for small mercies, though Snyman did get his recess.

These men were stone-cold ideologues. They were fully indoctrinated in the "total strategy" doctrine of former president P. W. Botha, a doctrine deployed to fight the so-called "total onslaught," meaning black resistance. But it was deeper than strategy. The Afrikaners of their ilk were fighting an epic, almost Darwinian battle "for the continued survival of the Afrikaner white people on the southern extreme of Africa," in Snyman's words. So blinded by white supremacy, they did not even seem to know when they sounded moronic. But none of them regretted what they'd done. None of them showed any remorse. Nieuwoudt's strange testimony, some months later, was typical:

Bizos: Did you consider the call by the [Black People's Convention] for democratic rights of all the people in South Africa a subversion?

Nieuwoudt: Yes, Mr. Chairman.

Bizos: When you wanted to call Mr. Biko a terrorist, it was because he was at the forefront of calling for the right to vote by all the people in South Africa in a unitary state?

Nieuwoudt: Yes, that is so.

Bizos: And you considered that equivalent to terrorism?
Nieuwoudt: Yes, because it had a military wing as well.

Nieuwoudt admitted beating Biko with a hosepipe. Siebert admitted the men had smashed Biko's head against the wall. During the "scuffle," Siebert testified, "all three of us then took hold of Biko and moved with him in the direction of the corner of the office and ran into the wall with him." Siebert tried to make it sound like an accident. But Bizos cut to the chase. He accused the men of using Biko like a "battering ram." And Snyman admitted that they lifted the clearly incapacitated and partially limp Biko up from the floor and shackled him crucifix-style against the door's metal security grille. They left him like that for several hours, to break his resistance some more.

Nkosinathi Biko, the handsome image of his father, sat fairly close to the men as these ugly details spilled out. He and his mother were just across the stage, at a long table of their own, next to Bizos. But the son rarely looked at his father's killers. Wearing headphones to hear their testimony translated from Afrikaans to English, he hung his head through much of the hearing. Biko's widow, Nontsikelelo, just looked disgusted. Here she was, listening to lies again, the very thing she'd vowed not to do.

But the New Brighton crowd was with her. "There can be no reconciliation without justice," proclaimed a placard held aloft by an otherwise silent protester. "Nieuwoudt you are a murderer. Go to jail," another placard read. Once in a while, the crowd hissed Nieuwoudt's name over and over, taunting him. "Notorious Nieuwoudt," some called him: the most hated cop in the Eastern Cape. At a different hearing, the mother of one of his victims lost it and screamed hysterically, "Nieuwoudt, you dog!"

Nieuwoudt, a red-haired man with long sideburns, applied for amnesty for ten murders. His killing was of the multidisciplinarian kind. He'd whipped and beaten Biko in 1977. He'd drugged and shot two other men, Siphiwe Mtimkhulu and Topsy Madaka, in 1982, then burned their bodies for six hours on a pyre and dumped the ashes in the Fish River. In 1985, along with Snyman, he'd hacked and shot the Pebco 3. Their remains, just ashes and fragments of bone, ended up in the Fish River too. And in 1989, Nieuwoudt blew to bits the Motherwell 4, a group of black police colleagues he believed were ANC spies. Nieuwoudt had already been convicted of murder in court for the Motherwell case. But in the strange practice of post-apartheid justice, a judge freed him pending an appeal of his life sentence.

Nieuwoudt's Truth Commission confession on the Mtimkhulu and Madaka murders revealed to the families what they had never known since the young men, both student activists, disappeared without a trace so many years ago. Mtimkhulu, twenty-two, was wheelchair-bound at the time of his death. He also had a pending lawsuit against police, alleging that they'd poisoned him in detention with thallium, leaving him chronically ill and handicapped.

Shortly before he died, Mtimkhulu had a son, Hlazo. By the time his father's killers were revealed, Hlazo had grown into a teenager quite haunted by his father's memory. At the 1997 hearing where Nieuwoudt had to publicly describe the killing as part of his amnesty bid, Hlazo Mtimkhulu fainted. But like so many families finally faced with the horrid truth, Mtimkhulu's parents were willing to sit down and meet their demon, Notorious Nieuwoudt. Strangely, Nieuwoudt, the stone-cold killer, wanted to express remorse to them. It was an odd ritual, these meetings between victims and their victimizers. A few had occurred since the TRC began, but none so strange as this. As he awaited word on his amnesty bids, the killer cop arranged a meeting with the family. A filmmaker traveled along to record the private event for a documentary, which was recounted in all the newspapers. Hlazo Mtimkhulu, the son, was not ready for this kind of meeting, and what happened that day resonated throughout South Africa when news of its conclusion leaked out.

"Thank you for the opportunity that I could meet you today," Nieuwoudt says to the family, according to published accounts. "I am grateful and thankful. I am here to seek forgiveness from the family for the hardship I have caused as a result of the apartheid regime."

"You know very well who I am," Joyce Mtimkhulu says in return. "My heart is full of joy that we can sit here today, facing each other eye to eye."

"With truth and sincerity, I come here today. This is where reconciliation starts," Nieuwoudt responds.

Hlazo lurked across the room near the kitchen, apparently seething. He couldn't take it. He picked up a vase and hurled it at Nieuwoudt, cracking the killer across the head, drawing the killer's blood. Maybe that was justice.

• • •

Nieuwoudt did ultimately receive amnesty for the Mtimkhulu and Madaka killings. But for all his other murders, the TRC refused to protect him from prosecution, as amnesty would have done. The TRC denied amnesty to all of the men who confessed to the Biko killing. In its final decision, the TRC said the officers' version of events "was so improbable and contradictory that it has to be rejected as false." In other words, the lies surrounding Biko's death continued.

As for the Mxenge family, their worst fears came true. The three killers who sought amnesty for Griffiths Mxenge's murder were granted amnesty. They had already been convicted for the killing in an ordinary trial, but they were able to convince the TRC that they had killed Mxenge on orders from their police seniors and in the context of a state philosophy that compelled them to do so, which was one of the amnesty requirements. Their amnesty victory legally nullified their convictions. That's what amnesty did. It wiped the slate clean on a case-by-case basis. And so Dirk Coetzee, a leader of the infamous Vlakplaas hit squad, named for a secret farm near Pretoria where its members trained and drank, would not be held accountable for Mxenge's murder. Nor would his co-accused, David Tshikalange and Butana Almond Nofomela.

Coetzee and Nofomela had made international headlines in 1989 as the first men ever to blow the whistle on hit squads within the South African police force. Apartheid's police attempted several times to shut Coetzee up; even sent a parcel bomb to kill their renegade comrade. Instead, it killed someone else. And the enigmatic Coetzee lived to tell his stories. He was a killer-cop-turned-whistle-blower who seemed to relish the opportunity to describe his macabre deeds. Who could forget his chilling TRC testimony about the tedious difficulties of burning fleshy sections of the human body?

But Coetzee failed to receive amnesty for a raft of other killings and conspiracies. And without amnesty, he became a potential target for criminal prosecution, should the state ever decide to hold trials of those denied amnesty, which was not at all likely, since they numbered in the thousands.

Apartheid's baggage proved a miserable tangle. In the case of the Cradock 4, the TRC denied amnesty for the six men, including Snyman, who sought it. And no one ever saw a trace of Sicelo Mhlauli's missing hand. That wasn't at all surprising. In the waning days of apartheid, its storm troopers and political leaders shredded documents and destroyed evidence at a fevered pace for fear they could be prosecuted after democracy's dawn.

8

The Elephants Fight

lying over the famous bend in the Zaire River, I could barely see the city nestled on its storied banks. Gaps in the lush rain forest offered only quick glimpses of the tall stone buildings, gray from mossy mold, with the minaret of a mosque donated by Libya peeking from the trees, along with church crosses. People on bicycles, the main mode of transport, slowly cruised the rutted roads near the silvery-brown river and its famous Stanley Falls. With its menagerie of rare and strange creatures, the irrepressible kingdom of the equatorial forest surrounded the city. Vines were monstrous, flowers were huge, and the towering, tangled trees formed an impenetrable canopy that cast the forest in perpetual dusk.

A city of 500,000 situated just north of the equator at the very heart of the continent, Kisangani's connections to the outside world were tenuous, at best. There wasn't even a functioning post office, not even an operational bank, and the Kisangani campus of the University of Zaire barely functioned as an institution of higher learning. The rain forest had swallowed the crumbled old roads from the capital, Kinshasa, long ago. In their absence, river barges ferrying everything from cars to monkeys were Kisangani's only link to the nation's largest city about 750 miles away. The town, once upon a time, had been a hub of river and rail commerce for the entire northeastern Zaire region. Breweries still churned out beer here, and the diamond trade flourished. The Lebanese diamond merchants, who ran mining operations in the region along with their Zairean partners, were the main source of commerce in the town. In times past, before elephants were largely killed off, Kisangani had been a way station for poached ivory as well. Diamonds and ivory and most other commodities moved through a black market, not through legitimate channels, making Kisangani a netherworld of rough and violent trade.

The city had become a place of literary legend. Novelist V. S. Naipaul's chilling masterpiece *A Bend in the River* unfolds against the backdrop of a postindependence Africa gone quickly dysfunctional in this big, isolated city. And it was the locale, as well, for Joseph Conrad's enigmatic novella *Heart of Darkness*, which sparked decades of debate over where the darkness actually lay: in Africa itself or the souls of the white men who tried to claim her. White men constantly "discovered" Africa down through history, as if the continent had no existence before their arrival. It was the ultimate form of denial: you only exist because we have found you. But so impenetrable was this central Zaire region that Europeans had been on Africa's coasts nearly four hundred years before finally getting through to the interior.

In the meantime, the Mangbetu and Zande people went about their business of conflict and coexistence in the traditional states that ruled this region and farther north where rain forest gave way to a more hospitable grassland climate. In the lush Ituri Forest east of Kisangani lived small hunting and gathering clans of Mbuti Pygmies. With Arabic slavers from the north and Swahili ones from the east pushing to the interior in the nineteenth century, Africa's disparate cultures rubbed shoulders, making Kisangani a symbolic African crossroads for years to come.

As our plane began its descent, I felt a flutter of excitement just to be landing in this infamous town, to be able to secure it as a dateline in my growing body of work. The more datelines I gathered, the more credible I felt as a foreign correspondent, not to mention the swashbuckling self-image I harbored as my travels broadened. I was eager to catch up with the foreign correspondent pals of mine who were more seasoned in this line of work than I. All Jo'burg-based, some were on the plane with me that day as we came in for a landing at Kisangani. They were Dele Olojede of *Newsday*,

Judith Matloff of the *Christian Science Monitor*, Marcus Mabry of *Newsweek*, and Ross Herbert of the *Johannesburg Star*.

We flew in because hundreds of thousands of war refugees were adrift in the region. Fighting had broken out that October along Zaire's eastern frontier with Rwanda, pitting the two countries' forces against each other. In the battles, a string of United Nations refugee camps that stretched for hundreds of miles inside Zaire had been overrun. Those camps housed Rwandan Hutu who'd fled their country after their country's genocide of 1994. Many among those "refugees" were killers from that slaughter and now combatants in this new war. But many more were ordinary people—men, women, children, old people. All were on the move, traveling beneath the lush jungle canopy, lost out there somewhere but believed to be moving in the direction of Kisangani.

From Kinshasa, the five of us journalists had hatched a harebrained idea that we'd fly to Kisangani and transfer to a smaller plane that would buzz the jungle so we could spot the missing refugees. Despite their huge number, the terrain was so rough, so inaccessible, and so overrun with hostile forces that the U.N. and international relief groups had been unable to figure out just where the refugees were. In our misguided valiance, we were determined to find them.

Commercial flights to Kisangani had been suspended because of the war, but we'd negotiated with the head of Air Zaire, José Endundo Bononge, to let us fly on one of his planes anyway. To iron out the details, we'd dined at his Kinshasa home, secured by bodyguards and filled with tiled rooms adorned with beautiful art and lovely photographs of his well-groomed children. The dust and stink and clawing poverty of Kinshasa's streets could not intrude on the hermetically sealed world of Zaire's elite class, like Endundo. Though surely Endundo had more important business to tend to than ours, he was accommodating. He enjoyed speaking to the foreign press, as did many of Zaire's elite. And Endundo sympathized with our efforts to write about his desperate country. After much discussion, our plan was set. We'd fly to Kisangani and connect with a small-plane operator who'd fly us farther east, to the town of Walikale, if fighting had not yet broken out there.

The plan had its risks—even more risks than we knew. But frankly, at the time, I was so pumped up at the prospect of getting closer to the action that the dangers did not sink in. Other journalists had gone to Kisangani recently without serious mishap, so I figured we could pull it off too. But one of my friends, Amma Ogan, wife of Dele and also a journalist in Jo'burg, thought we were nuts. She phoned from South Africa and tried to talk Dele out of going. Then she phoned me and warned that we were being careless and simply trying to win Pulitzer Prizes. I told her not to worry, that everything would be fine. And it was, at first. We each secured government passes to travel, at three hundred dollars a head, and finally boarded our chartered 727. The pilot, Captain Pascal Mwema, who'd studied in Texas and in Belgium, was quite amused to be ferrying a group of foreign correspondents. And we were quite amused to be flying in an otherwise empty ninety-eight-seat jet. The flight attendants served us full meals, complete with wine, and we settled into hours of silly chitchat and roaring laughter about everything and nothing.

Amma was right, of course. We were flying right into a maelstrom. As we finally landed in Kisangani, I had a sinking feeling that this was indeed a bad idea. I could see soldiers running toward our taxiing plane. In fact, soldiers were everywhere, in no particular order on the tarmac. Some troops wore uniforms, others were clad in little more than rags. Some were even barefoot. And all of them were angry and wired. An ugly crowd gathered down below as the rolling stairway was pushed into position against our plane's door. I dreaded the moment that door would open, for I had no clue what form of chaos would roar into the plane.

Quickly, we appointed Marcus our spokesman. He'd lived in Paris for several years and spoke perfect French. He'd talk us out of this mess, which seemed primed for hostage-taking if we didn't play it right. I braced for trouble. These troops were in full retreat from the fighting that had broken out three hundred miles to the east. They had marauded up the Kisangani road—yes, that stretch was navigable—stealing cars, aid agency vehicles, and food. Terrified local villagers fled into the forest for safety. Mobutu's army was in such disarray that rival divisions fought pitched battles against each other along Kisangani's streets and, of course, looted the place too.

It had been decades since Kisangani had seen such a spasm of violence.

During Belgian colonialism, when Kisangani was called Stanleyville, it was a hotbed of support for the charismatic and mercurial pan-Africanist Patrice Lumumba, the first prime minister during the 1960 shift to independence. After his assassination in 1961, Kisangani and the whole of eastern Zaire descended into chaos that climaxed with mass killings in 1965 perpetrated by pro-Lumumba rebels as well as by Belgian paratroopers and European mercenaries flown in on U.S. transport planes to help Mobutu Sese Seko's army put down the rebellion. Blood literally flowed in the streets of this unfortunate town, and now it was happening again. In fact, some of the same rebels who fought in the eastern rebellions of the 1960s were among those who'd launched this 1996 war to end Mobutu's three decades of power.

Mobutu's troops, the ones about to clamber aboard our plane, would not be happy, we surmised, to welcome a bunch of foreign reporters. But when the soldiers piled into the cabin with their awesome equatorial funk and foul soldier's breath, they really weren't all that interested in us. What they really wanted was to get as far away as possible from the war. Marcus talked us off the aircraft and onto the tarmac, where our contact, the small-plane operator, found us, herded us into a vehicle, and told us to forget about doing anything at all in Kisangani except staying alive until we could get out. He'd already been beaten that day at the airport. And a driver waiting for someone on the tarmac had been shot dead.

We headed to the Palm Beach, a small 1970s hotel right on the river's north bank. Despite its name, it was nothing fancy—two floors of large linoleum-tiled rooms and a spacious, well-stocked restaurant. The day of our arrival, the tripod-mounted machine guns awaiting action at strategic positions in and around the grounds were the hotel's most remarkable feature. We ran into a trio of British journalists at the Palm Beach who'd arrived a few days prior with the same bright idea—to search for the refugees. But they'd been taken hostage in Kisangani by soldiers who beat them, pointed guns at their heads, stole their money, and released them with a warning to leave the city. And now, at the Palm Beach, our traumatized colleagues warned us to get out too.

But it would take two bizarre days of diving for cover as bullets flew around the hotel, of sitting on the floor in the restaurant, of staying away from the windows for fear of getting shot, and attempting to make phone calls from the one satellite phone among us without soldiers seeing the device and stealing it. The whole adventure was a fiasco. We were able to interview only a few people—a local missionary, a French diplomat, and a Zairean businessman—all with stories of the mayhem that deepened by the day. Finally, when another plane came in, some friendly soldiers agreed to ferry us to the airport to fly out, back to Kinshasa.

We did not find the missing refugees. But they were still out there, a presence that would haunt Central Africa, even in death, for years to come.

• • •

"Refugees"—the very word suggested innocence and victimization. Of the 1 million Rwandan refugees who lived in those eastern Zaire camps in the care of the United Nations, perhaps most were indeed victims. But among them, too, were scores of thousands of stone-cold killers: soldiers, militiamen, and civilians who'd slaughtered their countrymen in the Rwandan genocide of 1994, then fled en masse across the border. The Zaire war of 1996 was a direct result of that genocide, whose domino effect would claim Mobutu, embolden a new clique of African leaders, rearrange power politics in the region, and expose, yet again, the international community's ambivalence and prevarication over the value of African life. From Africa to Europe to the Americas and the United Nations, diplomats debated the number of refugees and whether their plight warranted rescue. It had been this way for two years, since the genocide whose repercussions were shaking much of Africa.

Rwanda is a tiny country, a speck on the map of Africa, really. Its Hutu people were 85 percent of the population, while its Tutsis were a minority of about 15 percent. Historically, the Tutsis were pastoralists, owning huge herds of cattle and large swaths of land. The Hutus, on the other hand, were peasant farmers and often the clients of Tutsi patrons. But the social and economic distinctions between the two groups were mitigated by the fact that Hutus and Tutsis intermarried, practiced the same religions, and spoke the same language. Their coexistence was unequal, but not murderous. Until colonialism hardened the differences between them, there'd been no record of Hutus and Tutsis slaughtering each other.

During Belgian colonialism starting in 1919, the whites fastened onto a presumed Tutsi racial superiority. In the pseudoscience of racial classification that was all the rage in Europe as its period of African colonization commenced, Europeans who had seen the Tutsis were virtually intoxicated at the thought that their thin lips, narrow noses, slender physique, and tall stature suggested they carried a racial stock not of Africa. Certainly, so the colonists thought, the Tutsis were a different people than the squat, broad-nosed, and thick-featured Hutus. Imaginations ran wild. One Belgian colonialist even wondered whether the Tutsi people were survivors of the lost continent of Atlantis.

The Belgians made their racial theories a matter of colonial policy. Tutsis were preferred in all sectors of society—education, employment, land, and the church. And the previously porous boundaries between Hutu and Tutsi society—through social intermingling, marriage, and cattle wealth—were hardened. The Belgians issued identification cards designating each person by his or her ethnic group. The Hutus languished on the receiving end of the worst of the colonial policies, including forced labor.

It was only a matter of time till the better-educated Tutsis began sniffing around this new concept called liberation that was sweeping the continent in the 1950's. And their quest for African self-rule hit the Belgians like a stinging slap. After years of enforcing Tutsi superiority, the Belgians turned to the Hutus, empowering the Hutus, inflaming the Hutus with anti-Tutsi rhetoric. In a hastily arranged election in 1959, the Hutus rose to power in the U.N. trusteeship conferred on Rwanda as an intermediate step before independence. Full self-rule came in 1962, and the Hutu majority took up its place as the ruling group, seething with vengeance. Successive Hutu governments built a whole governing creed on anti-Tutsi hatred. Waves of anti-Tutsi pogroms and massacres occurred at regular intervals from 1959 onward, flushing columns of thousands of Tutsi refugees out of Rwanda, headed for neighboring Uganda. Paul Kagame, who would become pivotal in Central Africa as an adult, was a toddler when he walked with his family into

Uganda. He would grow up, fight alongside Yoweri Museveni to overthrow Ugandan dictator Milton Obote, and serve Museveni's government as an intelligence chief. But always, Kagame and his brethren nursed a dream of one day returning to their country.

The Tutsi exiles formed the Rwandan Patriotic Army (RPA) and launched a civil war against Rwanda's Hutu government in 1990, with Kagame one of the key leaders. By 1994, with a U.N.-sponsored peace accord in place that would assure power sharing between the two groups, extremist Hutu leaders bent on exclusive ethnic power had planted apocalyptic paranoia within the Hutu population. Tutsis would exterminate the Hutus, the propaganda said. Tutsis must be rounded up and killed. The Hutu army and militias drew up lists of Tutsis and moderate Hutus to be killed. Weapons were distributed to town and village leaders to prepare for the killing. On April 6, 1994, a plane carrying Rwandan President Juvénal Habyarimana and Burundian President Cyprien Ntaryamira crashed mysteriously in Kigali, the Rwandan capital. Widely believed to this day to have been the work of Rwandan Hutu extremists out to subvert Habyarimana's more moderate agenda, the deadly crash provided the signal, as it were, for a preplanned campaign of ethnic and political slaughter.

That very night, it began. Rwandan Hutus—mostly soldiers and militiamen—slaughtered nearly eight hundred thousand of their Tutsi countrymen in about ninety days. It was a systematic, calculated attempt to eradicate the Tutsi ethnic group and any Hutus who did not pursue the extremist line. It happened quickly and efficiently, not in a frenzy. Killers had hit lists. Soldiers threw up roadblocks so they could examine identification papers—that pernicious inheritance from the Belgians—and separate the Tutsis for killing. Village and town counselors led the genocide in the rural areas. Ordinary people did a significant share of the killing as well. They were compelled to kill by their leaders. They were forced to kill under threat of their own deaths. And many wanted to kill.

It was the most intensely rapid episode of bloodletting of the twentieth century, though certainly not unprecedented. Ethnic warfare in Europe had made Bosnia, in the former Yugoslavia, a vast killing field in the early 1990s, and would do it again later in the decade. But it was the methodical, decisive nature of the Rwandan killing that set it apart. And unlike Bosnia in the early 1990s, where the United States and its allies overcame their initial reluctance to intervene and finally mounted a massive peacekeeping intervention, in Rwanda the international community did nothing to stop the killing.

The United Nations' most decisive action during the Rwandan genocide was to pull out a peacekeeping mission already in the country. The United States did not want to even acknowledge that genocide was happening. Back in Washington, officials of President Bill Clinton's White House debated, behind closed doors and with administration lawyers, whether the word "genocide" should be used in public. They decided against it. To acknowledge that killers were trying to wipe out an entire people would, morally and legally speaking, require some action under the U.N. genocide convention. And the United States had no intention whatsoever of getting involved. Infamously, Warren Christopher, the secretary of state, authorized language that would acknowledge only that "acts of genocide" had occurred. The horrific body count of Rwanda would mount for two months before the White House would acknowledge that genocide was under way. It is easy to attribute this noninterventionism to what some academics call the Somalia syndrome. After eighteen U.S. servicemen had been killed in the Somali battles at Mogadishu in 1993, the United States developed an aversion to intervening in Africa. But on Rwanda, the Clinton administration wouldn't even support the formation of a U.N. intervention force manned by other nations.

The killing stopped only when Kagame's RPA swept through the country and flushed out the Hutu killers from the Armed Forces of Rwanda (now known as the ex-FAR) as well as the terrifying militia known by the Kinyarwanda word "Interahamwe," which means "those who work together." For extremist Hutus bent on ethnic cleansing, the "work," since the 1960s, had been deadly. With the RPA victory, a huge swath of Rwanda's Hutu population flooded out of Rwanda, including innocents as well as the killers. A million people surged into Tanzania to the south. A roughly equal number, about 1.2 million, fled west into Zaire.

The whole Hutu state fled: government ministers, generals of the ex-FAR, the Interahamwe, plus national bureaucrats and town and village officials. They took cars, trucks, buses, tankers, documents, currency, and arms.

In effect, the Hutu state transplanted itself, using ordinary Hutu people as convenient cover. People fled in the same village or commune formations in which they had killed. Even the innocents were forced to flee. The Hutu propaganda of paranoia told people that the Tutsis would surely slaughter them if they did not flee. And the United Nations mounted a massive humanitarian rescue mission for the Hutu "refugees," who included a significant number of killers, known in French, the lingua franca of the region, as *génocidaires*. The United Nations housed and fed them in a network of forty U.N. refugee camps up and down the frontier in the Zairean region of Kivu, along a vast lake of that name.

Predictably, the camps became heavily militarized. When ex-FAR and Interahamwe mounted routine military incursions against Kagame's new Rwandan government, the world did nothing then, either. The United Nations refused to even attempt to disarm the fighters in those camps or separate them from the civilians. The United States and other leading nations were loath to step in to so difficult a quagmire. Everyone knew what was happening. The problem had been studied and debated over and over. But it existed, for Western policy makers, in that abstract realm of paradigms and scenarios, not in reality. For two years, no one did a thing, as if nothing could be done. U.S. Assistant Secretary of State Phyllis Oakley captured the inertia aptly. Speaking of the fact that the international community was feeding and caring for both refugees and killers, Oakley said in early 1995, "We've all been aware of the moral dilemma. None of us has the means to solve it."

So the spiral continued. Mobutu's out-of-control regime, with its generals-turned-arms-traffickers, shipped arms to the Hutu camps, as did France. At the same time, Mobutu sent troops from his elite Special Presidential Division to provide security at the camps, where outbreaks of violence were routine. Mobutu was an old friend and ally of Habyarimana, the fallen Hutu president. Mobutu had even sent troops and arms to help Habyarimana's forces fight the RPA in the early 1990s. Though his corrupt and degenerate regime had fallen out of favor in the international community, Mobutu's stature suddenly soared with the refugee crisis unfolding on his soil. He was a power broker again, the go-to leader on a major African issue.

But hostilities were brewing up and down Zaire's Kivu border region, where the ideology of genocide found fertile ground. The *génocidaires* had common cause with their extremist Hutu brethren in Zaire. Even before the Rwandan genocide, the Zairean Hutus of the Kivu region had been purging Tutsis from the highlands of the agriculturally rich Masisi plain just west of Lake Kivu. The influx of more than a million Rwandan Hutu refugees into Zaire caused a simmering pot to boil over. The Zairian Tutsis, for their part, formed themselves into an alliance to fend off the ethnic cleansing. Among them, the Banyamulenge (people of the Mulenge hills), who had lived in Zaire for generations, were most prominent. In September 1996, Zairean officials in Kivu told the Banyamulenge that their citizenship was no longer recognized and they must pack up and leave the country. Local militia and the Zairean military backed up the threat with attacks on Banyamulenge settlements.

Finally, Kagame and his key ally, Museveni of Uganda, decided enough was enough. A fly on the rump of the Zairean elephant, tiny Rwanda made its move to quash the genocidal threat once and for all. With support from Uganda and Burundi, Rwanda and its Zairean Banyamulenge allies launched a war. They pulled in a mishmash of Zairean forces for the sake of local legitimacy. The dreaded Mai Mai militia, which for nearly a century had clung to the belief that rituals of water could protect its fighters from harm, threw their lot in with the Banyamulenge for a while.

A veteran revolutionary, Laurent Désiré Kabila, shook off his dusty revolutionary mantle and joined the war too. He'd fought against Mobutu in the 1960s and now, a lifetime later, he became the public face of a new movement called the Alliance of Democratic Forces for the Liberation of Congo-Zaire. Despite its name, the Alliance was very much a Trojan horse for Rwanda. Starting in October 1996, the Alliance swept through Zaire's eastern border regions from lakes Tanganyika to Kivu to Edward. With Rwandan troops as most of the muscle, they busted up the refugee camps, fighting both Zairean and Rwandan Hutu troops along the way. Each new battle set waves of refugees adrift. Some marched north. Others marched south. The most unfortunate of them all plunged west, forced by the *génocidaires* among them to push deeper and deeper into Zaire. By mid-November, a humanitarian crisis of huge proportions had unfolded. More than a million people were on the move.

The United Nations managed to cobble together the international will for intervention. Canada would lead. The United States would commit up to five thousand troops. The international peace force would feed the refugees and open humanitarian corridors to guide them back to Rwanda. The mission would not intervene in the fighting and would not disarm the combatants, but at least it would do something. And the United States seemed serious this time about helping. It established a logistics and communications base, which I visited, at Entebbe, Uganda, to coordinate the U.S. deployment.

But neither the Alliance nor its Rwandan patrons wanted international troops roaming around eastern Zaire, potentially fouling up their military strategy. In mid-November, the Alliance encircled and attacked the largest of the Hutu refugee camps, known as Mugunga, about fifteen miles from the Rwandan border town of Goma. In the chaos, the *génocidaires* based at Mugunga moved west, while the masses of refugees cowering at the camp headed east. In a refugee movement as torrential as anything the twentieth century had seen, a tidal wave of refugees clogged the road to Rwanda, heading back home. Over several days, roughly 600,000 men, women, children, elderly, and infirm hobbled back to their homeland for a very uncertain future.

Rwanda and its allies had succeeded. Now there'd be no need for international intervention. The United States, especially, breathed a sigh of relief. That both Kigali and Washington plied the same policy line seemed to give credence to theorists who believed the two countries were in strategic—if not operational—cahoots in the first place. U.S. State Department briefers back in Washington declared that the refugee crisis was substantially over. Those refugees who remained in Zaire, Rwanda claimed, were either the *génocidaires* or their families. The U.S. Embassy in Kigali, in a case of what some dubbed the rabid clientitis that afflicts diplomats too close to their host countries, parroted the Rwandan line.

Leaving Kinshasa behind, I'd arrived in Kigali by then, in time to hear the very loquacious political counselor at the embassy, Peter Whaley, and his ambassador, Robert Gribben, openly question the U.N. estimate of the refugee numbers. The U.N.'s figure of 1.2 million became the subject of huge debate, with Washington alleging that the original number had been inflated.

Further, some officials suggested that most of the refugees had returned to Rwanda. Gribben declared that "the bulk of the refugees . . . who want to come home have done so. There may be some that are staying behind because they do not want to come home." And clearly, people guilty of murder in Rwanda would not want to go back home—that seemed to be his implication. And the nature of the Rwandan genocide meant that the guilty ones weren't only the ex-FAR and the Interahamwe but also their relatives, their neighbors, just ordinary Rwandans. Among those hundreds of thousands of people who'd encamped inside Zaire, an untold number had blood on their hands. But what of the innocent refugees? What of the children, the elderly? The *génocidaires* leading the refugee columns were holding civilians as human shields and driving them farther west like cattle, into the equatorial forest.

Despite the Washington-Kigali line, the haunting question remained: if there were 1.2 million refugees in eastern Zaire to begin with and only 600,000 could be accounted for, what of the missing 600,000? U.S. aerial surveillance and satellite reconnaissance had spotted various large clusters of people in eastern Zaire, but officials said it was difficult to tell if they were Rwandan refugees or displaced Zaireans. And they were at the front line of a war. Getting to them would likely mean combat. No one in the international community had the stomach for that. Within days of the massive Rwandan refugee repatriation, the humanitarian mission fell apart. The United States scaled back to six hundred its original troop commitment of five thousand. For the refugees still marooned in Zaire, the writing was on the wall. Over the coming weeks, many Rwandans would find their way back to Rwanda. But most would languish out there, deep in the impenetrable rain forests, heading west as the war drove them, and left to whatever fate had in store.

● ● ●

BUKAVU, ZAIRE, LATE NOVEMBER

In a café on the Ruzizi River in the Rwandan town of Cyangugu, I dropped my fork, slapped some dollars on the table, and grabbed my bags. Bosco, my guide for the trip, did the same. Together, we sprinted toward the border post at the river bridge. The Rwandans and rebels who'd seized the Zairean town of Bukavu, on the other side of the river, were opening the town to journalists for the first time since they'd routed Mobutu's troops three weeks earlier and busted up the Hutu refugee camps. Refugees had scattered around the Bukavu region, adrift in the lush forest and caught in the growing war.

Along with a few other journalists, I'd held vigil for two days at this border crossing, in hopes of finally getting into rebel territory. And suddenly, the border was opening, which is why Jesper Strudsholm, another traveling mate, was standing by our car at the border post and hollering like hell for us to get there fast.

The three of us seemed an unlikely team, but that's the way it goes. Foreign correspondents have a way of forming alliances with each other for the sake of the job. Jesper, also based in South Africa, was a Dane who wrote for the Danish newspaper *Politiken*. We'd agreed to share the rather exorbitant fees charged by Bosco, a jack-of-all-trades businessman who earned extra cash as a driver, translator, and guide for foreign journalists. In hiking boots and rakish wide-brimmed leather hat, Bosco at first seemed suspicious to me. But I came to trust and respect him immensely because of his courage. I will use only his first name, which is pretty common in the area, for fear that otherwise he might have trouble amid the inflamed politics of his home region. Born and raised amid Africa's Great Lakes—Victoria, Edward, Albert, Kivu, Tanganyika, and Malawi—Bosco was a product of the politics, culture, and ethnic networks of the region. He could talk his way into and out of any scrape. Without such a "fixer" at your side, travel in rough terrain is virtually impossible.

At the border, Bosco jumped behind the wheel of the rented sedan and revved the engine as Jesper and I piled in. Up ahead, leading the convoy of four carloads of journalists and a few human rights and medical aid workers, Banyamulenge troops in a looted U.N. truck guided us out of Rwandan territory and up a slight hill into the ravaged town of Bukavu. The roads were empty but for a few brave souls. The fighting had forced local residents indoors or flushed them out to the bush to their deaths. True to the legendary pastoralism of the Tutsis, Banyamulenge troops were driving a huge herd of beautiful longhorn cattle through the town even as we arrived. Our escorts led us to the Hôtel Résidence on the town's main drag, where they stamped our passports with rebel visas and proceeded to tell us absolutely nothing. The rebel leader, Kabila, would come to address us "very soon," the rebels said. But in the meantime, we were forced to just sit tight. The arrival of dusk made it clear that nothing much would be happening until the next day.

A relic of the old Belgian colonial days, the Résidence had the eerie feeling of a haunted house. The hotel manager, Franck Mugisho, politely informed his new visitors that things had been idle at the hotel because of the war but that he would round up some staff to make a meal. Of course, with no phone service, this would mean sending a runner through town to find a few workers. Luckily, I traveled with a stash of protein bars, since I'd discovered much to my chagrin that I had a chronically bad stomach and couldn't hold down much regular food anyway, except bread, rice, and potatoes.

Later, I settled into my cavernous room, with its high ceilings and huge windows. It smelled of mildew. I eventually traced the smell not only to the bathroom, where the spigots ran rust-brown, but also to the bed and its dampness. I hit the pillow and a mildewy dust cloud exploded. But somehow I slept—fully clothed, with my backpack as a pillow. The next morning, I did the best I could of bathing, with splashes of bottled water and dabs of soap. Then I rejoined Jesper and Bosco downstairs on the veranda to plan our day.

"Fixers" do pretty much what their title suggests: they fix problems and make things happen. And that is what Bosco did. He secured our passes to move around the region. He managed to skirt the requirement that rebel escorts travel with us. He even finagled a Land Cruiser, since the little sedan couldn't hack the rough roads. Lord only knows to whom the cruiser originally belonged. Bosco did a deal with some businessman—three hundred dollars a day, cash up front—who no doubt had received the 4 × 4 as looted property when the rebels seized the town. That's the way things went. The whole region was topsy-turvy.

Humanitarian aid workers who'd entered Bukavu with us were receiving regular reports from their headquarters of the latest U.S. and U.N. projections on where the refugee masses were clustered or in which direction they were moving. One estimate said a mass of close to 200,000 people was moving north from Bukavu, on the west bank of Lake Kivu, toward the town of

Sake. To get to them would be a rough day of travel, with no guarantee of finding them or making it back to Bukavu by nightfall. It was a gamble, but one worth taking, since the double-talk from Washington and Rwanda on the "missing" refugees had by now become infuriating.

But it seemed our travels were jinxed shortly after we set out. Not far outside Bukavu, the three-hundred-dollar-a-day Land Cruiser blew a tire. We changed it. Then another tire blew a short time later. Luckily, it happened near a church mission that had a tire to spare, which we bought. And when the third tire blew, we doubled back to the mission, where a worker repaired it. My faith in the adventure wavered. I had no idea what I might be getting into. We were rumbling up a deserted road in a region awash with refugees, génocidaires, rebels, water-worshiping warriors, and looting army troops. Anything could happen, and whatever happened wasn't likely to be good. The region had become hell, which was precisely the reason we had to be there to act as witnesses. That is what we do as journalists. That is what we love.

Like a plate of platinum, Lake Kivu shimmered just beyond the trees on one side of the road. On the other, towering pines whispered and swayed in the breezes over the mountainous remnants of a range called the Mitumba. Geologically speaking, this region was Africa's Rift Valley, a cleavage in the continent's crust. How appropriate that Africa's strategic cleavages were tearing up the old balance of power up and down this same rifted region. If we could make it through, we intended to drive up to Sake, about one hundred miles north, near Goma. We took along our sleeping bags and gear in case we got lucky, or in case we got marooned.

Sometimes children emerged from scattered settlements near the road and ran along as we passed. They shouted, "Biskwit! Biskwit!" It seemed sadly endearing. They wanted biscuits, those nutritional crackers the U.N. workers handed out to the refugees—at least that is what I initially assumed. But the more I heard shouts of "Biskwit," the more the voices seemed angry. Local Zaireans had watched for two years while the United Nations fed the Rwandans but provided no aid to the local people. I'd brushed up against their resentment several days before. Mistaking me for a U.N. worker, a woman on another refugee road shouted at me, "Why do you give refugees biscuits and forget us?" Even the children felt this way. The shouts of "Biskwit" that trailed us sounded more and more like bitter taunts.

About sixty-five miles north of Bukavu, we rounded a bend and Bosco suddenly braked. Up ahead, a crowd of people stood in the road. They looked as startled as we did. But right away, we could tell they were refugees. They had bundles and sleeping mats. Grass and twigs clung to their clothing. Some were barefoot. They'd clearly just left the forest; some of them were still climbing down from an embankment. There were too many women and children among them to pose a danger, so we got out of the car to talk to them. Tentatively, a man stepped forward from the group. He brushed off his soiled blazer of blue pinstripes and whacked his hands at the twigs clinging to his wrinkled gray slacks. I was struck by his attempt to appear more presentable, though he looked as weary as a human could be.

His name was Jean Damascene Baragondoza. He told us he'd worked at a Kigali post office before he became a refugee. In his native Kinyarwanda, translated by Bosco, Baragondoza told a chilling story. There were seventy in his group, but they'd been part of a larger refugee column that filled the road as far as the eye could see as they marched up from a camp near Bukavu. The Interahamwe fighters had driven the refugees north and they had walked for a month.

They hoped they were going home to Rwanda, but the Interahamwe forced them off the road, turning them west into the mountains. Those who did not wish to go were shot. The refugees could hear a battle raging down in the town of Nyabibwe, between the Interahamwe and Banyamulenge fighters. With chaos breaking loose, Baragondoza and others found a chance to escape. "We had to hide, because we were all supposed to be in big groups together," Baragondoza said. Several families, including his own, crawled through the bush and remained hidden for a day, until the refugee column moved on. Then the escapees felt safe enough to return to the road, to retrace their footsteps back south to Bukavu. Many in his group were plainly sick. Their coughs sounded deep and tubercular. The children's noses ran with green mucus. One of the women was heavily pregnant.

"There are many bodies in the mountains," Baragondoza told us. "Can you tell people that we need help? We need something to eat. We are very tired. And medicine, we need." We told him we would write his message in our dispatches. He directed us onward, toward Nyabibwe itself. We shook hands and wished each other Godspeed.

Now we knew we were close—perhaps too close—to the war. Nyabibwe lay just a couple of miles ahead. We drove in silence. Bosco seemed extra alert. We had no idea what we would find there. As we edged closer, we could smell the smoke. The road descended into a clearing, a small idyllic valley ringed with cloud-kissed mountains. Rays of sun spread across the sky like golden brushstrokes, as if an artist had painted Africa in its glory. Bosco navigated slowly down a hill and around a bend.

We saw the first truck—burning, twisted. "Oh shit," Bosco said quietly. Then another truck and another came into view, plus buses and tankers and cars—more than thirty of them, pierced by rocket-propelled grenades, blown up, just wrecked. The apocalypse filled the road. We'd caught up with a major column of the ex-FAR and Interahamwe, the *génocidaires* of Rwanda, or what was left of them. With this many vehicles on the road, surely the refugees that moved with them were huge in number, as Baragondoza had described. And with this many vehicles moving through a deeply rural region where vehicles were rare, there was no way the U.S. Navy P-3 Orion reconnaissance planes flying over the region could have missed them. I knew in my gut that my government was playing games with these refugees' lives. But there at Nyabibwe, there were no refugees in sight. The only evidence of people in the surrounding hills was the constant report of automatic-weapons fire from shooters we could not see. "There are many bodies in the mountains."

Bosco steered the Land Cruiser off the road and rolled around the smoky wreckage. Up ahead lay the tiny town itself, or what was left of it. It, too, smoldered. People scurried around, some carrying bodies. Others ferried buckets of water to douse the embers of burned huts. Jesper and I jumped out of the cruiser to get down to business. Bosco warned us to go slow. We bounded forward, toward the small settlement. I sensed no threat; I saw no soldiers. But the glinting of metal caught my eye. I looked on the ground. Oh my God. Stopping in my tracks, I yelled for Jesper to stand still too. Unexploded mortars and grenades lay all around us.

Creeping now, we carefully edged forward, identifying ourselves as foreign journalists to the people we encountered in the town. A man appeared. He strutted toward us. His walk told me he was a man in charge, but his outfit looked quite silly. He wore Wellington boots, lime-green shorts, an orange mesh tank top, and a large semiautomatic pistol in a holster at his waist. Men with AK-47s flanked him.

"I am the commandant," he announced. We explained who we were. He did not reciprocate. Leading him on, I asked, "Are you the Banyamulenge?" "Yes," he said. "I am Munyamulenge." A red light flashed in my brain. Big lie that one. This guy's a Rwandan Tutsi, I thought. His English wasn't French-accented, like that of most Zaireans, and he commanded the language too well for a Zairean.

And then more lies. No, there's been no battle, he said. The ex-FAR and Interahamwe had destroyed their convoy and the town before the Banyamulenge got there. Automatic-weapons fire still rained down in the hills, but he said he had no idea what all that shooting was about. He made no sense. This war made no sense. But that's all we got out of him. The commandant made quick work of saying little, and then he sloshed off in his rubber boots. Townspeople, too, were reluctant to speak. The few people out and about kept their heads low. The shooting in the hills was constant for the hour we spent there. The lovely valley felt like evil, a place of slaughter in the African bush.

A light drizzle dripped onto the road to Bukavu as we drove back toward the town. I fully expected we'd come across Baragondoza and his escapees once again. There wasn't much we could do to help them, and that's not the journalist's role anyway. We roar into difficult situations to witness and record events, not to become players, unless it is morally unavoidable. Privately, I hoped we could give a lift to the very pregnant woman and to the sickest of the children. But we didn't see them again. They had vanished. I would like to think they scattered into the bush when they heard a vehicle approaching. I would like to think they were innocent refugees and not *géno-*

cidaires. I hoped they made it home alive, though that seemed doubtful, under the circumstances.

As we rumbled down the road, I thought of the fifteen thousand U.S. troops in Bosnia, the former Yugoslavia. The United States deployed them to stop the nastiness of European tribal slaughter. But the ethnic cleansing in Africa's Great Lakes region soared in proportion to Bosnia's. Rwanda had already lost nearly a million people in the 1994 genocide, and this new war in Zaire, where the killers were many and the victims were legion, would bloat the region's body count further. But in Washington's strategic calculus, this African tragedy did not matter. This was not Europe. The United States sliced and diced the notion of morality, again, and Africa came out the loser. The demise of the international intervention force for Zaire was an act of neglect as terrible as the West's cut-and-run policy during the Rwandan genocide.

Scores of thousands of people were massacred throughout Zaire during the war, across the length and breath of the vast country. No one knows for certain how many died; the hidden mass graves would remain just that. The United Nations would report many months later that one of the mass killings of 1996 happened in Nyabibwe that November.

● ● ●

GOMA, ZAIRE

Kabila rode on the coattails of all this killing. Though he'd been an anti-Mobutu "revolutionary" all his adult life, this wasn't his war. He didn't start it. He didn't fund it. He didn't even arm it or staff it, at least not in the beginning. Mobutu loyalists in Kinshasa called Kabila a marionette whose strings were pulled by Rwanda. The label bore some truth. But Kabila filled an important void as the public face of the rebel Alliance. He served as its chairman, and his presence made the rebel push far more palatable to Zaireans, at least at first. Though Rwanda and Uganda were the muscle in the early months of the war, Kabila gave the movement a veneer of credibility as a bona fide anti-Mobutu force.

For starters, Kabila was Zairean. Second, he wasn't a Tutsi, though many troops under the Alliance banner were Tutsis from Zaire and Rwanda. Third, he'd fought, way back in the 1960s, as a pro-Lumumbist. That made him welcome by the legions of Zaireans who still revered the memory and the aborted cause of the country's first elected prime minister. And finally, Kabila was untainted. He'd done no deals with Mobutu, at least none that were known. He hadn't collaborated with the dictator or been compromised by him. Instead, he'd spent nearly his entire life in opposition to Mobutu's regime. In the Alliance cities of the east in those early weeks of the war, Kabila performed his role to the hilt. Though people even in his own country knew next to nothing about him, his destiny, it seemed, had finally arrived. The war—someone else's war—gave Kabila the truest shot at Mobutu that he'd ever had, and he and his considerable girth filled Africa's center stage.

Built like a fireplug, Kabila sported a bald head, glistening-smooth chocolate-brown skin, and a seemingly jovial manner. His round cheeks seemed forever puffed in a grin, which, when he was angered, had a menacing way of crawling across his face. But he had an easy manner with the army of journalists clamoring to meet him in the rebel headquarters at Goma. Clearly, Kabila relished being the man of the hour.

Once, at the start of a massive press conference to announce a major wartime gain, Kabila entered the room and snickered "Ooo-la-la" at the size of the crowd. Then he bellowed a friendly "So how are you?" as if he and the crowd were old friends. Another time, I tagged along as he jovially led a bunch of journalists through one of the lakeside Mobutu villas the rebels had seized. With its chandeliers, marble floors, green velvet furniture, and huge Jacuzzis—one blue, one red—lined with carafes of bubble bath and cologne, and its carports of polished limousines, the villa bore testament to Mobutu's flamboyant consumption. Kabila made a good show of his outrage at Mobutu's excesses.

But who, really, was this man? If you'd ask him, he'd shrug his shoulders humbly and say, "I am just Kabila." His refusal to reveal himself struck me as suspicious the first time I met him, seated around his desk in another seized villa with five other journalists. This was a man quite skilled at cat and mouse, I thought, a man quite deft at hiding in plain sight. His main credentials—at least among the very few who knew anything at all about him—

were that, by the age of fifty-five, he'd spent his entire adult life opposing Mobutu. His revolutionary background was genuine. He served in a provincial assembly in his home region of Katanga during Patrice Lumumba's brief prime ministership in 1960, and fled the country after Lumumba's assassination the following year. In opposition to Mobutu in 1963–64, Kabila fought alongside other pro-Lumumbists, the most prominent of whom was Pierre Mulele, a minister in the ill-fated Lumumba government who left the country for military training and returned to lead a vast rebellion. In what came to be broadly known as the Simba Rebellion, the rebels seized several regions of the country—virtually all of the east, including Stanleyville (now Kisangani), and much of the southwest region of Bandundu. Kabila held a junior position in that war as a zone leader in the Tanganyika region.

After the Belgian, U.S., and mercenary intervention quashed the so-called revolution of second independence at Stanleyville, Kabila hung on. Deep in the Kivu region, his forces continued to fight in the Tanganyika hills around the towns of Fizi and Baraka. For the next decade, Kabila's Party of the Popular Revolution, a part-Marxist, part-Maoist group, ran a revolutionary fiefdom at Fizi-Baraka. But the revolution buckled, some accounts say, as Kabila spent more and more time trafficking in gold, diamonds, and ivory.

In 1965, the legendary Argentinean guerrilla Ernesto Che Guevara led a hundred-man contingent of Cuban soldiers to Fizi-Baraka to help Kabila further his revolution. But Guevara wound up disillusioned by the troops' brutality, their lack of discipline, their leaders' chronic absences. Kabila spent lots of time in African capitals, raising money, hanging out in bars, issuing communiqués, and chasing beautiful women, or so Guevara wrote at that time. Guevara was disgusted at the wasted opportunity and pulled his men out of Fizi-Baraka only six months after their arrival.

In his little kingdom, Kabila had become a warlord, in effect. The Bembe people who lived in his liberated zone were treated as mere vassals. They would later tell one of my *Washington Post* colleagues of Kabila's duplicity and brutality, including the burning alive of those who crossed him. And though Kabila opposed Mobutu, he did not oppose doing business with Mobutu's army. In a hands-off arrangement of convenience, both sides smuggled gold in the region.

Kabila escaped American attention until his movement took four westerners, three of them Stanford University students, hostage in 1975. Kidnapped in Tanzania where they were studying chimpanzee behavior with naturalist Jane Goodall, they were ferried across Lake Tanganyika to Kabila's mountain redoubt and held for several weeks. Eventually, their families paid ransom, reportedly about $500,000. The hostages were released.

In the 1980s, Kabila went into exile in the Tanzanian capital, Dar es Salaam. His revolution had all but withered. He lived high in Dar and his wealth attracted suspicion. Mystery seemed to follow him, no doubt fueled by his many aliases. "Raul Kabila," he sometimes called himself, or variations of "Collins," "Christopher," or "Mzee Mtwale." He had, by then, become just another exiled revolutionary with an uncertain future, swimming in the ferment of African conspiracy and disillusionment. But time did not wither his dream.

In 1996, Kabila emerged in the international spotlight as the potential liberator of Zaire. But he was an anachronism. Like a specimen from another epoch, his politics were frozen in the ideologies of revolutions past. In Goma, the headquarters for the new revolution that wasn't really his, he ordered Zaireans who wanted to work with his rebel Alliance to take "political ideology" classes. Those classes taught the same lessons—about class struggle, the state as an instrument of oppression, and the ignorance of the masses—that had been taught more than thirty years before at Fizi-Baraka. Kabila's people said such political lessons were a precondition for the country to hold elections. In the classes, students were issued a handbook, written by Kabila, that listed the mistakes of the old Simba Rebellion of the 1960s. They included: egotistical struggles among the leaders, tribalism, dependence on fetishes and mysticism, savage warfare rather than strategic thinking.

In yet another requisitioned villa, I asked Kabila's security strategist, Paul Kabongo, who'd returned from exile in Spain to be part of this war, how long the reeducation of Zaire would take. His answer offered another bad sign, though perhaps it was influenced by the strong drink that was never very far from many Alliance officials. With menace in his voice, Kabongo said, "The political education of a nation cannot be measured in time, in space. It is a long work."

· · ·

Eastern Zaire was hard duty. I stayed on the road that fall of 1996 for five weeks, and it wore me down. Physically, it was exhausting. But emotionally, it was withering. I had seen lots of suffering during my career, but I had not seen it by the tens of thousands, as was the case in Rwanda and Zaire.

Over at Sake, a small eastern Zaire town about fifteen miles west of Goma, the refugees were still streaming out of the hills and marching onto the Mugunga road and toward Rwanda. My fixer-translator for this leg of the trip was a young Rwandan journalist named Alec. We stood at the base of the road from the hills and talked to refugees as they came by, to hear of their struggle in the mountains and of the fighting they had witnessed. A small crowd gathered in front of us, and things seemed to be going well. I noticed, as I'd seen before in both Rwanda and eastern Zaire, that many of the men carried machetes. They were farmers, the people of this region, and machetes were as common as walking sticks. These refugees were bone-tired, sick, and just dragging. Their blades didn't threaten me at all.

But Alec, a Tutsi, had lost many relatives in the Rwandan genocide. He knew he was talking to people who might have been killers. As the crowd grew and wrapped around us in a circle, Alec became agitated. Though I do not understand the Kinyarwanda language, I could tell from his tone that he was speaking to them far more aggressively than he should, almost barking at them. I stopped him and asked what was wrong, what he was doing. He was telling the people not to stand behind him. He could not have these machete-carrying people encircling him, he told me. I suggested we pull back and take a break so he could collect himself. He was generally quite professional in his work, but this time the genocidal fear had overwhelmed him.

With about ten thousand refugees camped along the Mugunga road one day, I met an eighty-year-old man, Mihigo Enok, and his obviously ill wife, Kampere Louise. She had malaria. Sweat dripped down her face. Her feet were bloody. They'd been walking for more than a month. Enok couldn't carry everything, so they'd unloaded some of their belongings along the way. Despite the heat, he wore four shirts, two jackets, and had tied an orange plastic cup to the rope that served as a belt, next to the coat pocket that held a bottle for collecting water from streams. In their long trek, they'd been separated from the rest of their family. They'd had no food for two days. The couple seemed totally dazed as they moved on to join the thousands of refugees. Some who were too ill to continue the walk would be trucked over to Rwanda.

From my hotel in Goma, the Frontière, I returned to the Mugunga road the next morning. Refugees were still camped on the side of the road, still awaiting those relief trucks. To my shock as I walked along the road, I saw Mr. Mihigo and his wife. They saw me too. I greeted them. They looked utterly desperate, even worse than the day before. They had still not been picked up and transported back to Rwanda. I could not bear witnessing old people in such terrible straits. Something in me snapped. I ran to a relief worker. I think she was from the Red Cross. I demanded that the old couple receive food, water, and medical attention right away. I got so choked up I couldn't even talk. I was out of line. I'd let the situation overwhelm me. I don't know the aid worker's name, but she looked me straight in the eye and firmly told me to get hold of myself. Everyone among the thousands of people on that road was hungry and sick, she said. The old couple would be tended to in due time. It was the right thing for her to say, for everyone around us was desperate and no one person could be plucked out for special treatment. I went back to reassure the old couple that help would soon come. But the whole episode left me feeling depressed.

I battled that feeling often through the long months of covering the war. The story—and the things I had to do to cover it and write it—kept me in a state of constant turmoil. Three difficult weeks I spent in Goma again the following spring, in March 1997, were especially challenging. Getting information about the war was difficult enough, what with Kabila's rebels always playing cat and mouse with reporters. On top of that, the logistics of war coverage were incredibly complicated. Every day at the Frontière, I had to climb out my room's window and onto the corrugated metal roof to readjust my satellite phone antenna. The hotel had no telephone service, so my sat

phone was my only link to the outside. On it, I spoke to the office and trans-
mitted my stories. With power outages routine, I worried constantly about
keeping the phone's battery charged.

Every day, I ate nothing but starchy foods, but still got road sickness. And
when I sat down to write in the evening, the industrial-style fluorescent
lights running across the ceiling of my room attracted every insect in Africa.
The ones that looked like thumbs with wings really made my skin crawl.
Marcus, my traveling pal, took to bouncing on the bed like it was a trampo-
line and swatting the flying thumbs with newspaper. And if all that wasn't
bad enough, it was just my luck that a senior editor at my newspaper back in
Washington had studied the Congo crisis when it was unfolding thirty years
earlier and thought it reasonable to phone me one morning at two o'clock,
Zaire time, to suggest changes in my daily dispatch. The piece had already
been edited, but this senior executive wanted me to broaden the historic context.

It was a front-page piece describing how Kabila and some of his top aides
traced their ideological roots to the nationalism of Lumumba. Zaire's past
was truly its prologue. Many of Kabila's men had fought at Stanleyville in the
1960s, and they represented the Zairean aspirations of yesteryear, back when
the country had a chance to reshape itself. But those ideals had been lost in
the country's twisted history. I perceived these men as people stuck in a time
warp, having spent their lives nursing the wounds of the old struggle. Included among them was Anicet Kashamura, minister of culture and information in Lumumba's 1960 cabinet, who carried around the tattered pages of
the bulky memoir he said he was writing of his life. He hung out at the Frontière and spoke to me endlessly at the bar. I was proud of the article I produced from those interviews. No one up to that point had written of these
men in such a broad historic context and shown how rooted in the past this
new revolution actually was, notwithstanding Rwanda's modern-day agenda.

Then Zaire's third largest city, Kisangani, fell to the rebel Alliance, and
the press scramble was on to arrange charter flights into the newly "liberated"
town. Working by sat phone with the Associated Press office in Nairobi, I
and a few other correspondents arranged a charter flight that would pick us
up in Goma and fly on to Kisangani. Kabila's Alliance didn't want us to go.

But Goma airport officials gave the green light. As the small plane taxied for takeoff, some civilian rebel officials ran out onto the runway to stop the flight. The pilot leaned out from the cockpit and asked us what he should do. The eight of us on board hollered for him to just go, go, go! And so we took off. As we gained altitude, I had this strange afterthought: did the rebels really have antiaircraft artillery, as my U.S. sources claimed?

This, my second trip to Kisangani, was fruitful, and safe. People there hoped that peace would settle in. They hoped Kabila would bring far more stability than had Mobutu. I returned that evening to Goma, filed my story, and prepared to pull out of Goma within a day or two, as soon as I could finagle a seat on someone's plane. I learned of a flight to Nairobi and dashed to the airport hours in advance to alert the Alliance immigration officer of my imminent departure. Rebel immigration procedures were bizarre. To enter rebel territory, journalists had to turn over their passports and receive, in exchange, a pass to circulate. Even to leave rebel territory you needed permission, and only then would your passport be returned. I'd gone through this before and knew I'd get my passport back with no trouble. But it turned out that the Nairobi flight was filled. The next flight that day was to Kigali. Since I'd been given permission to depart for Nairobi, not Kigali, the petty little immigration man refused to hand over my passport. "I cannot give it to you." That's what he said, and he said it flatly, leaving no room for discussion. That's what set me off.

I banged my open palm on his rickety metal desk like a drum and yelled at him over and over to give me the X#?&%*X#-#X&% passport. I yelled till I was out of breath and hyperventilating. I vaguely remember the little immigration guy pushing his chair away from the desk, away from the stark raving lunatic before him. A German television reporter, another woman, came and put her arms around me and walked me away to pace the floor until I could catch my breath. But I got my passport, offering profuse apologies for my tantrum, and got on that plane. After two days in bed at the Hôtel des Mille Collines in Kigali, I returned to Jo'burg, unpacked, did laundry, packed again, and headed back to Zaire.

9

Mobutu's Fading Spots

hen Mobutu stepped into the threshold of his chartered DC-8 in December 1996, a deafening roar rose up over the N'Djili Airport tarmac. Kinshasa hadn't seen the president for several months. Rumors flew that maybe he had died. But there he stood, beaming and waving at throngs of his people, no doubt relishing a rare moment of glory. It would be his last chance to revel. The Zaire he had made in his own image and then devoured was slipping from his grasp with each passing day, each time the eastern rebel Alliance gobbled up another piece of his nation. Mobutu's Zaire was finished. Those of us who'd been in the east could sense it. Those in Kinshasa could only fear it. His famous diviners and West African marabouts (Muslim priests with supposed supernatural powers) couldn't stop what time had in store. As Mobutu stepped from his plane that December, he stepped onto the pages of history.

Despite his obvious excitement, he looked gaunt and frail. His spotted leopard-skin hat and his walking stick of exquisitely carved wood failed to conjure the mythic stamina and virility of the fabled "all-powerful warrior" he once claimed to be. Illness enfeebled him. At sixty-six years old, he arrived back in Kinshasa after four months in Europe to rest from surgery for a cancer that began in his prostate and spread to his bones.

His ruling party, the Popular Movement of the Revolution (MPR), bused in hordes of people for the sparkling welcome. By the thousands, they swarmed through the stinking, decaying airport and spilled onto the tarmac. Marching bands trumpeted. Drummers pounded. In unison, undulating women swayed their hips. And all around me down there where the red carpet awaited Mobutu's footsteps, jubilant people waved cheerful little flags that told a sad lie: "Father has come! Zaire is saved!" They wanted it to be true. They wanted Zaire to be strong and mighty. They wanted their leader, as reviled as he usually was, to restore the national pride, to be Mobutu the magician once again.

He stood in his limousine, waving his fetish stick through the sunroof, regaling the crowds who lined Kinshasa's streets. Up on Mont-Ngaliema, as if the good old days were back, Mobutu presided on the veranda of his presidential villa on the grounds of a military compound called Camp Colonel Tshatshi. Waiters circulated on the lawn below, around a great stone fountain, serving hors d'oeuvres. The entire predator class of Mobutu-aligned politicians milled about in anticipation, as did bemused members of the local and international press. Africa's most grandiose dictator was about to utter his first words in defense of his nation. It was, shall we say, far from rousing.

"Today, I am back in Zaire," he began, his voice sounding hoarse. He could not even bring himself to speak directly of the eastern rebellion, except for an oblique jab at those who "seized the opportunity of my illness to put a sword in my back ... My heart is charged with a moral debt to my people. I know what you are expecting of me ... Every time our country has been threatened in the past, I have never retreated. This time, again, I will not retreat." The Congo River rapids roared in the background. Pecking around the grounds, Mobutu's peacocks screamed out a few caws. And the words of the mighty Mobutu seemed just part of Kinshasa's strange noise.

In the coming days, he named a new top general. His government promised an all-out offensive to put down the eastern rebels. He hired Serb mercenaries from the former Yugoslavia. He reshuffled his government. But it all seemed business as usual. The new cabinet had the same old faces from Mobutu's revolving political door. He'd kept the reviled prime minister,

Kengo wa Dondo, whose history as a Mobutu crony did not endear him to the population.

Whatever goodwill the Kinois might have felt for Mobutu on the day of his triumphal return that December had vanished by the time he left in January to seek still more treatment for the cancer. Instead of cheers, catcalls greeted his motorcade. And when a new currency was introduced shortly afterward in an economy already hit with wild inflation, people refused to trade with it. Cruelly, they called the new notes prostate money.

Whenever Mobutu had been in this kind of trouble before, his foreign patrons bailed him out. Starting with President Eisenhower, numerous American presidents had favored Mobutu. The United States nurtured him, used him as a key bulwark against Soviet expansion in Africa, paid him handsomely for his services, and turned a blind eye to his mounting malfeasance. Even before Mobutu seized the presidency in his 1965 coup, the Americans and Belgians had bailed out his military in the separatist fight at Stanleyville in 1964.

Mobutu faced more internal military pressure in 1977 and 1978 in the southern province of Shaba, known also as Katanga. When Katangans who'd fought to secede from Zaire in the 1960s invaded Shaba from their bases in northeastern Angola, Mobutu's Western patrons flew to his rescue. Led by France, a multinational force fought back the first Shaba invasion. As a former Belgian colony, Zaire was the largest French-speaking nation in the world after France itself and a key to the French sphere of influence in Africa. When the second Shaba invasion broke out a year later, the United States jumped in as well. President Jimmy Carter justified the intervention with an accusation that the Soviets and their Cuban allies were aiding the Katangan rebels. But it is probable that U.S. economic interests were also at stake. Two-thirds of the world's copper and cobalt came from Shaba, and U.S. mining companies had significant interests in the region. So the Carter administration added U.S. muscle to the second Shaba intervention force, backing up French and Belgian commandos with air support to put down the invasion.

But by the 1990s, with the Cold War's end, Mobutu's usefulness to the West waned. With Zaire's foreign debt at $13 billion, its treasury emptied, its mining and other companies bled dry through corruption, Mobutu's international patrons turned the screws. They refused to secure any more loans to Mobutu's regime. They suspended foreign aid and made democracy a condition of its resumption. But democracy, Zaire-style, produced gridlock, in which Mobutu remained the main beneficiary. Democracy, Zaire-style, was a bunch of politicians inextricably stuck in the mud of a tangled, corrupt, and grudge-driven system. From that mire, the politicians who'd been part of the Sovereign National Conference that was to form a new political system looked up in 1996 and saw a rebel movement bearing down on them, threatening to eclipse them. Many within the Zairean political class did not grasp how their world had been upended.

As if he remained a viable political leader, Etienne Tshisekedi, the leading opposition figure who'd been named prime minister by the Sovereign Conference, continued to stubbornly lay claim to that high office even after Mobutu ousted him from the post for the third time. From his home, where supporters routinely gathered in the streets, Tshisekedi held press conferences and issued statements through the spring of 1997, as if he were an important player. He wanted Laurent Kabila's rebels to respect his standing and include him in whatever plans came with Mobutu's ouster. Kengo wa Dondo hung on too. He managed the financing of the war effort, until Mobutu ousted him that April and accused him of looting the government's war chest. Kengo fled from the country, a very wise man.

The situation looked grim for Kinshasa's fat cats. Ever so quietly, they began ensconcing their wives, girlfriends, and children in the Hotel Intercontinental, the city's main hotel, even sending them off to South Africa and Europe for safekeeping. Mobutu's capital felt like an empty circus tent—no more highfliers, no more magic tricks. It became a city of waiting, the Zairean interregnum. On the sweltering streets, the city seethed with demands for change. Protest marches and citywide boycotts became regular features of everyday life. In the cool cocoon of the Intercon, Mobutu's political class postured and gossiped and conspired to save their skins.

And the European and Arab expatriates boated on the Congo River, taking sumptuous food and fine wines along for luncheons on the river's sandbars. This was a part of Kinshasa life I'd never seen, until one Sunday when I accepted the invitation of a European diamond trader to go out on his boat and have lunch with a few others. As a buffer against the diamond trader's chronic flirtations, I asked Dele, my pal from *Newsday*, to come along. In a speedboat, we roared across Malebo Pool, which felt as vast as a large lake. We weighed anchor, so to speak, on a large sandbank and off-loaded folding tables and chairs for our lunch of shrimp, salad, and champagne. Expatriates zoomed past on their Jet Skis. Zaireans glided by in their dugout canoes. Our host stripped down to his skimpy swimming trunks and set off to water-ski. I had no intention of showing any flesh, and had even declined the diamond trader's offer of a skimpy bikini he just happened to bring along. I remained the spectator, not a participant. The stark display of inequality on that river—rich versus poor, white versus black—made me uncomfortable. There was something debased about the expat existence.

To them, Zaire was just a playground. The diamond dealers from Britain, Belgium, and Lebanon clearly viewed Zaireans as an amusing mass of dysfunctional people. For them, the country's mess produced great drama, great diplomatic gossip, great diamonds and gold, but little else. It was a netherworld, an African fantasia. Servants were plentiful. Money flowed unrestricted. Government was nothing but a wink and a nod. And beautiful women were welcome attractions in the absence of the wives and families the expatriates left back home.

But their days of plunder were about to end. By April 1997, one of the most resource-rich countries on the globe had *no cash* left in the central bank (none except for the equivalent of $120 million worth of "prostate" currency that none of the city markets would accept). And with the diamond and gold mines of the east and central regions falling into rebel hands, little hard currency was coming into Kinshasa. The problem was dire. Unpaid, poorly fed, and ill equipped, the Armed Forces of Zaire (the FAZ) was primed for *le pillage*. They'd rioted over lack of pay twice, in 1991 and 1993, literally tearing big cities apart. In Kinshasa that spring of 1997, speculation swirled about whether and when they'd riot again.

But the problem of the war effort went beyond pay for the army. By then, Angola had entered the war on the side of Rwanda's Alliance and poured in troops to defeat Mobutu's army. The FAZ didn't really want to fight anyway. And even if they wanted to, they weren't properly trained to wage war. And even if they'd had the proper training, they didn't have enough serious weapons. Their generals, you see, made a pretty penny in the sale of weapons to the UNITA rebels down in Angola, among other buyers on the arms market. And the weaponry that remained had largely decayed for lack of maintenance. Before the war, the army's broken-down fleet of a dozen 1950s-vintage tanks had to be parked during a military parade. There were some helicopter gunships in the arsenal, but no local pilots knew how to fly them, a diplomatic defense attaché told me.

With the FAZ in such a debased state, it's no wonder the eastern rebel Alliance found its advance toward Kinshasa so peaceful. The FAZ fled from most potential battles, but not before looting whatever they could on the way out. Considering Zaire's size and reputation for brutality, the war had unfolded, miraculously, with but one major battle. At Kisangani that March, the FAZ, its mercenary allies, and the remnants of the Rwandan Hutu ex-FAR and Interahamwe fought for a day against the Alliance and lost. Kisangani was the turning point of the war. The fall of Zaire's third largest city, the seat of the so-called government counteroffensive, made it absolutely clear that the rebels really could take Kinshasa. And they kept on marching, straight across Africa. Though other diplomats and local residents were verging on hysteria as they anticipated an assault on Kinshasa, the defense attaché was blasé. "The war is over," he said. "It ended at Kisangani. It's just the rebels moving from place to place."

Mobutu held on, despite declining health. On bad days, he received visitors in bed at Camp Tshatshi. While reassuring Mobutu that they could retake territory and win the war, some of his generals secretly sent their families and valuables out of the country. Even the Terminator, Mobutu's trusted security adviser, had spirited his own family away. One of Mobutu's sons, twenty-seven-year-old Mobutu Nzanga, arrived that spring to stand by his father during the ordeal. A handsome and quite dapper young man who lived in Morocco but also shuttled between Paris and Brussels, he seemed out of his depth amid the cutthroat sport of Kinshasa politics from which his father had shielded him. He was one among sixteen Mobutu offspring, including two who were deceased. Designated the family spokesman, he was quite a contrast to another brother sticking close to the father in those final days, Mobutu Kongulu, an army officer known by locals as "Saddam Hussein." He had a reputation that struck fear.

I spoke with Nzanga many times in those final weeks. In light of his father's desperate situation, Nzanga's easy manner and openness to journalists at first surprised me. Naturally, his function was to spin the news, to doctor the Mobutu legacy. And who could begrudge him? That's what a son should do. He felt aggrieved at the way the press, including me, had portrayed his father, so giving him a voice in my coverage seemed the fair thing to do. And it couldn't hurt to have a source as close to Mobutu as a son presumably would be. I got the sense in some of our talks that his platitudes, his earnestness, were actually sincere, though perhaps it is more accurate to say: sincerely misguided. Over and over during those final weeks, I raised the question of his father's seemingly unavoidable resignation. Nzanga routinely reacted as if the very thought was an absurdity.

We spoke at length one Saturday, ensconced behind lush foliage in a far corner of the Intercon's poolside café. He portrayed his ailing father as deeply hurt by the rebellion, but resolute in his commitment to remain head of state. Yes, his father knew the depth of the crisis. Zaire was on the verge of exploding as troops backed by foreign governments swept across the country. But for the sake of Zaire's integrity as a nation, his father felt duty bound to hang on, to resist the pressure to resign. "He would feel it would be treason if he did it now."

"When I tell you President Mobutu is a real patriot, it's not because I'm his son," Nzanga insisted. "He hopes he really gave Zaire pride." He was referring to the campaign of the 1970s, called *authenticité*, in which African names, customs, and styles of dress were given primacy over the European. For Nzanga, it was an issue of pride, and he spoke bitterly about the international ridicule that had rained down on his father's Africanism campaign. "Outside, people laughed at it. They *laughed* at it. But if you think about it, it was a way for the Zairean people—after years of colonization, of being told they were no good because they were black, they were nothing—to give them pride. And so I hope the Zairean people will be grateful."

The country had been ground into medieval poverty. The economy had shrunk to its pre-independence productivity. Annual per capita income was

$150. One hundred fifty dollars! And Mobutu, all the while, was accused of stealing between $150 million and $400 million a year through the 1980s from the country's mining revenue. How on earth could Nzanga possibly think for one minute that Zaireans would feel gratitude? He was, alas, the good son.

But the objective fact was this: Zaire turned on Mobutu with a vengeance. People wanted him gone. They awaited Laurent Kabila, the rebel leader, as their liberator. And soon they would have him, for better or worse. Mobutu could sit tight and watch Kinshasa snatched from under his feet, perhaps with terrible bloodshed, even his own death. Or he could do something he'd never been forced to do: negotiate for his very survival. He had no cards left to play.

* * *

POINTE-NOIRE, CONGO REPUBLIC, MAY 1997

The decks of the SAS *Outeniqua* steamed in the equatorial heat. Confined to the upper deck with about a dozen other correspondents as part of the ship's security lockdown, I paced the rails—watching, waiting, and writing.

On the quay down below, a convoy of dark sedans with tinted windows pulled up. Its passengers piled out, and I spotted some of Mobutu's top men. Honoré Ngbanda Nzambo ko Atumba, Mobutu's chief security adviser, the Terminator, was down on the quay, as was Gerard Kamanda wa Kamanda, a lawyer by training, a foreign minister, and a key Mobutu insider, chomping on a cigar. After days of wrangling over venue, the show would finally begin. Mobutu agreed to negotiate an end to the war. He would meet his nemesis, Kabila, for the first time.

Only a few days earlier, President Clinton's administration sent a delegation to Kinshasa headed by Bill Richardson, the U.S. ambassador to the United Nations, who told Mobutu he had no choice but to step down. President Nelson Mandela pressed Mobutu as well, in an effort to secure what the Americans called a soft landing once the rebels reached Kinshasa. But Mobutu's health had been on the decline. By early May, he was too ill to fly to South Africa for talks. So Mandela decided to bring a neutral venue to

Mobutu. Mandela dispatched the *Outeniqua,* an eleven-story, 21,000-ton South African naval supply ship and icebreaker, whose name in the South African Khoikhoi language means "bearer of honey." Normally, the ship plied the frigid South Atlantic. Now it would see duty in the steamy heat of Pointe-Noire. The plan called for Mobutu and the other guests to board the *Outeniqua* at Pointe-Noire. Then the ship would steam out to international waters, where Kabila would chopper aboard. Kabila refused to board in Pointe-Noire itself, for the Congo Republic president, Pascal Lissouba, was a Mobutu ally. Kabila feared for his life if he tarried in Lissouba's territory. Talk about a logistical nightmare. The stakes were high enough already without the extra hurdle of getting all the players in place.

Mandela, still Africa's most towering figure, staked his substantial credibility on the affair. He worked from the successful South African template of compromise. The relatively peaceful settlement to end apartheid grew from good-faith negotiations. In finding a common ground—the preservation of South Africa—old enemies hammered out a formula for political reconciliation. That the bitterest of enemies—South Africa's ruling whites and its oppressed blacks—could hash out a nonviolent end to their struggle seemed a remarkable turn of events that many, most of all Mandela, hoped could be a model for negotiations elsewhere. Success at the talks would be a great coup for South Africa, the presumptive new power on the continent. And Mandela had come to Pointe-Noire for the sake of an old idea that his nation's rebirth had made new, the idea of an African renaissance. That's what peace in Zaire would help foster, for there could be no renewal in Africa if the country at its very heart, the linchpin between Africa's disparate regions, was spewing chaos onto its neighbors.

But I had my doubts. Mandela's model struck me as nontransferable to the Zairean context. The protagonists—Mobutu, Kabila, Rwanda, Uganda, Angola—did not strike me as players among whom a common ground could be found. And Zaire had no tradition of good-faith compromise. In fact, its political and diplomatic tradition was quite the opposite, of bad faith and duplicity, of shakedowns and payoffs. That was the Zairean way. I had the nagging suspicion that the South Africans were out of their depth. Maybe those analysts were right, the ones who said that Mandela and company, having spent so many years cloistered within apartheid's ferment and alienated from the dynamics of the rest of Africa, weren't up to speed on the new power politics reshaping the continent. The talks would be a test of South Africa's foreign policy skill, and Mandela brimmed with confidence as he received a hero's welcome by the 120-man ship's crew. U.S. Ambassador Bill Richardson boarded as well, as did U.N. envoy Mohamed Sahnoun. But down on the quay, Mobutu's entourage looked troubled.

The Terminator and Kamanda studiously counted the thirty-one steps on the stairway up to the ship's deck. They slowly climbed from deck to dock, looking glummer. The *Outeniqua's* first diplomatic disaster: Mobutu's prostate cancer and its complications made him too weak to board ship on his own. The diplomats and naval logisticians put their heads together. One idea that floated around ship would have spelled certain collapse of the talks. No way would Mobutu agree to be winched up on deck in a cagelike container like so much cargo. Obviously, the idea went nowhere.

Finally, the crew constructed a makeshift vehicular ramp that allowed Mobutu and his friend, President Lissouba, to drive directly into the ship's hold. Mobutu and Lissouba had different origins—the latter was an elected leader, unlike the dictator of Kinshasa—but they would have similar endings. In pursuit of their own strategic aims in middle Africa, the Angolans who were after Mobutu would soon set their sights on Lissouba, for he, too, supported the Angolan rebels, UNITA. Angolan President José Eduardo dos Santos had sent troops into Zaire not so much to help Kabila as to shut down the arms pipeline that Mobutu's regime had run to Angola's rebels. Dos Santos had been fighting the rebels of UNITA leader Jonas Savimbi for decades and saw, in the Zaire war, an opportune way to flank Savimbi's forces. Though Rwanda started the war, Angola would be pivotal to its finish. No wonder that Kabila, as he awaited his rendezvous on the *Outeniqua*, was in Angola with dos Santos.

That night, with all parties on board and ready to talk, the *Outeniqua* pulled anchor and churned out into international waters. Mandela's deputy president, Thabo Mbeki, took off from the ship's helipad to meet Kabila and escort him back for the talks. As the ship plowed through the waves, it occurred to me how thoroughly the chickens had come home to roost for

Mobutu. The Angolans wanted him gone so the Zairean-UNITA link would be severed. The Rwandans and Burundians wanted him gone so they could root out the genocidal Hutu forces plaguing both their nations. In addition to supporting Rwanda, the Ugandans threw in because Zairean territory harbored antigovernment Ugandan rebels. Whatever the talks might produce, Central Africa was seeing an unprecedented realignment of power.

And speaking of realignments: We journalists were standing on deck watching the brightly lit oil derricks on the horizon get closer and closer as the *Outeniqua* steamed toward them, when ever so slowly we noticed the vista change. The *Outeniqua* was turning around. And Kabila wasn't on board. Mbeki choppered back to ship with a new list of Kabila conditions: Lissouba had to go; Kabila would not board ship with Mobutu's pal on hand. Ditto for Richardson, whose tough talk on rebel atrocities had angered Kabila. From an advance man already on board, Kabila learned of the random figures in Mobutu's delegation, some of whom turned out to be armed aides posing as presidential journalists. They'd have to be ejected from the ship or be disarmed in a tighter security lockdown before Kabila would come on board. The no-show embarrassed Mandela deeply. The old man was livid, his aides said. How dare Kabila do this to him. Through that Friday night and Saturday, feverish negotiations via satellite telephone were whizzing up and down the African coast.

I'd flown from Pretoria aboard a South African military transport (four hours on a pitching plane) thinking it a one-day jaunt. So I'd packed far too lightly for what turned out to be a weekend held hostage to diplomacy. I don't mean to belittle the effort, for I believed then and now that Mandela did what he had to do. But the hassles involved, especially for us journalists, were beyond belief. When not eating or sleeping, we were confined to the deck at the ship's bow, amid its cables, coils, cranks, drums, winches, and ship's grease. That's where South African diplomats briefed us with the scant information they were willing to reveal about the difficult diplomacy under way. We had to use ship satellite phones to communicate with our overseas offices and transmit our dispatches. When one of Mandela's satellite phones broke down and his aides requisitioned the press phone for presidential use, we journalists turned on each other in a shouting match over who could use our one remaining phone and when. We were so loud, so ugly, that a South African official intervened. Mandela, he said, could hear the ruckus.

For meals, the crew marched us through the hot, musty bowels of the ship, past the giant sauna down in the hold wallpapered with a Russian birch forest scene, and to the "mess." There we were fed food that is best described as clumps of goop in big vats. I exaggerate, but only slightly. And at night, the six women correspondents among us were put up in one cabin meant to bed two sailors. They'd graciously moved out to make way for us in their quarters with the tiny, moldy shower, which I, for one, did not touch. In my clothes, I slept on a banquette at the small dining table. Others slept in the bunks or on the floor. The male journalists, meanwhile, slept al fresco up on deck, struggling for comfort in canvas stretchers more flimsy than cots. The pressure got to everyone. One of Mbeki's junior aides made a spectacle of his own. He drank late into the night and early morning, then charged up on deck a raving maniac. He roused the sleeping journalists with demands that they be placed under guard and searched. We never saw him again that weekend. Rumor had it he'd been confined to quarters.

The *Outeniqua* felt like a floating circus. And that was sad indeed. Mandela's people were fuming at Kabila's seeming disrespect of Africa's elder statesman. One Mandela aide called Kabila "mad"; another called him a "cowboy on the loose." I half expected Mandela to pack up and leave. He'd have been justified if he abandoned the effort, I thought naively. Why expend his moral capital on a lost cause? As the hours ticked by that Saturday afternoon, Mobutu left the ship, though he stayed close by, in Pointe-Noire. But Kabila kept stalling, all through the day. He wanted all Mobutu's family off the ship. He wanted all Zairean security men disarmed. He wanted Mobutu to board the ship first for yet another voyage to international waters.

And Mandela stayed. He'd committed himself to this course and would not just walk away from it. Zaire was too important to African peace and stability to let it slide deeper into chaos without heroic efforts to stop it. Plus, Mandela had a kind of leverage that could make Kabila respond. The fact is, an unknown and questionable leader like Kabila couldn't afford to burn the bridge to South Africa. Mandela reached Kabila via satellite phone and delivered an ultimatum, as paraphrased for me later by one of his aides: "You come here now, or I'm leaving. I'm not prepared to accept those conditions. I'm rejecting them now, even without talking to Mobutu!"

The threat worked. Late that night, Kabila flew aboard with Mbeki. As Kabila strutted down from the helipad and across the deck, wearing the kind of guayabera shirt favored by the likes of Cuba's Fidel Castro, that menacing grin spread across his face. The next morning, Mobutu returned to the *Outeniqua*, accompanied by his wife, Bobi Ladawa, as well as a daughter and two sons, including Mobutu Nzanga.

The delegations met for eighty minutes, then emerged grim-faced. It had not gone well. They took up position at a long table for a formal presentation to the hostage press. I nestled myself atop a high coil of anchor cables. Though typically charming in such ceremonial events, Mandela seemed dour. He would take no questions. He would make no small talk. There would be no glad-handing and backslapping. Mandela squinted in the noon glare. Mobutu required assistance to walk, and leaned on a crisply dressed military attendant who saluted him dramatically as Mobutu sat down to Mandela's right. Wearing the ever-present leopard-skin hat, he stared straight ahead from behind thick black-framed glasses. Either from pique or from the discomfort of his illness, his face sagged in a pout. That is how Mobutu made his last appearance on the international stage: clearly defeated. To Mandela's left, Kabila looked like a very self-satisfied man just playing along with this charade. After all, whatever any peace deal said, his forces were about a hundred miles from Kinshasa. They did not need to negotiate.

When all was said and done behind closed doors, Kabila and Mobutu exchanged diametrically opposed proposals for a handover of power. Kabila wanted all power for his Alliance, with a cease-fire coming only thereafter; Mobutu wanted a cease-fire up front, with power transferred to a transitional authority that would stage elections. He would resign only once a new president was elected. It was an utterly ludicrous position, considering the balance of forces arrayed against him. But by then, Mobutu seemed to be just going through the motions of holding on. Nothing had been achieved in the talks, but Mandela did not say this. He couldn't say it. Instead, he intoned gravely that each side would consider the other's proposals and meet again soon. Ever the statesman, he stroked the two characters on either side of him, saying he was honored to serve as a broker between "two of the greatest sons of Africa."

It was a completely futile show of pomp and diplomacy. I'd hoped that Mandela and his moral authority would somehow eclipse the venality of Congo's morass, as represented by the roguish characters beside him. But forces far stronger than Mandela were at play in the Congo, and Mandela's authority and powers of persuasion would have but limited effect. The diplomatic show aboard the *Outeniqua* wasn't really about Mandela, Mobutu, or Kabila at all. It was about Rwandan Vice President Paul Kagame, whose tiny nation was propelled by a postgenocide survivalist instinct that had been the raison d'être for the war in the first place. It was about President Yoweri Museveni of Uganda, Kagame's patron, who'd become a key African power broker. And it was about dos Santos of Angola, whose army would miss no opportunity to hit at the allies of the UNITA rebels. None of those men were present on the *Outeniqua*, and yet they—not Mandela—were dictating the course of events. Mandela had been in contact with these men or their representatives repeatedly in the weeks before the talks and definitely knew what roles they were playing. But South Africa's intervention could not alter the course that had already been set in motion.

In the old days, the troika of powers that manipulated Zaire was Western: the United States, Belgium, and France. But now, with the West having largely lost strategic interest, Africans took up the mantle of the troika. Kagame, Museveni, and dos Santos would reshape middle Africa through firepower, not through a well-intentioned notion called an African renaissance. Mandela held the moral high ground, but Zaire's crisis, down in the valley of realpolitik, wasn't about morality at all. Based on raw power, Kagame, Museveni, and dos Santos, for better or worse, were creating a new world order in Africa.

10

Exit Mobutu

I knew the end was nigh when "Mr. King," my interrogator from the airport, turned from foe to friend and started feeding me secret information. He was shifty, oily, and scary, and I never knew his real name. He told me to call him "Mr. King," and so I did. When he'd ring up my cell phone that May to tell me of the latest bigwigs to fly into exile and what valuables they'd taken with them, I did not even bother to ask how he got my cell phone number. He worked for one of the intelligence services, so of course, he could find out whatever he needed to know.

On an earlier trip to Kinshasa, Mr. King had detained me, along with my Jo'burg pals Judith Matloff and Ross Herbert, and seized our passports. Taking us deep into the airport terminal, he sat us at a table in a dank room with a lightbulb dangling overhead. With a great show of menace, he demanded to know why my passport was green while Judith's and Ross's were blue. Of course, I had no idea why and didn't care to even think about it. It was just the prelude to the deal. We solved the mystery of the green passport with greenbacks, *le petit cadeau*: thirty dollars. At war's end, I laughed each time Mr. King phoned, and I discovered, after my own reporting, that his facts were mostly right on target. Mobutu's cronies were in full flight.

But even more crucial events were unfolding up at Camp Tshatshi among the Mobutu crowd. Mobutu had held on to the remains of his old friend, the slain Rwandan Hutu president, Juvénal Habyarimana. Habyarimana's death aboard a downed plane in Kigali, Rwanda, in 1994 was the trigger that presaged that country's genocide. Mobutu apparently felt his loss keenly. They were close friends—so close, in fact, that Mobutu somehow gained possession of Habyarimana's remains and had them buried at the Mobutu mausoleum in Gbadolite. But several days after the *Outeniqua* talks, apparently realizing his time was running out and fearing Habyarimana might be defiled by the rebels, Mobutu ordered his old friend's remains dug up and flown to Kinshasa. In one of his final bizarre acts as president, Mobutu presided over Habyarimana's cremation.

That evening came the worst news of all. The army chief of staff and defense minister, General Mahele Lieko Bokungu, informed Mobutu that all was lost. Kinshasa could not be defended. Mahele urged Mobutu to flee while he still had the chance. Early Friday morning, with no fanfare and no announcement, Mobutu and his family, plus a planeload of their belongings, took off from Kinshasa, en route to Gbadolite. Late that night, Mobutu Nzanga rang my cell phone. He sounded tired and sad, but strangely chatty. Perhaps he'd been traumatized by the day's events. But he was still sharp enough to speak for twenty minutes and put a heavy spin on this most disastrous day for the Mobutu family.

"The president didn't resign today," he said emphatically when I used the r-word yet again. He claimed his father was *not* going into exile. "No, that's not the case. But I think, you know, there's a military situation. It will depend on the course of the situation." He took a deep breath, sounding as desperate as he should, when I asked him about the family's next move. "I don't know. I don't know. I'm more concerned about his health." That was my last conversation with Mobutu Nzanga during the Mobutu era. I actually felt sorry it had turned out this way for him. (His family did indeed fly into exile, and that September Mobutu Sese Seko would pass away in Morocco.)

That same night of my final chat with Nzanga, Kabila's forces blasted through Kinshasa's eastern line of defense and seized N'Djili Airport. The commander of Mobutu's elite presidential troops fled across the river to Brazzaville, leaving behind soldiers who were fighting mad about the capitulation.

Mahele, the defense minister, had held talks with at least one U.S. diplomat on ways to avert catastrophe when the rebels marched into the city. He went up to Camp Tshatshi early that Saturday morning to calm the troops and counsel them not to fight the rebels. But someone put a gun to his head and blew his brains out. The most infamous of Mobutu's sons, Mobutu Kongulu (aka Saddam Hussein), may not necessarily have been the triggerman, but all observers believed him to be in league with Mahele's killer. Kongulu wanted the blood of the men he believed had deserted the great leopard.

My cell phone rang at 3:00 A.M. Saturday. Paul van Goethem, a Belgian correspondent based at the nearby Memling Hotel, phoned to warn me that Kongulu was rumored to be at the Intercon in a blind fury and with tanks. I jumped up and headed out to my balcony, which overlooked the hotel's entrance. I heard no commotion. I saw no tanks. The night seemed strangely calm. I caught a few more hours of sleep. At 6:30 A.M., I headed out, pressing casually for the elevator. The doors opened. My heart stopped. I faced this: five men, swathed in bandoliers of bullets, holding Uzi-like machine pistols, with thick-bladed knives strapped to their thighs. This is what Paul had tried to warn me about. Saddam Hussein's henchmen were still on the loose.

I couldn't just cut and run. That would seem suspicious. I didn't want these guys chasing me through the Intercon hallways, maybe shooting me in the back, or worse. So I stepped into the elevator, as if life were normal. I chirped a quick "Bonjour." They did not respond. With my back to the barrels of their guns, I made laserlike eye contact with a handy spot on the floor. Never has an elevator ride seemed so long.

Finally, the elevator landed in the main lobby. The doors opened onto a scene of pandemonium. The high-and-mighty Mobutuists were evacuating. Men shouted and scrambled around. Women in a shambles—hair all over their heads, no makeup, not at all stylish as the Kinshasa way—dragged crying pajama-clad kids and bulky suitcases across the marble floor. Outside, panicked people piled into a waiting armored convoy that would take them to the river. The ninja stood guard. A photographer raised his camera to capture the episode. I thought they'd shoot his head off. He lowered the camera.

I stood against a wall, quietly amazed to watch this microcosm of the fall of the old Zaire. They were a class of people who, as individuals, may have been perfectly fine, God-fearing folk. But as a collective, they represented all that had turned Zaire into a nightmare, Africa's nightmare. Kongulu himself finally fled too. He left a couple of tanks and his Mercedes-Benz at riverside before jumping onto a speedboat, heading for Brazzaville. Scavengers picked over, stripped, and burned the vehicles. Across town, Likulia Bolongo, the last prime minister, fled to the residence of the French ambassador, then himself caught a boat to safety. Other Mobutuists begged at least one Western embassy for asylum, to no avail. As a diplomatic source told me that day, "We don't want to have a Saigon."

A trickle of advance rebel units slowly became a torrent as thousands of rebel troops streamed into the city Sunday morning. The marching troops, some barefoot, some in flimsy flip-flops, some with the faces of preteens, snaked along the broad boulevards. People waved palm fronds—a symbol of peace. They wrapped white bands around their heads as a sign of welcome. A woman ran out of her house with boxes of Cocoa Puffs cereal, which the rebel troops devoured. One of the rebels shouted, "Clap your hands! You are liberated!" and the people within earshot on the street clapped on cue.

I cruised around with a few other journalists, escorted by a U.N. security officer. Gunfire crackled here and there, bursting the odd quiet of the empty streets. Crowds surrounded the vehicle, shouting, "No French! No French!" or "Kabila is our liberator!" Bodies lay scattered about, though the Red Cross later put the death toll of Kinshasa's seizure at fewer than three hundred, out of a city of 5 million. At the port, Ngobila Beach, some of Mobutu's soldiers flagged down our vehicle. At first, I thought we'd be shot or taken hostage. But they merely asked the U.N. officer what they should do, where they should go. He told them to put down their weapons and surrender and they'd be all right.

From his redoubt in the southern city of Lubumbashi, Kabila declared himself president and renamed the country the Democratic Republic of Congo. But until his politicos arrived a few days later, the power vacuum led to more mayhem. Looting, rioting, hijacking of cars: for a brief period, it seemed there could still be anarchy. Crowds jammed the streets around Mobutu's Camp Tshatshi, where the most frenzied looting took place. I never got there; the crowds swamped my car and I could not get through. But witnesses told me later how residents swarmed through the gates of the military compound, stealing everything, anything, including the swimming pool slide. Even a few journalists grabbed mementos of the Mobutu days. The place was completely stripped of all belongings, except for Mobutu's diapers. In his ailing state, he'd been reduced to that.

• • •

It hadn't seemed possible for the ambiance of the Intercon to get more bizarre than the tragicomedy of Mobutu's final days. But a theater of the absurd to beat all was ushered in that first week after Mobutu's fall. I'd never watched a rebel army march in, take a major capital city, then set up political headquarters at a swank hotel. Congolese from the Alliance, including Tutsis who'd been purged from the city when the war began, filtered into town. Rwandans and Ugandans were on hand too, even a smattering of Ethiopian and Eritrean civilian advisers. The hotel that once echoed with French and Lingala now filled with English and Swahili. Africa's east had come to its west, as if the continental plate had shifted. I ran into Alec, my young friend from Rwanda, a devout pan-African idealist and a Tutsi, who'd arrived to help establish links with Kinshasa youth.

It is a miracle no one in the Intercon was killed. Troops were everywhere, and from everywhere. There were plenty of Tutsis, no doubt many from Rwanda, and also the Banyamulenge. There were the Katangan Tigers, the Congolese exiles from Katanga who'd lived in Angola since their failed bids at Katangan secession in the 1960s and 1970s, who returned to fight with Kabila's Alliance. Most troubling, there were too many Kadogos ("small ones" in Swahili). These were boys and teens recruited as child soldiers who hailed from the east of the country or from the midsection. Some had never seen a place of such opulence as the Intercon. The rumor made the rounds of a Kadogo who went into a panic when the elevator he stepped into began to move. He'd never been in one before. That sounds kind of cute, doesn't it? But it wasn't cute.

These kids knew little discipline. And they were as heavily armed as their adult comrades-in-arms. At the breakfast buffet, it was best to just stand back and hope for whatever crumbs were left. With a vengeance, the troops tore through the croissants, eggs, assorted meats, and fruit. Balancing their plates with their ever-present AKs, their gun barrels pointed every which way. The hotel was like a gas leak. It could blow at any time. There were too many factions, too many guns, and too many cheeky Mobutuists still afoot. Even Mobutu Kongulu's chief aide, a suave young man in a flowing robe, thought he could stay on with no trouble, chatting with journalists, sitting right out in the open—until he disappeared. Kabila's soldiers arrested him, so I was told, for carrying a grenade.

The scene outside was even more surreal. To get into the hotel, you had to prove residence, be well connected, or be in possession of a weapon. In the clamor to get in, a mural of desperate faces pressed against the plate glass, on-lookers, well-wishers, glad-handers, and job seekers. By the dozens, they stood in long lines that snaked along the hotel's curved drive and down the sidewalk. Some were lucky. I spotted at least a couple of the old Mobutu retreads saun-tering through, on the make again. With a new government in town, new deals could be cut, new alliances made. Bernardin Mungul Diaka, a former prime minister, marched through with an air of presumed importance, two security men by his side. In a mansion where goats lounged on a tiled veranda and fish swam in man-made ponds, Mungul Diaka had lived in the political wilderness since Mobutu fired him after a month in office in 1991.

But politicians who'd been part of the Mobutu years were now passé. In-stead, it was the new era of the old Lumumbists. Exiled lawyers, doctors, pro-fessors, had streamed into rebel territory during the war, and now Kinshasa belonged to them. Even Lumumba's daughter, Juliana Lumumba, returned from a lifelong exile in Belgium. Her brother, François Lumumba, had re-portedly already met with Kabila. Pierre Mulele's daughter, Jeanette Mulele, whom I had tracked down and met earlier in the war, emerged from wartime hiding. She was only twelve years old in 1968 when Mobutu lured her father back from exile with a promise of amnesty for his rebel activities, then had him tortured to death. At one point, the entire family, including the children, was arrested. Ten years later, in a 1978 sweep of the opposition in the Kwilu region southeast of Kinshasa, the troops killed her mother along with many other Muleles. Reduced to pauperism, the remaining Muleles were too poor even to flee into exile. So "problematic" was her family name, she told me, that no one would marry her. With Kabila's rebels approaching but Mobutu's troops still in town, she lived her final days of the Mobutu era in hiding and in utter fear that Mobutu's troops would try to settle scores with the remaining Muleles. Kabila, she told me, "is continuing the work of my father." While young intellectuals and students began gathering at the Mulele compound in the Bandalungwa neighborhood awaiting word on Kabila's plans, the entire city bristled with anticipation of his arrival.

In the meantime, the Alliance quickly scrapped all previous talk about democracy. Forget about political activity; there would be none of that. Kabila slapped a ban on all political parties. Kinshasa's nonviolent opposition, as Mobutu's local opponents had been called, were deeply offended. They'd been awaiting Mobutu's demise since the early 1990s, when he initiated a charade of democratization.

Kabila finally arrived in Kinshasa, amid cheering, waving throngs who lined his route from the airport along Boulevard Lumumba. But it seemed far from triumphal. He arrived after dark, within an immense cordon of security vehicles, saying not a word in public acknowledgment of his victory or the capital's high anxiety. And when he named a government a couple of days later, the honeymoon that had barely begun just about ended. Kabila snubbed the most popular political figure in the city, Etienne Tshisekedi, whom the Sovereign National Conference had once elected as prime minister. Some newspapers had predicted Tshisekedi would be named vice president or prime minister. But neither position existed in what Kabila said would be a "presidential regime." A bullheaded man with an immense political following, Tshisekedi called on his supporters not only to protest the new government but also to ignore it. That very day, less than a week after Mobutu's demise, the first anti-Kabila protests broke out. Hundreds of angry youth marched and shouted, "Kabila! Dictator!" They were angry at the snub of Tshisekedi, but also angry at the presence of Rwandan Tutsi troops on their streets. "No Rwandans," they shouted. There was supposed to be freedom, a new beginning. But already, Kabila's troops were firing in the air to disperse protesters. It was a harbinger of things to come.

On the business front, the Alliance made a show of calming the jitters of the business community in a mass meeting of executives held at the Intercon. Business leaders, afterward, expressed some cautious optimism about Kabila's devotion to a stable environment. Though Kabila was a wild card and no one could say which direction his regime would actually go, many business leaders felt they could safely stay on after Mobutu's fall and work with the new order. "We are here to make this country work," José Endundo Bononge, the airline executive and, by May 1997, also the head of the nation's Chamber of Commerce, told me after meeting Kabila's Alliance.

Then the new troops began looting leading business figures. The very day of Kabila's arrival, troops raided Bemba Saolona, one of the wealthiest men in the country. Not far from the Intercon, they stormed his home. At gunpoint, they forced Bemba to lie on the ground while they stole his Jeep, his Mercedes, his cash, and his weapons. They didn't throw him in jail that time, but later they surely would. Fat cats from the Mobutu days suffered the same fate throughout the city. The new ruling Alliance dubbed their wealth "ill-gotten gains" that needed to be seized. But the truth was more base: a massive settling of scores was under way, a redistribution of wealth from one faction to another.

Still, for many ordinary people, a giddy sense of change infused Kinshasa with a festive atmosphere. Hopes were incredibly high among many ordinary people of a city that had been ground into desperate poverty. When Kabila's troops marched into Kinshasa, Mary Nzenza grabbed her malnourished children and joined the crowds running in the street to hail the liberators. A mother of seven and a subsistence farmer on a plot of land right in the city center, Mary embraced Mobutu's fall as the moment she was released from the prison of her old life. She would be free, she hoped, free to thrive after the long tyranny of Mobutu had closed all opportunities for people like her.

At the age of fifty-three, Mary had no job and only rarely had eaten any meat since her husband, a sporadically paid government clerk, died twenty-eight months prior. To get by, she cultivated the cheapest of all crops, a leafy plant called *matimbele*, for sale to other poor folks who could afford nothing else. Like legions of others, she farmed right in the middle of the city, on the side of the road. That is where I met her, as she worked like a serf in the Mobutu kingdom.

Though education was supposed to be public, it went the way of all other institutions in Mobutu's Zaire: another way for bureaucrats to get bribes and "fees." Nzenza couldn't afford to keep sending her oldest children, Tonton and Joceline, aged fourteen and thirteen, to school. The depth of the family's misery—and Congo's as a whole—was evident in Joceline's protruding bones. She had the physique of a refugee. Routine bouts of malaria only worsened Joceline's condition, Mary said. The two youngest girls, Mafuta, five, and Labanzandia, three, had malaria too. Their neighborhood, where kids played ball with garbage bound with string, was like a mosquito breeding farm, with no sewage system to drain away the standing water and waste. Like people all over the city, the kids suffered from intestinal amoebas and chronic diarrhea from Kinshasa's untreated water system.

To Mary, all this was Mobutu's doing. He'd robbed her of life and freedom. He'd helped only those close to him, those he could use. But Kabila held out a new hope, a very real hope. That is why she ran out into the street. "I was happy, because I was a prisoner for a long time. I was happy because I felt I was no longer in prison. So let the one who has come change things. We like him a lot. We are happy. Let him also make us happy."

Her wish for life in the new Congo went like this: "I want to be given enough money to continue my business, continue working in the field, produce more than I am producing, because if I'm working I can sell more and I can get more money, feed my children, send them to school.

"If Kabila fails to change things, people will curse him," she warned prophetically.

All parents, everywhere, want the same things. But few parents, except in the world's poorest places, are forced to scratch, claw, and grovel the way Mary had to. The old Zaire had been reduced to a nation on the take—either out of greed or from pure desperation. Mary and her skinny, barefoot children fit in the latter category. When I arrived that day to her tiny home that had no chairs, she sent a neighbor to run and fetch something for me to sit on. I insisted that standing was fine, but off the neighbor went. Mary laughed and said, "Maybe you can buy me a chair." I laughed along. But she was not joking. When I pulled my notepad from my bag, she hit me up again, asking point-blank for money in return for her interview. I explained that I did not work that way; that I did not pay people for their interviews. She agreed to speak to me anyway. "Maybe you can find a husband to give me money," she said, and we laughed together again.

But of course, I am too soft a touch. If ever the old African adage was true—when the elephants fight, the grass suffers—Mary and her family proved the point. They were fragile blades of grass. I had hundreds of dollars on me, and I could not allow myself to just walk away from this forlorn family without making a contribution. When Mbongo and I went out to the car, I handed him a wad of cash—a small fortune in Zaire—and asked him to go back and give it to her, for the sake of the children.

• • •

JOHANNESBURG

It would be an understatement to say I felt dispirited when I finally left Congo-Zaire. The war had ended; a chapter had come to its close. But I couldn't shake it. It was winter in Jo'burg when I returned and late at night I'd sit in front of the fireplace in a funk. I felt helplessness. I'd crossed a line. Writing Africa just didn't seem enough. Part of me wanted to do more, not just to smuggle words out of people's lives and write them onto the front pages in the hope they would have an impact on an American public that did not care enough and whose view of Africa was too often the voyeur's. I cringed at the thought that somewhere back in Washington, readers had consumed my dispatches as confirmation of their disgust at Africa's straits. I'd wanted those readers to be moved, to care, to question, not to turn away.

Certain images kept running like newsreel in my memory: Jean Damascene dusting off his dirty blazer and stepping forward to speak for the wandering refugees. The orange plastic cup dangling from Mihigo Enok's rope belt. The angle at which the grannies bent, supported by their walking sticks, to scavenge through the remnants of emptied refugee camps. Gunfire echoing in those glorious hills around Nyabibwe, where bodies I could not see kept falling and falling. They did not have to die. But those who could have saved them decided their lives were of little value.

Somehow I felt responsible. I felt journalism had failed. Late at night sometimes, I'd reread my dispatches. If I'd written more searingly, more elegantly, perhaps more angrily, could I have made a difference? Could I have roused Americans to demand more from their government, the world's only superpower, than its rush to abandon the U.N. peacekeeping force at the beginning of the war? Would the people who were massacred have been saved? Of course, they would have, if the world hadn't stood by and if we journalists had hit harder, dug deeper, and yanked Washington's chain for coddling its Rwandan allies and training the Rwandan army that then marched into Congo-Zaire for post-genocide revenge.

After the war, the Congo story became mired in allegations and investigations of the massacres, like Nyabibwe, that were perpetrated across the length and breadth of the country. Many of the lost refugees were slaughtered. The death toll was put at scores of thousands. The United Nations hammered at Kabila's new government to cooperate with the massacre investigations, since he was, after all, the head of the rebellion. But the reality was that Rwanda's troops led the war. Kagame admitted this to one of my colleagues shortly after the war ended. He said his troops planned and largely executed the military campaign. Once the body counts and mass graves were revealed, it was obvious that the war against Mobutu was also a Tutsi campaign of retribution for the 1994 Rwandan genocide committed by the Hutu *génocidaires*.

Weeks after the war, internal U.S. Pentagon documents came to my attention. They laid out the extent of U.S. military involvement with Rwanda. During the war, U.S. defense officials had repeatedly assured Congress that the training in Rwanda was of the relatively innocuous kind. They called it classroom-style training intended to professionalize Rwandan troops and inculcate in them a deeper understanding of human rights. But the documents I received showed that the training included psychological operations as well as U.S. Special Forces tactical exercises that clearly would be geared to combat techniques. Not that I'm blaming America. It was the Africans who did this killing, after all. But the situation was far more complex than it had once seemed. Far from being a war with an unstoppable, almost inevitable momentum, it was a war that could have been calibrated by the obvious leverage the United States could have applied to rein in the Rwandan army, if it had cared to do so. All the attention of human rights investigators and the U.S. State Department was focused on Kabila to account for the massacres. Rwanda, whose fighters led the Zaire campaign, clearly got a pass.

11

Lyrics of African Lives

HUPULA VILLAGE, NAMIBIA, JUNE 1997

 half-moon bathed the tiny village in a faint light, lengthening the shadows of the trees at the edge of the wilderness just beyond a clearing. This place was called Hupula, but its name appeared on none of my maps. Nestled deep in the wetlands of Namibia's northeastern Caprivi Strip near the confluence of the Kwando and Chobe rivers, Hupula is where I found myself in June 1997. It was a place that defined remoteness—the perfect place to lose myself, even rejuvenate myself, after the Zaire war and the emotions it stirred. Life went on. My work went on. Hupula was no vacation spot; it was just an ordinary place of African life, where an ordinary African story was unfolding.

There were round thatched huts behind tall reed fences that formed a series of courtyards spread across the sandy ground. On the outskirts of the village, near the cattle pens and small fields of maize, barking dogs shattered the evening hush. The villagers of the Mayeyi clan listened for a moment, but realized that the barks did not carry the dogs' familiar alarm. No predator was approaching, not this time.

Aglow in the firelight, I sat with the Hupula villagers around a blaze that crackled beneath the evening meal, a thick stew of vegetables and a gritslike cornmeal known as pap, very much a staple in the southern African region.

The Mayeyi greeted me warmly and welcomed me to their village. I had come at the suggestion of Janet Matota, a Hupula resident who worked with my guide and travel companion, Margie Jacobsohn, a Namibian archaeologist-turned-conservationist. Margie ran a nonprofit group that worked with villages like Hupula to help them conserve nature while also thwarting the rampaging elephants and ravenous lions that ate their livestock and crops. Graciously, Margie took me to a few Caprivi settlements to help me learn of the life on this battleground in the age-old struggle between man and beast.

In the pecking order of the clan, the elderly village *induna,* or headman, Isaya Ndubano, was the first to speak. His voice was deep, his delivery the rapid clip of the Siyeyi language, as he told of the times when life was easier. I had listened to many elderly Africans tell of the lives and times in which they lived, and in their lyrical phrasing, their ironic musings, I heard the poetry of ordinary Africa. I don't want to exaggerate and overromanticize the experience, for the ordinary life I witnessed and recorded was often bitterly hard and suffocatingly limited in a material, temporal sense. But that is precisely why the renderings of life I heard from countless people seemed so rich. Their perceptions and their words struck me as if I'd found blazing blossoms growing amid rocky ground. The narratives related by the elderly were especially enthralling, nurtured as they were by the wisdom of age and of struggle.

Maybe I was just prone to love to hear stories. I've always been that way. But the things I was told had a value beyond what I placed on them. Out in the wider world, where Africans are often viewed as mysterious and foreboding, the words that people loaned me to tell my stories brought to life Africa's normality and humanity.

Ndubano and his clan were poor subsistence farmers, but they were quite astute about the possibilities and contradictions of their world. They were humble but dignified people attempting to eke out a living in circumstances whose challenges were strange to me in their specifics, but also felt universal. I visited Hupula for just a day and a night, insinuating myself into their world only briefly, but its effect on me was like a balm. This was the

Africa of which I'd wanted to write: ordinary Africa, real Africa, not Africa at war.

When he was a boy, Ndubano began, the elephants were fewer and easier to manage. Villagers had time-tested methods to control the beasts. His forefathers told him, "When the elephant is passing by, just climb in the trees and use a bow and arrow." And if the fields were under attack, Ndubano recalled, "They used to beat the drums and light fires." And it worked, for a time. Man and beast carved out a truce. But the huge African elephant range that encompasses parts of Namibia, Botswana, Zimbabwe, Zambia, and Angola seemed, by 1997, more overrun with elephants than when Ndubano was a boy. Though Africa's elephants had been hard hit by ivory-hungry poachers who cut their continental numbers so low as to cause the elephant to become an officially endangered species, the southern African range had been rejuvenated. Law enforcement had made southern Africa relatively safe from poaching, compared to the East African range where poaching was still dwindling herd numbers. And with more than 170,000 elephants afoot, the population of the southern range was stable.

They stomped across borders and through fences. They forded rivers and climbed hills. They found their way straight to the small plots where subsistence farmers like Ndubano nurtured crops of maize. Most of the eastern Caprivi Strip was communal farmland, but that same region also supported some of Africa's highest elephant densities too. Kipi George, another older gentleman of the Caprivi and a headman of the Kxoe Bushmen, told me later, "They are our shadows, like the trees."

The villagers of the Caprivi devised new methods to combat the elephants. They used "game guards," men specifically designated to keep watch over fields. Jacobsohn's group funded the guard project. Eustice Mabbi was one of them, and he joined us around Ndubano's fire, telling of his frustrations with the limitations of the project. Guarding the fields helped, in some cases, but there weren't enough guards to cover all villages every night, and not enough of the guards were armed. Even when they did have guns, they could only shoot in the air, because the elephants' status as a protected species meant they could not be killed. The elephants proliferated so much that they become bold or, as Mabbi put it, "rude and stubborn."

"Now," Ndubano continued, "you can beat the drums. They don't run. You can light the fires. You can shoot in the air. They don't run."

As for the lions, the villagers' barking dogs were the best defense. At least the barking would sound the alarm, and villagers could race out with fire to ward off the predators. But not everyone kept his or her cattle penned up at night. Many of the farmers were old people whose younger relatives—the ones who could help them manage the herds—had moved into towns or to the capital, Windhoek, to find jobs. In a nearby village, there'd been a big lion attack just the previous month, when five lions set upon a herd and took down one of the cows. Villagers and game guards tracked the lions and were able to shoot at least one of them. But the battle was daily and constant and getting more and more difficult to sustain. Crop yields were way down, leaving families with less to eat, less to market. Women were often afraid to go to the river to collect reeds for their courtyard fences, palms for their baskets, and water lilies that had become a staple in the stews.

Charles Mukuba, an elderly farmer from the nearby village of Sangwali, could not accept that the elephant held protected status while humans suffered. Some of the elephants should be shot, he said—not all, mind you, just the ones the local people called PAs, or problem animals. "They are just like people," Mukuba said. "They also realize what death is." Killing just a few, Mukuba believed, would send a powerful deterrent message to the elephant herds.

"I know that the government cannot allow me to shoot the elephant to kill. But after the elephant has finished my crops, can I go to the government and the government compensate for what I eat tomorrow? If the elephants finish my crop, to whom can I go to explain? To whom can I go for assistance?" They were rhetorical questions Mukuba had asked himself many, many times.

Jacobsohn's and other groups were trying to help the Caprivi villagers turn the elephants to their advantage. The Namibian government had agreed to proclaim certain areas as conservancies so that the local people could receive revenue from the wildlife and eco-tourism that attracted tourists, especially foreigners. All sorts of proposals were being fielded for tourism lodges, arts and crafts centers, game viewing and the like.

The conservation push got a boost when a U.N. convention on endangered species decided to downgrade the protected status of elephants in Namibia, Zimbabwe, and Botswana because of their success at wildlife preservation. The downgrading meant that those three nations could sell off the huge stockpiles of ivory they'd been prohibited from selling because of the elephant's endangered status. And the proceeds of those sales would be funneled back into people-centered conservancy and eco-tourism ventures. But the conservationists' vision of man and beast co-existing in the Caprivi was a long way off, if ever it would emerge. In the meantime, families hunkered down with less to eat, less to sell, sometimes depending on the kindness of neighbors. I could not solve their problem, but now I understood it enough to tell it.

Bedtime arrived. The families drifted off to their courtyards. Margie and I pitched our separate tents and rolled out the sleeping bags. There was no space for visitors in the courtyards, for Janet Matota, one of Margie's conservation aides and our hostess at Hupula, had recently had a baby, and a relative had moved in to assist her. Ndubano's people assured me that no lion would come after me while I slept; that the cattle were the only prey. Nonetheless, Margie gave me the drill. If I heard any noise, I should keep perfectly still so as not to attract attention. As for the bathroom, well, there wasn't one. The bushes and trees would have to do. Normally, I could handle it. I'd done bushes and trees before. But with lions on the prowl in the dark of night? No way.

I was petrified.

I barely slept. I listened to the night, just about all night long. I lay perfectly still. I held my breath in fear when I heard a breeze whisper in the trees. When the dogs briefly barked, I went into virtual shock. I imagined what it would be like to attempt to fight off a lion. Somehow, no doubt exhausted by fear, I dozed just a bit toward sunrise. I'm sure if my hosts at Hupula knew I'd been scared to death inside my tent they'd have gotten a good laugh. Living with this peril had become routine for them. Now I'd gotten a taste of that existence, and I had not handled it well. I felt like the "silly American," just as my friend, Nonhlangano Beauty Mkhize, had laughingly tagged me back in South Africa a long time ago.

• • •

DRIEFONTEIN, SOUTH AFRICA

An older woman and widow, Beauty hosted me at her home during my travels in 1990. She lived in a traditional Zulu kraal, or fenced compound, at a settlement called Driefontein not far from the South Africa–Swaziland border. Also close by was the grave of her husband, Vusumuzi Saul Mkhize. He had been a leader in this community that had been targeted for a forced removal under apartheid's laws, but had resisted the government. During a community meeting in 1983, a white police constable shot Saul Mkhize dead in front of Beauty and a large crowd. The constable had been tried in court, but acquitted, despite the evidence of witnesses to the cold-blooded killing. Beauty and her son, Bongani Paris Mkhize, who was eighteen when his father died, had to live with their pain and bitterness and go on with a difficult life.

In her own way, Beauty took up Saul's mantle. Though a woman in a staunchly male-centered culture, she became a community leader just as Saul had been. She involved herself in land disputes, legal disputes, working closely with law groups from Jo'burg that helped rural people sort out their problems with the apartheid state. That is how I met her: her reputation as a simple yet strong-as-a-tree woman preceded her, and an antiapartheid lawyer took me out to Driefontein to meet her.

Driefontein was incredibly beautiful—lush and green, with hills that rolled gently and cattle that grazed endlessly. Beauty's small herd—the wealth of rural Africa—was penned up not far from the main house at night, but during the day a herd boy named Sandile took them out. I walked with him one early morning to see the start of a traditional day. Beauty's borehole, or water pump, was a short distance from the house. Seeing her go and fetch water each day and return with a full bucket on her head, I decided that I should learn to carry water on my head as well. At the pump one day, while

Beauty was giving me instructions that she laughingly knew were pointless, a gaggle of young girls from the settlement covered their mouths and giggled sweetly as I drenched myself over and over. That is when Beauty laughed too and called me the "silly American."

And I made a silly fool of myself in Driefontein again, in 1994, when I visited the impoverished household of the Mthembu family. Kaizer Maseko, a local youth, took me there as part of my research into rural living. The extended Mthembu family, fourteen of them all told, lived in a kraal similar to Beauty's, where they grew corn (called mealies in South Africa) as well as a few cows and chickens.

When we arrived, we found Flavia Mthembu, a twenty-year-old, applying fresh mud in elegant swirls to the outside of the round hut. Her father, Alfred Mthembu, took a break from cutting wood for repair of the thatched roof that had been damaged by recent rains. Kindly, Mr. Mthembu invited me into the main house. There were two sparsely furnished rooms. The main one, painted pink, had only a wall clock, a television set, an ironing board, and two chairs. As Kaizer translated, we sat and talked of the Driefontein life and the hope that South Africa's freedom would bring. Then his wife, Elsie Mthembu, walked through the door. In her arms, she carried a loose newspaper-covered bundle. She extended it toward me as she approached. The bundle began moving. It was a live chicken. Mrs. Mthembu offered it to me as a gesture of welcome into her home. It was a traditional form of hospitality, though her family could scarcely afford to part with a chicken. Her offering struck me as deeply humbling, to see one so poor make such a richly human gesture. But at the same time, my mind raced. How could I escape this chicken? The idea of a chicken flapping (and worse) around my rental car repulsed me. No way could I take a live chicken with me. I was in a full-blown cultural panic.

With Kaizer translating, I thanked Mrs. Mthembu for the lovely offering and tapped my palms together in the traditional way of appreciation. I explained quite apologetically that I was traveling a lot by car and could not take a chicken along. Mrs. Mthembu's pleasant face turned to bewilderment, as if I was slighting her in the worst way. I kept trying to explain. Kaizer kept

translating. She stood there holding the chicken for the most excruciating series of minutes. Eventually, she acquiesced. She took the chicken back outside.

"She was dejected, but I think she understood," Kaizer told me later. He
wouldn't say so, but I knew what he was thinking: I should have accepted the
chicken. I could have given it away, but at least I would have spared Mrs.
Mthembu the odd refusal of her offering. My friends Yunus and Cajee
Mushooda, the Indian storekeepers and activists with whom I was spending
the night, told me I could have brought the chicken to them and they'd have
cooked it. I could have taken the chicken to Beauty as well. But none of that
came to mind when I found myself face-to-face with the bird.

My efforts to know ordinary life were those of an earnest traveler. I was
just passing through, most of the time, but I tarried long enough, often
enough, in enough places, to gather up a store of knowledge that gave me a
respectful sense of basic African life. I'd seen plenty of what was reflected in
the dire statistics on Africa—its deep poverty, its immense suffering, and its
high mortality rates. But there were no statistical measures for graciousness
and humanity. I gathered up my own barometers in the people and the narratives I carried with me.

• • •

LUSAKA, ZAMBIA

In that way, I held on to Julia Malembeka. How could I possibly lose her?
She was an effervescent and petite woman of forty-three whose face seemed
always poised to smile, whose speaking voice sounded like a song. She hardly
seemed the package that would contain a firecracker, but that is what she
was, in her own sweetly optimistic way. She knew how to make good things
happen and she knew, even at an early age, that certain obstacles existed to be
overcome.

Tradition pertaining to women and their secondary role vis-à-vis men
puts a powerful brake on women's development and betterment in much of
Africa. Girls, especially in the poorest countries and in rural areas, are encouraged to be domestic—to marry, procreate, and serve their families. Julia's

family in Zambia was no different, but this particular girl-child grew up to want more.

"I come from a family where my father believed girls should just be married off and boys should go to school. But I said no. I am going to school." She finished high school and took some college courses. She married and had a son, but also went off to work. For nearly eighteen years, she'd been at UNICEF, where I met her at her secretarial desk in 1995. The job gave her a window onto a world that offered resources and tools for community development, and what she learned on her job dovetailed nicely with the needs of her township north of Lusaka, called Kabanana, population eight thousand.

Development became her passion. Kabanana (meaning a place where there are bananas) needed so much. Roads, health clinics, telephone service, schools. But the most basic of amenities stood at the top of the list. "Water," said Julia, "actually is a headache." For reasons no one in Kabanana knew, the water to the tidy little homes in the township had stopped running five years prior. The water was supposed to be provided by the city of Lusaka, but the country's economy had been ground to dust by years of mismanagement. The water taps of Kabanana were one of its casualties.

Without running water, the women of Kabanana, including Julia, were forced to go back in time, to revert to the old custom of walking to nearby streams to fetch water in large buckets. Or they paid young boys to fetch water for them. The water would sometimes be dirty, but at least it was water. So Julia and several other women decided enough was enough. No one could figure out which politicians to appeal to because a batch of city councilors had recently been fired and the mayor had resigned. An election campaign was to begin soon, said Julia, chirping out the most cynical of assessments: "That's when you will see the politicians come to tell you about development which they will never bring."

So the women formed a cooperative. They called it the Kabanana Site and Service Women's Club. Bypassing her own employer for ethical reasons, Julia wrote international finance and donor agencies to ask for grants for the water project. And it actually worked. The Kabanana program received enough funding to purchase the equipment. At a site near the township's police post, workmen drilled for water and rigged the electricity to pump it up to a huge new water tank connected to taps for the townspeople. It wasn't like having indoor taps, but at least it was right there in the town. For a small fee, Kabanana's residents could have access to water without hassle. To raise more money to maintain the new system, the women's club threw barbecues and sent solicitations to the banks and businesses of Lusaka.

"If we use our own initiative to raise money, then the club will keep on working without depending on the donors all the time . . . We were hoping to have another borehole drilled, but our money was stuck in Meridian Bank. So we are bankrupt." That bank had collapsed, and depositors' funds had not been returned. So the women kept raising money, kept writing those letters of appeal.

Julia and her colleagues had nothing against their men. But the women—since water is supposed to be women's work—wanted to do the site and service project on their own. The only man they employed was a security guard to watch over the pumping station.

"Our culture indicates that when you are in the presence of men, you just let the men talk and you listen," Julia explained sweetly. "But it is us who carry water on our head. We all work, but when we get home, it is women who have to care for the house while the men read the paper.

"It is women who go to vote, and we elect men who don't think about our concerns." Even in the local PTA at the town's one high school, the women elected a virtually all-male slate of officers, even though most PTA members are women. "I was fuming." Julia laughed as she told me this. She would have run for a PTA office, but arrived too late to stand.

With their women suddenly stepping up to take a lead on the town's main problem, some of the men harrumphed. They thought government should have managed the water project. They thought that men—any men—should have been in charge. "But we stood our ground and said no ways. So we are running that program as women." And anyway, the men couldn't complain too terribly loudly. "They have no choice," Julia said, laughing. "They are drinking clean water! Their shirts are cleaner!"

Julia and her women had even more ideas for development in their town. There were health problems, transport problems, and the general isolation of the place. "We hope to have a clinic too. We have no clinic. And the roads too. We hope that one day we'll have the phones. Then you can pick up the phone in Jo'burg and reach me at my home. They are dreams," she said, her voice rising like a balloon in the sky. But it is people who often make dreams come true.

Julia and I parted, and I vowed to stay in touch. The next time we had contact, I had some very good news. A few weeks after my article ran in the *Washington Post* and the *International Herald Tribune*, readers responded. From around the world, from Oakland, California, to Paris, France, people wrote the paper to find out how they could help Julia and her valiant women. The Samaritans numbered only a half dozen, but they were from development organizations or water-related groups. I forwarded the letters to Lusaka, where I knew Julia would be elated. Her eyes had been opened to a whole new realm of possibility when it would have been so easy to just sit by and accept that dirty old water.

• • •

BEIRA, MOZAMBIQUE

I could not imagine the storms that pummeled and tossed the big ships off the Mozambican coast, then crashed them onto the shore. They were huge ships—commercial fishing trawlers, mainly—all rusted and barnacle-encrusted, reaching up from the sands of Beira's Praia Nova like monuments to defeat at sea.

The Indian Ocean could be wondrously terrible, and yet men like Francisco Chivamo made peace with it. I met Chivamo at the Praia Nova one day in 1996 as he toiled in the shadow of the defeated ships. He bent over a trunk of the night's catch—six hundred pounds of prawns—that he was busy packing in ice for his buyer. Chivamo lived on the sea. His father and father's father did the same. And when his three-year-old son grew old enough to cast a net, he, too, would find his life on the sea. Chivamo would take his boy, Manuel Francisco, out on the Rio Buzi near its Indian Ocean mouth and teach him to haul in the prawns that were the lifeblood of the family name.

"The sea is good for people who know how to deal with the sea. I use the sea as my place of work. I get fish there. I swim there. So the sea, for me, is my life. Our life is the sea. Our life is fishing to provide for our future." His three brothers were just down the beach, packing their catch as well.

Though Mozambique had been an agriculturally rich country of cashew, cotton, sugar, and tea, its production had been depressed by the seventeen-year civil war from which the country emerged in 1992, with the peace cemented in elections two years later. Farms had been decimated, roads ruined, rail lines blasted to smithereens, and millions of people uprooted from their homes by the war that left schools and clinics destroyed and the land sown with mines. Postwar Mozambique was one of the world's biggest charity cases, almost completely reliant on international aid and on credit from the World Bank. On the bright side, the country had sunk so low from the war that just about any economic activity represented growth. Investment began pouring in, fueling an impressive economic growth rate of nearly 7 percent by 1996. Not at all bad for a country in utter ruins.

Slowly, the country began to redevelop. Maputo, the capital, sported refurbished hotels and outdoor cafés on broad boulevards lined by brilliant red and yellow flamboyant trees and lavender jacaranda. The northern regions began producing again, though the absence of functioning rail lines and roads to move the maize crop meant much of it would rot. Beira, the nation's busiest port, was being upgraded to handle more of the regional traffic from landlocked southern African nations which long had used Mozambique as a corridor to get exports out to sea. And Mozambique turned more and more to the ocean for its sustenance as it put the war years behind it. What the land could not provide, the sea would: precious export revenue, mostly from prawns.

Out in the ocean, where vessels flying flags of European kings and Arabic sultans once sailed this coast with spices and slaves, I could see ships trawling for shrimp and prawns along the rich Sofala Bank. Its shallows stretch from Beira to the town of Nacala on the northern coast, where Muslim minarets are as prominent as Christian spires. Along with Mozambique's small commercial fishing fleet, large operations from Japan, Portugal, Spain, and South Africa plied those waters too. And small though they were, local operations like Chivamo's fueled the fishing economy as well.

A thirty-year-old father of two, he learned to fish when he was eleven. The sea became his way of life. Until a couple years before I met him, his operation had been threadbare. He went out onto the Rio Buzi in his dugout canoe, carved from a tree and propelled by paddles. Then he bought a larger wooden boat, which he named for his twelve-year-old daughter, Laurina Ulombo. And he fully expected to do so well as to afford an even larger boat to expand his operation even more.

Thoughts of bigger things to come filled Chivamo's days as he and his dozen workers clambered aboard the *Laurina Ulombo* to head out for the casting of their giant nets, 250 yards long. "I think about increasing my life, to become better in my life," Chivamo said of his thoughts aboard ship. "I think if I get more money I will buy a big boat. I will work with two boats. Then I can get more fish to increase my life."

Sometimes they hauled their nets all day, all night, and into the next morning. By lamplight the fishermen worked, filling the time with songs, sung slowly and softly, as they waited for the sea to increase their lives, to make their empty nets full.

12

Winniephobia

Winnie Madikizela-Mandela moved like royalty. She didn't walk so much as glide, surrounded by her lawyers, her daughters, and her retinue. The narrow, cramped hall in the Mayfair section of Jo'burg was overheated that November 1997, by a Southern Hemisphere summer. But Winnie seemed cool and serene. Strands of pearls draped the neck of her cream-colored suit. Her tinted eyeglasses with the sparkly frames lent mystery to her coy smile. She cut a striking figure, as usual, and all eyes in the room devoured her. They were admiring eyes, hateful eyes, and eyes of complete fear.

Could she really have been party to murder? I asked myself this question. I'm sure many others in that hall asked it too, for that was the reason we were there: to hear the Truth and Reconciliation Commission examine Winnie's alleged role in abduction, assault, torture, and murder. I tried to imagine her actually punching and whipping young comrades, even a pregnant woman, as her accusers claimed she had. It seemed hard to conjure a vision of a Winnie so treacherous and cruel as to plot the ways and means of murder of her own people at the height of their struggle against apartheid.

She was "mother of the nation," for Christ's sake, the wife of the imprisoned Nelson. She was the raging flame of the antiapartheid struggle, the woman who could not be broken. Lord knows the state tried, in a decades-long struggle against the woman who more than any other figure in South Africa at that time symbolized total defiance.

For the nearly three decades of Nelson's imprisonment, apartheid security forces hounded her. They tailed her. They banned her. They tapped her telephone. They threw her into solitary confinement for seventeen months. They denied her a bath or shower. They gave her inedible food. She suffered malnutrition and fainting fits. One of her lawyers of that time wrote later that she wavered between "sanity and insanity" during that confinement. Over the years, police planted spies among her friends. They arrested and detained her over and over. The courts banished her to a small town and restricted her movements. Two of her homes were firebombed. But Winnie emerged from apartheid's storms fierier than ever, always agitating, organizing, and protesting. Over and over, from the ashes of her rumored demise, she rose like a phoenix, her fist high in the air, her speech laced with threats, both veiled and blatant, of the fire yet to come if apartheid did not end. That's why so many black South Africans loved her: the Afrikaner could not break her.

And yet, something must have broken, somehow, someway. Apartheid must have taken a deep psychological toll. How else to explain the madness that she allowed to surround her, even if—I say *if*—she didn't participate in it? Winnie's domain within the antiapartheid struggle became, by the late 1980s, a hidden world of paranoia and brutality. People around her tended to die. If they did not die, they lived battered and tortured. By the 1990s, the murders and assaults had piled up. Her foot soldiers had been charged with various crimes. She herself was tried and convicted for kidnaping in 1991 in the case of four youths abducted in 1988 and beaten at her home, including a fourteen-year-old named Moeketsi "Stompie" Seipei. His body surfaced in 1989. His throat had been slit.

Whispered innuendo and headlined slander filled Winnie's world; fact blended with fiction and the political intrigue of a new nation shadowed her every move. And still Winnie prevailed. She had the Mandela name, the cachet as the ultimate victim, the steeliness of a warhorse of the struggle, and a massive following among South Africa's impoverished people. For years, a vast conspiracy of silence within the ANC had rendered her virtually untouchable—until that November.

Finally, Winnie would be called to account. She would be confronted with testimony and evidence suggesting her involvement in killing. People like Tutu, who had spent a lifetime admiring her, would place her on the hot seat. Winnie had been charged with no crime, nor had she admitted any wrongdoing, not ever. The TRC did not operate as a court of law. But Winnie was on trial nonetheless—morally, politically, historically. And so was the liberation movement that had become the ruling party of Nelson Mandela.

The probe was bitter and sensational. But it had to be done. For the sake of the TRC's credibility, it had to live up to its mandate as an unbiased seeker of the facts that languished beneath the many fictions of the apartheid years. Plus, too many mothers and fathers who once supported Winnie had pleaded with the TRC to find out what had happened to their missing and presumed-dead sons.

To those parents, Winnie had gotten away with murder. But to her hardest-core supporters, it was Winnie who was the victim—being persecuted yet again. For her political rivals, the truth probe opened an opportunity to see Winnie publicly smeared and neutralized once and for all. The hearings were like a Ouija board on which you could read all manner of insidious conspiratorial dynamics in the politics of the liberation struggle and the "new" South Africa it had created.

Some two hundred journalists descended like vultures on the small community center wedged among the Indian shops and cafés of the Mayfair community. People I'd never seen before—reporters from the American television networks who'd shut down their Africa bureaus—were suddenly on hand to report. From day one, three of us formed a little clique: myself, Charlayne Hunter-Gault, based in Jo'burg at that time for National Public Radio, and Suzanne Daley, bureau chief for the New York Times. For nine days, we spent nearly every lunch break at a local Indian restaurant arguing and rehashing the merits of the testimony. It was an effective balm against each day's insanity. I for one never wanted to have to report on Winnie Mandela this way.

The hearings were held inside the Jo'burg Institute of Social Services, which became center stage in the most intriguing of all morality plays, filled with stories of Winnie and murder and mayhem. Forty-three witnesses testified. The numbers contained the gravity of it: eighteen murders were investigated, with Winnie potentially linked to eight of them.

Winnie's supporters demonstrated outside on the sidewalk, waving banners and singing songs of their heroine. Hawkers sold plates bearing Winnie's face (and Nelson's too). In the ladies' room one day, some of Winnie's supporters accosted the mother of a murder victim. Another day, a clutch of young men in battle fatigues and red berets marched in single file and took up seats along the back wall. The tension in the hall shot up like a geyser. The place was abuzz with mutterings and whispers. Who are they? What do they want? The men were Winnie's comrades, it turned out, and their very presence scared the wits out of some witnesses. A man who took the stand to testify against Winnie demanded official protection for his family before he'd say another word. And routinely, day after day, Tutu and his colleagues decried the death threats that anti-Winnie witnesses claimed they'd been receiving, directly from Winnie herself.

The press, of course, took heaps of criticism, both in South Africa and abroad, for being voyeurs salivating over an incredibly scintillating story. From friends back home, I knew that some black Americans especially were apoplectic that Winnie, an icon even across the ocean, was being victimized. But the criticism did not phase me. I'd reported enough on Winnie over the years to know that she was a far more complex and conflicted person than her one-dimensional international image suggested. She herself had wanted the hearing held in public, not behind closed doors, as the TRC originally proposed.

And Winnie's accountability was *huge* news. No two ways about it. Everyone knew that thousands of white Afrikaner soldiers and cops had murdered and tortured black people during apartheid. Everyone knew that the apartheid state was morally bankrupt and itself a crime against humanity. What everyone did *not* know was that at the heart of the noble antiapartheid movement, one of the world's most famous women had become a rogue, a volatile force. So magnetic was her charisma that people claimed they killed in her name. So potent was the mayhem around her that some of her own comrades within the ANC seemed frightened of her.

The Reverend Peter Storey, a respected Methodist leader and former president of the South African Council of Churches who was involved in the 1980s efforts to tamp down the violence around Winnie, described elegantly just what we all were witnessing.

Speaking to Tutu during the hearing, Storey said: "This week, for the first time, there is a probing beneath the surface of the skin of South Africa's shame. The primary cancer will always be and has always been apartheid. But secondary infections have touched many of apartheid's opponents and eroded their knowledge of good and evil. One of the tragedies of life, sir, is it is possible to become like that which we hate most, and I have a feeling that this drama is an example of that."

Winnie greeted her many subjects as she moved through the hall. Some of the parents and siblings of the dead were there watching her. Winnie seemed oblivious to the gravitas of the occasion. She shook hands. She waved. She pinched cheeks. She behaved as if she were being hailed, not hounded for murder. I sat on the aisle, stunned by her imperious performance. I'd tried numerous times to interview her, to no avail, but had written of her many times. Suddenly, she passed right before me. "Hello, Mrs. Mandela," I said. She simply smiled down at me, a face in her crowd, and rubbed my cheek as she drifted past. How strange that felt. How eerie—both motherly and menacing all at once. I flushed. I felt embarrassed. I hoped none of my colleagues were looking. For just an instant, I'd felt her strange and sinister charisma. I did not know what kind of woman had touched me.

● ● ●

"This is not a circus!"

Tutu shouted from the head table, trying to calm a noisy stir in the crowded audience. Day after day, he threatened and cajoled. To him, a man of the cloth, the decorum and dignity of the truth-telling process must not be breached, no matter how strange the subject at hand. And the subject this day was strange indeed.

A bizarre witness entered the hall, the most bizarre witness of all. He wore manacles and handcuffs. A loose knot of police surrounded him. He held a miniature red soccer ball high in the air and mugged for the cameras. *Click-click-click*—the cameramen snapped away. They virtually crushed one another to get a good shot of this freakish-looking character. And he *was* freakish. Jerry Richardson was his name, and murder was his claim to fame. Brought in from prison, where he was serving a life term for the murder of young Stompie, Richardson on most days stuffed his chunky arms and body into a gold-colored football jacket he had long ago outgrown. The jacket still bore the name at the center of the storm, a name that had evoked terror in Soweto in the 1980s. "Mandela United Football Club," it read, named for Winnie Mandela.

Richardson had once been the team's coach, though neither he nor his players actually played much football. Instead, Richardson served as the killer in chief among a squad of young men who served as footballers-turned-bodyguards-turned-enforcers for Winnie. They were wayward young comrades, often on the run from police. Winnie took them under her wing, and they, in turn, devoted themselves to her type of struggle. Richardson told the TRC he would have done anything for her. And he did. He protected her. He looked out for her. He worried for her, in his disturbed way. And Richardson, like others, called Winnie "Mommy."

"I loved her with all my heart. I would have done anything for her. When other people got into the lift [elevator] with us, I wondered why they got inside the same lift, because I did not want anyone to touch Mommy and I was worried that they might touch Mommy. Only myself could touch Mommy. Not anyone else. I loved her."

When she needed someone removed, he killed for her too, or so he claimed. When the young Stompie was beaten so badly at Winnie's home that a decision was made to finish him off, Richardson took care of it. He slit the poor boy's throat. And when Winnie needed an alibi during her kidnaping and assault trial to claim she was not even in Soweto at the time of the Stompie beating, Richardson and others backed her claim that she was away.

But these many years later, Richardson's affection had turned vengeful. He was angry with Winnie for abandoning him. He had gone to jail for Winnie, and what did he get in return? He'd applied for amnesty for Stompie's murder, and in so doing claimed that the earlier Winnie alibi had been a lie. In his testimony before Tutu's hearing, he went for the jugular, though this time with words: "*I killed Stompie under the instructions of Mommy. Mommy never killed anyone, but she used us to kill a lot of people. She doesn't even visit us in prisons. She used us!*"

The more Richardson talked, the clearer it became that Winnie had surrounded herself with people who were truly unhinged. (Richardson's lawyer told the TRC his client had an extremely low IQ.) Many of the witnesses were a motley, messed-up cast of characters: the driver, the nutty aide, the numerous youths who passed through her world. But the victims of Winnie's club spoke, too, in words that were both chilling and believable. A host of clergymen and political activists who once tried to rein in Winnie's waywardness also sat before Tutu's commission to account for why they failed so miserably.

Taken together, their words painted a portrait of Winnie as a dangerous menace within the liberation movement at a time when a victory in the antiapartheid struggle seemed within reach. In the late 1980s, Nelson Mandela, though still in prison, had begun tentative talks with the apartheid state, as had his comrades in exile. Pressure within South Africa mounted precipitously too. Oliver Tambo, the ANC president in exile in Lusaka, Zambia, had called on party supporters to make the apartheid state "ungovernable." And the people responded intensely, meeting state terror with a terror of their own.

The liberation struggle in some ways became a street war, pitting black antiapartheid fighters and ordinary people against the white security forces. It also pitted various black factions against each other. "Comrades" enforced struggle codes of conduct against one another, and people deemed sellouts became easy targets for the "necklace"—a burning tire around the neck. Recently returned to Soweto from a bout of banishment in the small faraway town of Brandfort, Winnie capitalized on the militancy. In a 1986 speech that sent chills down the spine of South Africa's whites, she held a box of matches in the air and declared, "Together, hand in hand, with our boxes of matches and our necklaces, we shall liberate this country."

To the world, Winnie Mandela was the face of the Mandela name at a time when Nelson could not be seen. And she was, truth be told, perhaps the fiercest comrade of all. She wore khaki fatigues, plus boots and a beret. She ran a network of operatives for MK, the ANC's underground guerrilla movement. A former social worker—in fact, South Africa's first black one—she mediated in disputes among bands of youthful activists and rogue gangs. And all the while, police kept her in a tight net of surveillance and harassment.

A group of disaffected youth and young men began to coalesce around her. She called them her football club, even purchased track suits emblazoned with the new club's name, Mandela United Football Club (MUFC). They congregated in the yard of the small Mandela home, sometimes sleeping over in her little outbuildings. They mixed, from time to time, with MK fighters who were passing through. Richardson and his Mandela United squad recruited other youths through abduction and torture. Comrades who did not want to join were viewed as suspicious, even sellouts. Comrades who didn't toe the club's line were sometimes tortured, even murdered. Strange rumors filtered around Soweto of the football club using knives to carve the letter *M* on the bodies of its victims, then pouring battery acid on the open flesh. The club became such a threat in the Orlando section of Soweto that people began complaining about it to leaders of the ANC's internal surrogate, the United Democratic Front (UDF).

In mid-1988, a rival group of youths set fire to the Mandela home. It would once have been an unthinkable act, considering it was the home of the nation's imprisoned hero, Nelson Mandela. But the fire was a measure of how bitter Winnie's community had become. Leaders of the UDF, alarmed at the mayhem that Winnie seemed to spawn, set up a Mandela Crisis Committee to handle their Winnie problem. The committee sent word to Nelson in prison, telling him of the strange doings with the so-called football club. And he personally urged Winnie to disband it. But she didn't. Winnie, by then, accounted to no one. She moved her home base from the burned-out house in Orlando West to a larger one, complete with Jacuzzi, in Soweto's Diepkloof section. And the body count climbed.

Dudu Chili, also an activist in Soweto, at first worked with Winnie and respected her as a leader. But the disturbing turn in Winnie's behavior pushed many of her women comrades away. "She was behaving like a goddess, like someone who was untouchable and could harm anybody," Dudu told me. "She seemed to be a person who didn't have a sense of conscience, of guilt, of shame."

Dudu came to fear Winnie. Dudu's son, Sibusiso Chili, was being hounded and threatened by the football club. Dudu went to Winnie to talk over this harassment. As Dudu claimed, Winnie told her that because Sibusiso refused to join the club, he had been labeled a sellout. It scared Dudu badly, for sellouts, as everyone knew, usually ended up with a necklace. The Chili family watched and waited for another shoe to drop on them.

In the meantime, the football club zeroed in on other targets. At the end of 1988, just before the new year, the football club abducted four youths from a Methodist church residence and took them to Winnie's new home. They were the young Stompie, plus Thabiso Mono, Pelo Mekgwe and Kenny Kgase. They'd been taken from the church on the pretext that they needed protection from a white clergyman who'd sexually abused them. But that turned out to be a lie told by one of Winnie's followers.

Word of the abductions spread through Soweto. Dudu Chili learned of it and began phoning church officials and civic leaders, including the highly respected Albertina Sisulu, wife of Walter Sisulu, one of the ANC leaders sentenced to prison with Mandela. Few people knew what was actually happening at Winnie's house. But the activists knew that the footballers were violent. And they were. The four youths were subjected to a kind of kangaroo court in Winnie's garage. They were grilled on why they'd allegedly slept with the white priest. On top of that, Stompie was accused of being a sellout. The beatings were so severe that the youths screamed. Richardson and his goons sang freedom songs to drown out the noise.

Thabiso Mono told the TRC of the ordeal: *"Jerry said someone must bring a chair for Mommy. Mommy should sit on the chair."*

> *Mr. Makanjee, a lawyer: Who was "Mommy" that was being referred to?*
> *Mono: He was referring to Mrs. Mandela.*
> *Makanjee: Did Mrs. Mandela then enter the room?*
> *Mono: Yes, she arrived in the room. When she arrived in the room she questioned us why we allowed a white priest to sleep with us. We did not ap-*

prove of that [meaning the boys denied it]. And then she asked Stompie why was Stompie selling out people. Stompie disagreed with that information. And then she started hitting us with fists, one by one. After that, the whole group joined in the assault.

Makanjee: After you were assaulted with fists, what happened?

Mono: After the assault with the fists, the whole group joined in the assault. They kicked us. They lifted us up and we were thrown to the ground. After some time they started hitting us with sjamboks [rawhide whips] . . . Mrs. Mandela started hitting me with a sjambok.

Richardson's testimony fleshed out the horror:

> *We started torturing the youths in the manner that the Boers [Afrikaners] used to torture freedom fighters. The first thing that I did to Stompie was to hold him with both sides, throw him up in the air and let him fall freely onto the ground. Mommy was sitting and watching us. I think we threw Stompie about seven times in the air and he fell onto the ground. He was tortured so severely that at some stage I could see that he would ultimately die . . . There are a lot of things that we did to Stompie. We kicked him. We kicked him like a ball.*

(Stompie's mother, Joyce Seipei, a simple, rural woman, wept in the audience as Richardson spoke.)

On New Year's Day, 1989, the Crisis Committee met with Winnie to press for release of the abducted youths. Winnie stonewalled. She claimed the youths were not being held against their will. She would not produce them. The Crisis Committee, in its tragic weakness, did not press further. Even as they were negotiating with Winnie, Stompie's fate was sealed.

Richardson, in his TRC testimony, described what happened in early 1989 after he dragged Stompie out of the Mandela house and took him to an open field:

> *I slaughtered him like a goat. I put garden shears through his neck and the garden shears penetrated through his neck.*

(Mrs. Seipei broke down completely and had to be escorted from the room.)

The rest of the captive youths were held and forced to participate in football club actions. On January 3, 1989, Richardson took them on an attack against Lerothodi Ikaneng, a former football club member who'd escaped. As he'd done with Stompie, Richardson stabbed Ikaneng in the throat. But the youth survived.

> Ikaneng: *They lifted me up and dropped me into some reeds and a swamp there, and I could hear footsteps fading away as they were walking away from the scene. That's when I decided to drag myself and go get some help.*

Dudu Chili's family went on full alert. Ikaneng was best friends with Sibusiso Chili, Dudu's son. Sibusiso had resisted attempts by the football club to force him to join them. This, in the strange logic of the footballers, made Sibusiso a sellout, along with Ikaneng, the defector.

Meanwhile, on January 6, a boy's decomposing body was discovered in a Soweto field. It took several days for the body to be definitively identified, but in the meantime Soweto was rife with the rumor that one of the abducted youths from Winnie's home had been found dead. A couple of days later, another of the abducted youths surfaced. He had escaped and sought help, with clear evidence of the physical abuse.

The Crisis Committee now pressed Winnie to release the other youths, to tell what had happened. High-profile members of the Soweto community met with Winnie, including Nthato Motlana, the Mandela family physician since the 1950s. Although he was a doctor and Soweto was abuzz with talk that the abducted youths had been severely beaten, Motlana told the TRC that he did not ask to see the youths during his visit to Winnie. In a strange moral splitting of hairs that left the truth commissioners stunned, he insisted that seeing the youths was not his brief. His only task was to secure their release. Motlana clearly wanted to keep a safe distance from the nasty mess, both when it was happening in 1989 and when he testified eight years later.

The Crisis Committee itself went to Winnie's house and demanded to see the youths. She permitted them to, and they saw fresh wounds on the young men's bodies, which the youths explained away as cuts and bruises from falling out of trees. The Mandela attorney, Ishmael Ayob, was deployed to discuss the Winnie matter with Nelson during a January 13 visit to him in prison. The next day, Ayob returned to Soweto with a firm demand from Mandela: the abducted youths must be released *now*. And two days later, Winnie released the youths to Motlana, who, in his minimalist approach to the crisis, did not even bother to ask why Stompie was not among them. The reason, though, was clear, as much of Soweto then suspected: Stompie was dead.

The Chili family remained on alert. A friend with sources in Winnie's camp warned the Chilis of an imminent attack. On February 13, the ambush came. In the melee that followed, one of the football club members, Maxwell Madondo, died. And Sibusiso wound up in jail.

That same month, having weighed the political implications of their actions and investigated the abduction cases, some of the country's leading activists took the once-unthinkable step of distancing themselves from the wife of their supreme icon. Murphy Morobe, a former Robben Island prisoner and a leader in the UDF, delivered the group's public condemnation of Winnie. He urged people in the movement to shun her, a fact she would never, ever forget.

"We are outraged by the reign of terror that the team has been associated with," Murphy told the world in 1989. "Not only is Mrs. Mandela associated with the team, in fact the team is her own creation . . . We are of the view that Mrs. Mandela has abused the trust and confidence which she has enjoyed over the years." Even the ANC in exile—Nelson Mandela's ANC—weighed in, saying in typically obtuse language, "It is with a feeling of terrible sadness that we consider to express our reservations about Winnie Mandela's judgment . . ."

But several days later, the football club struck again, with the final assault on Dudu Chili's family. Having been swept up in the police dragnet following the Maxwell Madondo killing, Dudu was not home when men with guns surrounded her house. They threw petrol bombs through the windows and sprayed the house with gunfire. Three of Dudu's relatives were inside. Two were burned, but survived. The third did not make it. Finkie Msomi, a thirteen-year-old niece who was like Dudu's daughter, was hit by an AK-47 round inside the house and fell into the blaze.

Dudu Chili: I was very hurt that this thing happened to me, especially that it happened with the football club which was connected to Mrs. Mandela. I never thought a thing like that can happen and I always thought Mrs. Mandela was a strong powerful woman and if she had the responsibility of the football club she could have managed to control them not to do the things that they did to the community.

That is what Dudu said to the TRC. To me, a few days earlier, she used much stronger words. "She is a monster," she'd said of Winnie. Dudu was a woman who'd been forced by fear to move out of Soweto and who still looked over her shoulder. I worried that she might cause herself more trouble if she was quoted as being so bitter.

"Monster" was a pretty harsh word, I told her.

"I know it is. You can write it down. I'm not ashamed to say that."

• • •

Despite the trail of death and tears associated with her goon squad, Winnie maintained her revered spot among the icons of a liberation movement that did its best to sweep her violence under the carpet. When Nelson Mandela finally walked free from prison in February 1990 after twenty-eight years, Winnie stood by his side. The ANC decided to rehabilitate her by absorbing her more purposefully into the organization. Toward the end of that year, it gave her a senior position, in charge of the party's welfare budget. And when she went to trial in 1991 for the kidnaping and assault of Stompie and his friends, Mandela stood by her side. The ANC portrayed the case as yet another form of harassment against Winnie by the apartheid state, though many of its leaders knew full well the truth.

In the end, she was convicted of both kidnaping and assault by a judge who dubbed her an "unblushing liar" and sentenced her to six years in prison. But she remained free pending an appeal, in which the assault charge was dropped and her sentence reduced to two years, suspended. Later in 1991, at their party's triennial conference, ANC members elected Winnie to their governing body—as if nothing had happened.

But Winnie was a liability to Mandela. Longtime rumors about her ro-

mantic dalliances became real to Mandela when he learned that she continued being unfaithful even after his release from prison. And on the criminal
front, things were looking grim as well. Two witnesses who'd backed her
alibi during the Stompie trial publicly reversed themselves and accused Winnie of direct involvement in the violence. In March 1992, Mandela called a
press conference. In tones that suggested his personal pain, he announced his
official separation from Winnie, while at the same time praising her commitment to the liberation struggle and her long sacrifice in its name.

Indeed, Winnie remained the movement's magic bullet, still able to speak
to the pain and impatience of the masses of black South Africans as well as
the militancy of the youth. Most important, Winnie still drew massive
crowds. During the campaign for the 1994 election, in which she was a parliamentary candidate, Winnie proved a magnetic stump politician. Once the
ANC swept into power as the ruling party, Winnie became a legislator in the
new Parliament and received an appointment from her estranged husband,
now president, as a deputy minister of arts. Later that year, she was among
the top five vote-getters for the ANC's executive body.

But she remained willful. She kept popping up in the news with various
odd business ventures—diamond deals, casino deals, tourism deals—and
she thumbed her nose, so to speak, at party discipline. She even took to crit-
icizing the new government in speeches in the nation's squatter camps, chid-
ing her estranged husband for not housing the poor. Finally, after nearly a
year of her troublemaking, Mandela fired her from the cabinet after she vio-
lated policy and took an unauthorized overseas trip. And ever so quietly, later
in 1995, he filed for divorce.

* * *

In his steely, gravelly voice before a packed room at the Witwatersrand
supreme court, Mandela's words dripped with bitterness and anger. His
statements during his divorce trial that March of 1996 stunned the courtroom into silence. Rarely had anyone ever heard Mandela speak with such
emotion. But most striking of all, the Nelson Mandela known for his
staunch reluctance to discuss personal feelings or reveal personal matters was
fully and freely airing embarrassing intimate details of his marital pain.

To win a divorce, the law required only that he prove he'd been separated for more than a year, which he had been, and that adultery had occurred, which the wayward Winnie did not contest. But Mandela went much further, as if attempting to publicly wound Winnie in the way she had so infamously wounded him. On the witness stand, he accused her of committing "brazen infidelity" even after his release from prison. He revealed that he learned of a letter she had written to a lover, whose contents he diplomatically described as "incompatible with a marital relationship." He complained of her rejections. "Ever since I came back from jail, not once has the defendant entered my bedroom whilst I was awake." He told the court he tried to talk to her, to persuade her of the need for intimacies between husband and wife. "But not once has she ever responded. I was the loneliest man during the time I stayed with her."

In the courtroom's public gallery, his words stunned us all into silence. Gone was the legendary romance of Winnie and Nelson. The lovely words they once wrote to one another—that her heart went with him when he was sent to prison; that she kindled a thousand flames inside him during his Robben Island loneliness—were now mere footnotes to history. If anyone doubted his commitment to the divorce, the final blow to the marriage came when he thoroughly debunked the possibility of any mediation. His voice virtually bellowed as he declared, "If the entire universe tried to persuade me to reconcile with the defendant, I would not. I am determined to get rid of the marriage."

They had wed in 1958, two years after Winnie, an attractive twenty-two-year-old social worker, caught the eye of a lawyer sixteen years her senior. Then a rising star in the long tradition of the ANC, Nelson's first marriage, to Evelyn Mase, a nurse and mother of their two children, had fizzled into estrangement and divorce over the gap between his revolutionary politics and her staunch religion (Jehovah's Witnesses). Winnie and Nelson became a celebrated couple in the struggle. Together, they had two daughters. But they shared freedom for only four years before he was caught, jailed, tried, and sent away. Winnie had been left to fend for herself in the maelstrom of apartheid and its constant repression.

For many, their reunion in 1990 was a harbinger of the victory to come.

The Mandelas as South Africa's first couple were awesome, for the brief time the world saw them together: he the undefeated icon, she the fiery heroine, reunited after decades of enforced separation and poised to lead their nation to its promised land. Instead, they ended up in court, with small clutches of fretful supporters milling about on the sidewalk outside, some in tears at the thought of the Mandela marriage coming to an end.

Inside, Winnie tried to win a postponement. She pleaded with the court to allow her to consult traditional Xhosa tribal leaders who might mediate in the marriage, though Mandela rejected any mediation. She also wanted to present evidence she said would prove that the discord in her marriage resulted from disinformation sown by her old apartheid enemies, though Mandela scoffed at the notion that any kind of dirty-tricks campaign was shaping his feelings. With no warning, she even fired her lawyer and begged the court's forbearance. Winnie seemed humble and defenseless. "My case cannot be closed, my lord. I seek the sympathy of this court. There is nothing I can do on my own."

But the presiding judge, Frikkie Eloff, president of the regional supreme court, saw it as a ploy and urged her to present her own case.

"Mrs. Mandela, the case is in your hands now. You have the right to address me, to tell me why you conclude there should not be a decree of divorce."

"This is no ordinary case," she said. "There are other relevant issues."

"Is that all you wish to say?"

"Yes."

And a short time later, capping a second day of testimony, Eloff ruled. He officially dissolved the marriage of Nelson Rolihlahla Mandela and Winnie Madikizela-Mandela.

But Winnie, as usual, rose yet again. Though her press was persistently bad and her political struggles within the ANC legendary, enough women still supported her to catapult her into the presidency of the symbolically powerful ANC Women's League early in 1997. And from there, the league nominated her to become deputy president of the party itself, which, if successful, would have made her a shoe-in to become the country's deputy president in the next election. Winnie was attempting her big move up the political ladder, but ANC leaders would block her at each step.

In one of her rare press interviews, she appealed directly to the black masses, pressing all the hot-button issues of the day. She took the ANC to task for the country's high crime rate, saying "the ANC is seemingly not in control. The criminals are in control." She criticized the ruling party for not acting quickly enough to provide housing to the millions of homeless, for straying from its liberation mandate, and for fearing her because of the grass-roots support she could easily claim. As if taunting leaders of a party in which her ex-husband was still the head, she accused the ANC of "Win-niephobia."

Upping the ante in what South Africans called a nasty "slanging match," the party responded with a published broadside of its own. It accused her of exhibiting the "political waywardness of a charlatan" who "tends to believe that everyone is against her and therefore resorts to strange behavior to at-tract attention." As for her contribution to policy in the new political terrain, the party characterized her role as "silence, silence, and more silence."

Against that backdrop, Winnie apparently believed she could credibly claim that the TRC probe had been motivated by politics, though I didn't at all believe it.

. . .

Day nine of the marathon TRC hearing, the moment all South Africans had awaited: Winnie took the stand. She looked very much the social worker, as if she'd dressed down a bit to appear more ordinary in a simple navy-blue suit. The same woman who had snickered and whispered while witnesses wept, who called her former driver senile, and who sarcastically signaled by circling her finger at her head that another witness was loony—that same woman seemed a portrait of humility.

She spoke softly. At first, I could barely hear her. In a strangely abbrevi-ated examination, her lawyer—the same one she'd fired during the divorce proceedings—led her through a series of inane explanations, coupled with an extraordinary string of denials. Winnie saw no evil, heard no evil, did no evil, suspected no evil, even when people were beaten half to death on her property. She portrayed herself merely as a selfless leader attempting to me-diate and guide the fractious youth of Soweto, to help them unite for the common goal of liberation. Her efforts, she said, led to the formation of the football club as a unifying activity.

> The various youths came to seek refuge in my house. Originally when I returned from Brandfort, I found a state of chaos within the community. Youths were fighting amongst each other and these were youth organizations, democratic youth organizations . . . They were fighting with gangsters and I brought them around a table to discuss those problems. And that is how they came to stay at my house. They were on the run from the police for one thing or another.

But the woman who reveled in her role as "mother of the nation" and the firebrand of the liberation struggle claimed she had no responsibility whatsoever for the actions of the youths who occupied the outbuildings and back rooms of her property: "I did not have any direct control over those youths who came to seek refuge at my place."

That, to me, was like a hammerblow chipping away a huge chunk of her heroic status. Winnie would not take responsibility for any part of the reign of terror hatched from the football club's redoubt at her home.

Did she order the death of Stompie? "That is ludicrous and the worst lunacy." Did she arrange for the murder of Dr. Abubaker Asvat, a local doctor friendly to the struggle, who allegedly had been called in to examine the dying Stompie? Two men convicted of Asvat's murder told the TRC that Winnie hired them to do it. "Those boys couldn't possibly be speaking the truth that I hired them to kill a close friend of mine." Did she order the deaths of Lolo Sono and Sibuniso Tshabalala, two other murdered youths? "That is ridiculous!" Did she parade a beaten Lolo Sono before the boy's father and claim he was a dog to be dealt with, as the weeping father testified? "I have no idea why he is making up that fabrication, save to say I suppose he is on the bandwagon to lead these false fabrications." Did she personally strike blows at Phumlile Dlamini, a pregnant rival for the affections of a man? "I regard that statement as totally ludicrous."

On and on it went. She even denied the abductions for which she was convicted in 1991 and said she saw no injuries on the youths who were beaten on her property, though other witnesses—even a doctor—had seen the lacerations and bruises on their faces and bodies. She grew testier under cross-examination and lashed out arrogantly in sparring matches with her interrogators.

"I will not tolerate you speaking to me that way!" "I hope I am not expected to respond to those ramblings." "I gave you my answer . . . If you don't like it, too bad." And to one lawyer who warned that she could be subject to criminal prosecution for one of the episodes of abduction and murder, she declared icily, "You are most welcome to proceed with any action if you so wish."

The spectacle was chilling. Winnie, in fact, accused just about everyone of lying, including the clergymen and the political leaders, among them two very senior government officials who'd tangled with her back in the bad old days of the football club.

"Yes, it is true that most of the witnesses who testified here are lying. As far as I am concerned, Jerry Richardson is lying. As far as I am concerned, the two youths who claim that I gave them money to kill Dr. Asvat are lying. As far as I am concerned, Morgan's [the driver's] ludicrous statements made before you here are a pack of lies. I can go on and on and on."

And she spat ethnic venom at South Africans of Indian descent. Over and over, she questioned the citizenship of Indian lawyers, though through her life she'd had a few Indian lawyers herself. She lashed out at a so-called Indian cabal within the liberation movement. And as for Murphy Morobe, the man who had the courage to push forward with a moral stand against the Mandela football club in 1989, she mocked him there at the truth hearing.

Morobe was a generation younger than Winnie and grew up near her house, in her shadow. He was one of the leaders of the famous 1976 Soweto uprising. He served time on Robben Island with Nelson Mandela. While most of the liberation leaders were jailed or in exile, Morobe was among the internal movement leadership that attempted to keep the struggle in focus. Unlike some others who could not see their way clear in the Winnie Mandela saga, Morobe had a sharp and fully operative moral compass. At the very time when the movement was poised to win its victory over apartheid, he knew that Winnie's deadly shenanigans could derail the process. I'd interviewed him before the truth hearings and asked how to reconcile the competing images of Winnie that so many people held. Memorably and wisely, he said simply, "The closer you are to the fire, you feel the fire differently."

Winnie tried to scorch him. She had not gotten over the condemnation of 1989. Before hundreds of people at the TRC, she tried to smear his credibility, even his manhood. Spitting it out as an ethnic slur, she called him "Murphy Patel" and claimed that comrades in the movement thought Indians controlled him. Winnie's bursts of bile mounted over the nine hours of her testimony. She was vindictive, vengeful, and crafty. Frankly, she was scary.

Tutu seemed almost in pain as he listened to her. Winnie was disdainful not only of her accusers but of the whole truth-telling process, though she herself had asked the TRC to hold these hearings in public. Tutu viewed the truth-telling process as a kind of spiritual journey from sin to repentance to redemption. In his faith, he believed that even the most evil characters could still be redeemed. But not once did Winnie express the least bit of contrition for, at a minimum, aligning herself with people who were deadly. Never once did she express regret for the lives that were lost. Not even once.

Finally, at the hearing's end, Tutu spoke directly to the heart he assumed she still had. He invoked the historic bonds between the Tutu and Mandela families. They lived on the same street. Their children attended the same school. Winnie was godmother to one of his grandchildren. He recalled visiting her during her banishment in Brandfort.

"I have immense admiration for her and there is no question at all that she was a tremendous stalwart of our struggle, an icon of liberation who was banned, harassed, under surveillance, banished, with her husband away serving a life sentence, and she had to bring up two girls. . . .

"I acknowledge Mrs. Madikizela-Mandela's role in the history of our struggle, and yet one has to say that something went wrong, horribly, badly wrong."

And then, for the sake of healing and reconciliation, he literally begged Winnie to apologize: "There are people out there who want to embrace you. I still embrace you because I love you and I love you very deeply . . . I beg you, I beg you, I beg you, please. I have not made any particular finding from what has happened here. I speak as someone who has lived in this community. You are a great person and you don't know how your greatness would be enhanced if you were to say sorry, things went wrong, forgive me. I beg you."

Winnie sat silently for a moment, as if deciding how to respond. And in that explosive silence, he told me later, Tutu prayed for God to work his magic.

Then Winnie spoke: "Thank you very much for your wonderful, wise words. That is the father I have always known in you. I am hoping it is still the same. I will take this opportunity to say to the family of Dr. Asvat how deeply sorry I am. To Stompie's mother, how deeply sorry I am. I have said so to her before, a few years back, when the heat was very hot. I am saying it is true. Things went horribly wrong. I fully agree with that. And for that part of those painful years when things went horribly wrong—and we were aware of the fact that there were factors that led to that—for that I am deeply sorry."

Critics lashed Tutu for appearing to appease Winnie, for virtually dragging that apology out of her. And yet, had he not done it, there may have been no public expression of regret from her, not even for the children who were harmed.

She returned to her "normal" life as an absentee parliamentarian, as a speaker on the stump at home and abroad, as a "mother of the nation" with a strong tinge of disrepute. She lost her bid to become the ANC deputy president, but she'd have lost that in any event. Within the ruling party, Winnie had hit her glass ceiling.

The threats of criminal prosecution came to naught. Though technically it was possible that at some point she could be brought to book for human rights abuses, no one in South Africa believed that would happen. Her innocence and guilt would simply be one of many chapters in the fraught history of the liberation struggle, perhaps its most tragic chapter, but just one slice of a much broader story.

In its final report, issued nearly a year later, the TRC said:

- "In all probability," Winnie did assault Dlamini, the pregnant woman, on more than one occasion.
- She knew of the murder of Dlamini's brother, Thole Dlamini, and tried to cover it up by sending potential witnesses into hiding.
- She knew of the kidnapping of and assaults on Lolo Sono and Si-

buniso Tshabalala, who were held hostage in her garage for several days of beatings. "The commission finds, therefore, that Madikizela-Mandela must take responsibility for the disappearances of" the two youths. Their bodies have never been found.

- During the beatings of Pelo Mekgwe, Thabiso Mono, Kenny Kgase, and Stompie Seipei, "Madikizela-Mandela was present at her home and not in Brandfort as submitted in her trial, and . . . she was present during the assaults and initiated and participated in the assaults . . . In all probability she was aware of Seipei's condition and failed, as the head of the household, to take responsibility by arranging medical treatment . . . The commission finds that Stompie Seipei was last seen alive at the home of Madikizela-Mandela and that she was responsible for his abduction from the Methodist manse and was negligent in that she failed to act responsibly in taking the necessary action required to avert his death."

- "The commission finds that Madikizela-Mandela was involved in and responsible for the attempted murder of [Lerothodi] Ikaneng."

- "The commission finds that the MUFC was involved in a number of criminal activities in the community, including killing, torture, assaults, and arson. The commission finds that Ms. Mandela was aware of the criminal activity . . . The commission finds that members of the football club operated from Madikizela-Mandela's house and that she had knowledge of the club members' activities and/or authorized and/or sanctioned them."

But Winnie would press on. Winnie always did.

13

With Impunity

ieter W. Botha ranted and raved. What else could he do? He had no more power, he was eighty-two years old, and he'd been dragged into court for thumbing his nose at a truth commission whose work he truly loathed. In the well of a tiny courtroom where he'd sat on a special cushion because of a bad hip, the former president stood and addressed the press in his trademark bellicose style. He looked wild-eyed. He wagged his finger at the TV cameras. Bald and waxy-skinned, Botha was literally spitting mad. Droplets kept landing on my notepad and hands, but that was a small price to pay for the pleasure of this moment.

By January 1998, Botha's angry predicament inside the George magistrate's court was probably the closest I would ever come to witnessing any senior Afrikaner politician of the apartheid days held legally accountable for his behavior. Botha presided over some of apartheid's harshest years. He served as prime minister, then president, from 1978 to 1989—a time when state security measures were at their most brutal. But Botha wasn't admitting to anything. In his eyes, he had done no wrong. Despite disbelief by the TRC and by a broad swath of the South African public, Botha claimed no responsibility for the assassinations, massacres, abductions, tortures, and bombings that were the heart of apartheid's power.

Senior officials had fingered Botha. The only apartheid-era cabinet minister to apply for amnesty, Adrian Vlok, claimed that Botha approved the plan to bomb the headquarters of the South African Council of Churches in 1988, on suspicion of antiapartheid activity. A police general claimed Botha ordered the bombing of the Congress of South African Trade Unions in 1988 as well. And documents of Botha's State Security Council, the brain trust of apartheid, showed that his government crafted a policy to "remove" or "eliminate" its adversaries.

Retired colonel Eugene "Prime Evil" de Kock, the convicted multiple murderer and killer extraordinaire of the old apartheid state, vented his spleen at Botha during the George trial. De Kock even claimed Botha conferred on him the police Star of Excellence for the 1982 bombing of the ANC exile headquarters in London. He called leaders like Botha cowards for not owning up to their deeds.

"They want to eat lamb," de Kock said contemptuously, "but they don't want to see the blood and guts."

Botha refused to respond to any of the allegations, and the TRC, being something other than a court of law, really had no way to force him to. The commission succeeded only when people wished to cooperate with it; it could only uncover truths that people helped it find. And with the wholesale shredding of intelligence, police, and military documents during the last apartheid government, headed by de Klerk, the exercise of truth-telling and reconciliation depended almost completely on perpetrators' willingness to talk.

But Botha refused even to talk to the TRC. When the TRC subpoenaed him, he ignored it. In a compromise to take account of his age and ill health, the TRC submitted written questions to him, which he answered in a seventeen-hundred-page document that explained apartheid and the siege its leaders faced from the black masses. But it did not address issues of culpability. One truth commissioner called the Botha document an act of more "confession avoidance." Personal pleading by Mandela himself would not budge Botha. So the TRC took the ex-president to court, charging him with contempt.

That's how we ended up in the George courtroom. It was a relatively minor charge, and yet it had huge symbolism. After the long years of apartheid violence and abuse, Botha became the first and only apartheid-era president ever to be prosecuted, albeit only for this relatively innocuous crime.

Living along the lovely Cape Coast at the base of the Outeniqua Mountains, Botha spent his twilight years fuming and seething about history's cruel turn. An old man incapable of reconciliation or just unwilling even to try, he was locked in an unreconstructed time warp, stuck in the halcyon days of his old white state. His old black enemies were now running the country. Also led by a black man, the TRC just kept nipping at his heels. And he found himself hauled into court to stand trial in a case presided over by a black judge.

Starved for news after a boring thirty-minute pretrial hearing in the George courtroom, the press corps climbed over tables, chairs, and one another to gather at his feet, to gaze on this relic of South Africa's past.

"I am not prepared to apologize," he bellowed and spat. "I only apologize for my sins before God . . . I stand with all those who executed lawful commands from my government in our struggle against the revolutionary communist onslaught against our country." All those were the hot-button words old apartheid leaders used to describe Mandela's ANC and other liberation groups, which Botha declared were making a mess of their shot at governing. "I'm still concerned about the onslaught. What I prophesied came true!"

He seemed delighted to be the center of attention once again. He even deadpanned that we journalists should salute him. But he still seemed as scary to me as he'd been on television when I'd seen him back in the 1980s, wagging that finger and railing on about crushing the "terrorists."

We threw questions at him and he sparred deftly. He tried to argue that the word "apartheid" can "easily be replaced by a positive term: good-neighborliness." At first I thought he was being cruelly sarcastic. But when he heard a few of us chuckle, he barked, "Who's laughing?" He scanned the crowd as if he'd do harm to the offenders. People should beware of awakening the wrath of the tiger within the Afrikaner soul, he warned. But one of the Afrikaner journalists flippantly informed Botha that there are no tigers in Africa. The sorry old president snapped, "If there were, *you* wouldn't have been one of them."

After calling the TRC a "circus" and a "witch-hunt," he coined a new slur: the "revenge and retribution committee," he called it, out to humiliate the Afrikaner. Those kinds of accusations always galled me. If the new South Africa really wanted revenge and retribution, humiliation would have been the least of the Afrikaners' worries.

* * *

Lots of embittered Afrikaners hurled insults at the TRC and tried to smear Tutu's work. It was the natural response, I suppose, for people watching all that was terrible about their old way of life being unmasked before the world. It was the natural response of people who did not believe that terrible things had happened at all. And to be frank, the criticism of the TRC was also a natural response for the guilty whose misdeeds were being exposed.

But of all the Afrikaners who lashed out and complained about the TRC's probing eye, one above all surprised and disappointed me most. I suppose I was just naive to think that F.W. de Klerk could actually go the distance in the historic walk to South African freedom he'd initiated with his reforms in 1990.

The last president under apartheid, the man who secured his place in history when he freed political prisoners, opened up the political system, and earned a Nobel Prize with Mandela in 1993 for their joint stewardship of South Africa's transition, de Klerk drew his line in the sand when it came to the issue of the truth. I'm not accusing him of lying. I'm not accusing him of anything. It's just that de Klerk's truth did not comport with the truth of apartheid, and that was plain and painful for all to see.

In an eagerly awaited 1996 TRC appearance to lay out the broad context in which his apartheid government operated, de Klerk consistently claimed he had never been party to or even aware of any government decision to commit human rights abuses. He acknowledged that terrible things happened, and he apologized, broadly speaking, for the pain and suffering those things caused. But in quite earnest tones, he said he had no idea *how* such terrible things could have occurred. Though he was a cabinet minister and then president during the height of the apartheid-era conflict, he said he knew nothing.

Truth commissioners later revealed proof that he'd attended a 1986 cabinet meeting in which plans to "eliminate" apartheid's opponents were discussed. But in a linguistic debate that broke out routinely in TRC hearings, de Klerk denied that "eliminate" meant to kill. Truth officials said de Klerk's testimony wasn't credible. And Tutu said de Klerk's claims made him want to cry. On that basis, de Klerk decided the truth body was biased against him.

He and his National Party—the old party of apartheid—withdrew all cooperation with the truth body and filed a lawsuit against it in 1997. Imagine that. The great reformer, the man feted as a hero, went to legal war against one of the key institutions of the new democratic era. Tutu's commission had treated him unfairly, de Klerk claimed, by suggesting publicly that de Klerk was not telling all he knew. The lawsuit was settled, with the TRC agreeing to a public apology to de Klerk for its public expressions of disbelief. But de Klerk continued to believe that the TRC's approach was actually polarizing the country anew.

Frankly, I'd heard de Klerk complain about polarization by blacks even before the TRC launched its hearings. Fascinated by the Houdini act required for de Klerk to try to wrestle free of the apartheid albatross, I'd interviewed him back while he was campaigning in 1995 for the National Party in upcoming local government elections. De Klerk was the National Party president then and also held one of two deputy presidencies in Mandela's government of national unity, another institution to foster reconciliation.

But even then—only eighteen months after the transition to democracy—he complained to me that the ruling ANC seemed "obsessed with race" and too focused on the past. Yes, he admitted, the legacies of the apartheid era needed to be rectified. "But the way to rectify it is to look forward and to do what needs to be done now. Everything in the so-called apartheid era was not bad." This to me was the good part. I enjoyed hearing old Nationalists try to defend apartheid. It seemed to confirm my belief that many of them weren't as changed as they tried to appear.

De Klerk explained that the apartheid era fostered Christian values, strong families, and a strong work ethic. Surely, South Africa needed such values, he said, not seeming to realize that he had created a double standard: it was fine to look to the past for apartheid's "not bad" elements, but not fine to look to the past for apartheid's terrible repression, as he'd accused the ANC of doing too often. And the tone with which he said it, the "so-called apartheid era," seemed to deride those who used the term. Revisionism, I knew, was at hand. And it kept spilling out. "My party stopped using the word 'apartheid' twenty-five years ago," he claimed. I worried that my face registered my utter disbelief at his words. Sure, "in many respects," apartheid left "a legacy which needs to be rectified, and my party is not defending apartheid," he said. But the ANC "must now stop blaming apartheid" and stop practicing "the constant emotive revival of the apartheid ghost."

I often thought of his words when his battles with the TRC began. De Klerk seemed to have a beef with the new era well before the TRC came along. Even before the ugly accounts of truth were told, de Klerk was rapidly running from the past and running as well, I'd venture to say, from the kind of reconciliation being offered with such magnanimity. His unreconstruct-edness stunned me. But it shouldn't have. He'd been so hailed as a visionary earlier in the decade that I sometimes forgot this crucial fact. De Klerk started his period of post-1990 reforms in the belief that he could hold back the push for a one-person-one-vote democratic system. And now, in light of his battles with the new dispensation, it appeared that de Klerk and black rule were an ill-suited match.

In the space of a year beginning in 1996, de Klerk withdrew from the unity government in which he'd stood with Mandela. He took his party into parliamentary opposition. He denied knowing anything whatsoever about apartheid-era atrocities. He sued Tutu and his commission. And then, ac-knowledging the baggage of the past that continued to drag down his party, de Klerk in the summer of 1997 stepped down as National Party president, turning it over to a younger breed of men. He resigned from Parliament too and receded from political life in the new South Africa he'd helped create. But allegations of his knowledge of or complicity in apartheid-era abuses continued to dog him as the press got hold of secret documents seeming to implicate him and as more security officers told the TRC, often with no evidence, that de Klerk, as president, must have known.

• • •

Whites who had presided over state terror or who actually committed it accused the TRC of persecuting them. Even whites not involved in apartheid's mechanics, those business and professional people who'd passively supported and benefited from racial exclusion, began to criticize the TRC for dredging up the past. (As if the past had died for all those widows and orphans that apartheid created.)

They grumbled among each other at dinner parties. They did not attend the truth hearings, a fact that Tutu noticed each and every time he convened such a gathering. The denial of white South Africa was so strong as to be aggressive. To embrace the truth-seeking process, to support it, would have suggested they had done something wrong, and white South Africa resented the mere suggestion of wrongdoing.

The idea that whites needed to reconcile with their black countrymen did not resonate within white South Africa. It was as if these whites believed they had atoned for the past by handing over power and allowing blacks to rule. In effect, South Africa was asking the victims of apartheid to forgive their abusers, while the masses of apartheid's white beneficiaries went on with their lives as if they'd had nothing at all to do with the nasty mess of the past.

Mandela and his team talked of building a new national consensus, and some whites fully embraced the new democracy of black rule. Whites were 12 percent of the population, but many of them found a comfortable niche in the new, relatively open society. They welcomed the end of South Africa's global exclusion as a pariah nation. They held posts in government, even within the ANC, which had been multiracial for several decades. In business, with the push to integrate the economy, whites and blacks were doing deals as never before. And blacks and whites were working side by side in various civil society groups intended to help South Africa change.

But in the main, blacks and whites occupied separate worlds physically as well as mentally. Most whites seemed to be digging in to hang on to what they had. Opinion polls showed consistently that, at worst, whites were on the defensive, or, at the least, feeling unmoored. The world as they had known it was no more, and society no longer favored them exclusively as it once had.

In their gated homes with the swimming pools and tennis courts, they "whinged." That's the South African word for "whine." In the executive suites, they fretted. On their farms where black workers still lived in hovels, they hunkered down, in the belief that the crime wave rocking the nation was a form of racial redistribution, though crime was far worse in black areas than in white ones. They feared their place of privilege would be eroded, their quality of life lessened. The new measures intended to redress the past and give blacks a better shot at the country's opportunities threatened some whites and sent them deeper into rejectionism.

Tony Leon, head of the small but economically powerful Democratic Party and a bulldog of a parliamentary critic of the government, accused Mandela of the "reracialization" of South Africa, as if racialism had suddenly disappeared in 1994. How was South Africa to chart its progress in redress-ing the past if it did not monitor issues of race? Sometimes I got the feeling that these white critics didn't really want the past to be redressed.

Mandela reminded his white detractors that electoral power for the black majority was not enough. In a 1998 speech to Parliament, he said, "Contrary to the disdainful assumptions of some honorable members, these communi-ties [nonwhites] are not satisfied with holding the flag of freedom whilst op-portunities and the resources of the country are held by others. They demand a place in the sun."

And in a little-publicized speech at a business breakfast, Winnie Madikizela-Mandela, the president's former wife, explained "transformation" in blunt, simple terms. A "second revolution" was sweeping South Africa, she said, in which the concerns of the black majority must inevitably become central in the economy and in the workplace. Whites must decide, she said, whether they will help create change or fight it.

"The truth and reality in South Africa today is no longer European or white, but African and more often black. Unless the African is placed at the center of transformation and the national agenda, our country will not be stable or productive."

All those present had heard this assessment before in one form or another, but Winnie's presentation seemed to hit like news of a death. I'd tagged along for this speech, in my ongoing quest to bag a Winnie interview and also to see how the white business community would receive her. After her speech, no smiles could be found in the room. The white businessmen did not appear happy with what they'd heard. Later, David Gleason, editor of a financial magazine, told me he was actually pleased to hear such plain talk. "Frankly, it's a good thing we finally heard it. Now we can really have a fight!" He laughed, but he was not joking.

In education, the white buzzword became "standards," as in: we must not integrate too fast, or educational standards will drop. In the workplace, the major peeve was affirmative action, though the sad fact of South Africa was that few blacks held the skills required to move wholesale into the workforce. Anton Carlson, a technical planner with the state-run phone company Telkom, told me he'd lost a bid for promotion and claimed affirmative action was the cause. That policy of black upliftment, he said, is "attacking my dignity." And of the overall government plan to uplift blacks through the provision of new housing, Anton pressed the stereotypical button of black lawlessness. Why waste the money? he said. "They burn each other's shacks."

White economists worried over the direction of policy and how the dynamics of race would affect it. Graeme Bell, a banking executive, told me, "We've got to help with the management, and if people listen to us because we've had the experience, we can move forward. But there's this attitude of: 'You're white. We can't trust you.' We've got to take a few slaps as a result of the situation."

The nuances of white angst were often more interesting than the angst itself. The end of apartheid had teased out some sharp, new distinctions within the white minority. In politics, the Afrikaner politicians—with the exception of de Klerk—often proved far more willing and able to make peace with the new order than did the English-speaking white liberals. The liberals, many of them secret supporters of the ANC during the days of apartheid, had once spoken out and protested for an end to racial repression.

Not all of them were fighting for majority rule or a system of one person, one vote, but at least they were fighting on the right side. White liberal lawyers represented ANC political prisoners. White liberal scholars inside the country or in exile wrote persistently of apartheid's failings. But when democracy finally came, some of these liberals began protesting the failings of Mandela's new government. Nothing wrong with that, for the failings were many. But the manner in which their protests were couched led some blacks to believe the liberals were arrogant, condescending, and unwilling, when the chips were actually down, to accept a nation ruled by blacks. Leon, the Democratic leader, seemed perpetually apoplectic under black rule, as if Mandela could never do anything right.

Helen Suzman, the legendary voice of white liberal opposition during apartheid, occupied a strangely dual role under democracy. She maintained a close friendship with Mandela, a friendship begun when she was among the few white politicians who visited him in prison and pressured the apartheid government to improve prison conditions. But even as her channels of communication with Mandela, the new black president, remained open, she alienated other blacks with her warnings that transformation of the universities could lower education standards if carried out too fast. Some blacks felt she was suggesting that blacks weren't up to snuff. Like other white liberals, Suzman often found herself at odds with the new democracy.

"We're finding a very difficult time," Suzman said wryly in her patrician voice as her black maid served us tea in the dark wood-paneled study in her home where we met. White liberals, she said jokingly, are an "endangered species."

Dennis Davis, a legal scholar at the University of the Witwatersrand, offered me what he couched as the inside scoop on white liberal South Africa. Davis, a jittery, quick-witted white man, was cuttingly smart and known for offering biting commentary. The basic white liberal refrain, unspoken but real, he said, was: "You black people don't know a bloody thing about running a country!" We laughed. I believed his rendering of white thought was true. Mandela and his team were sophisticated, well educated, and capable. But for many whites, they remained suspect and subpar.

A steady trickle of whites began emigrating. Though numbers at that time were hard to come by, experts believed the number was lower than before the 1994 election, when a big exodus of whites occurred in what some jokingly called the "chicken run." However small their numbers, though, the government was paying attention. Any drain of white professional skills in a nation in desperate need of expertise was viewed with alarm.

● ● ●

I spent more time than I'd have liked racing from one racial outbreak to another. Always they flared in the small towns and rural outposts of the Afrikaner platteland, where farmers wore khaki, their wives wore lace, and both sexes carried weapons. Those regions were the preserve of conservative, hard-core Afrikaners who owned vast tracts of land and lorded over their domains as if apartheid had scarcely ended. Life on the platteland remained terribly unequal, and nowhere was this more apparent than in the schools. The black schools, in the small townships or farm-labor settlements, lacked all educational amenities except pencils and tablets. They had virtually no textbooks, or textbooks so old as to be a detriment to black children's mental health, with their blatant racism. No playgrounds, just rough fields. Often not even any plumbing or enough desks.

Democracy, with its promise of equal education, sent black children streaming out of their townships and into previously all-white schools. In the cities, such integration had gone relatively well. Up the street from my house in Jo'burg, black and white students in their crisp uniforms flooded the streets after classes, sometimes clubbing together.

But out on the platteland, there was trouble. There, schools that had been exclusively Afrikaner, with lessons taught in the Afrikaans language and with all the amenities any school could need, including lab equipment and swimming pools, suddenly faced an influx of black students. The Afrikaner parents in episode after episode went ballistic. In one case, in the creepy little trucking town of Vryburg, parents attacked black high school students with baseball bats. The rural Afrikaner was having a hard time with the concept that Afrikaner culture and history could still thrive in a mixed-race environment: that's what I originally thought, and I assumed they could be taught or shown how diversity need not be a threat. But the more I delved into these conflicts, the more I realized that Afrikaner culture was so entwined with racial separatism that it seemed impossible to reconcile it with concepts of equality and democracy.

In a scene reminiscent of Little Rock, Arkansas, in the 1950s, police in the odd little town of Potgietersrus (we journalists called it Poltergeist) had to escort black primary-schoolers through a phalanx of angry white parents who did not want such children in their Afrikaner school. The Potgietersrus *laerskool* (lower school, or primary school) was a public institution, but had been an Afrikaans-language school since its inception. The new constitution guaranteed that students could be educated in the language of their choice, and already the *laerskool* had an English-speaking class for the 10 percent of white students who needed it.

But language, really, wasn't the entire issue. The Afrikaner parents, in reality, felt that the introduction of black students would dilute the thick Afrikaans culture of the school and strike yet another blow at what they felt was their embattled culture. They'd lost their government. They'd lost their exclusive franchise. And now they'd lose their schools? The parents took a harsh stand.

There was something thoroughly engaging in the dramatic, graphic bluntness with which these folks expressed their culture. That I was a black American did not seem to cause them to mince their words or pull their punches. People made some pretty racist statements to me in interviews, but I did not take it personally. To them, it wasn't racism anyway. To them, it was manifest destiny: the Afrikaner culture, many of its hard-liners believed, was superior to African culture and God had made it that way. I'd heard this kind of racism before back home. Hell, I'd *experienced* this kind of racism. And it never ceased to amaze me.

"I'd like to speak to you about the heartfelt emotions," Karen du Plessis said to me, her voice a low, rolling Afrikaans rumble. I met her in Potgietersrus, at the height of the conflict. Not the stereotypical Afrikaner matron, she wore fashionable blue jeans, dainty bracelets, and tasteful makeup. But she was every bit the hard-core plattelander, prepared to do battle with the government and the courts to preserve racial exclusion at her daughter's school.

"We as Afrikaner parents are but a small part of the great Afrikaner nation." While small in number in South Africa, "we make up for it in determination." They didn't look for trouble, she said, but "in this case it came looking for us. We are not prepared to sacrifice our Afrikaans culture. Why can we not have the right to protect our Afrikaans identity? We feel our identity is being murdered." If too much integration occurred, the mathematics of South African demographics meant the Afrikaner would be swamped. "Yes. It has to be exclusive, if the other people, by sheer numbers, will threaten the culture."

But there was more; I suspected as much. Though they would be in separate classes, the black and white children would still be "intermingled" at the school. She said it as if describing a revolting occurrence: intermingling. She'd heard talk of a black boy at another school trying to kiss a white girl. If the situation at Potgietersrus wasn't resolved to her liking, du Plessis said, she would pull her eight-year-old daughter out. "Because she's a girl, I'm worried about problems with black boys." The old black sexual boogeyman was preying on her Afrikaner soul. But it was good copy, a helluva good story. I did not want to mock her, but I sure felt gratified to hear such a graphic explication of Afrikaner fears.

Then she shocked me even more. She raised the name of Dr. Martin Luther King, Jr. "I want to quote something he said," something like: the ultimate measure of man is not where he stands, but where he stands in adversity, she explained. Looking straight into my eyes, almost pleading with me to see her side, she told me that I should understand the Afrikaners' plight, considering that I am a minority in America just as the Afrikaners are a minority in South Africa.

With the loss of power, the erosion of racial exclusion, the incursions of the black children into their schools, the Afrikaner felt pain, she said. I remembered another Afrikaner woman in Potgietersrus who shouted at me, "You can't understand! You don't want to understand." But actually I was starting to get it. I asked du Plessis to describe how she felt, and she growled, "A gouging in our hearts."

As the little black children walked hand in hand with their parents into the Potgietersrus school, angry white adults could do little but stand back in the face of a hundred cops, armored vehicles, and police dogs ringing the school. President Mandela had thrown his weight into the affair, urging both sides to be sensitive to the other. No one harmed the black children, some of whom were already crying as they walked into a school where empty class-rooms would greet them. The Afrikaner parents, by and large, kept their children at home, then went to the school to browbeat other parents to do the same.

Trying to stay focused on the task at hand, Maureen Molamu, a black mother, walked her nine-year-old daughter, Johanna, into the school without incident. Later, Molamu told me that the whites, in time, would realize they had no choice but to get in line with the aspirations for upliftment of their black countrymen. South Africa's demographics would make it impossible for whites to exist in isolation.

"It's not over yet, not at all, because obviously some will take their kids out of the school. They will go to another school. But we are coming there. We are going to that school where they are taking their children. So where will they end up? In the sea?

"I am stuck with them. They are stuck with me. We have to accept each other."

The South African reality.

14

The Scramble for Congo

GIKONGORO, RWANDA, MAY 1998

renched sideways, perhaps to deflect the blows, their heads bore deep gouges where the machetes had struck. Some of the corpses were missing hands, legs, and feet. Their jaws were frozen in silent screams, the effect of rigor mortis, I presumed, pulling their jaw muscles tight. They were adults. They were children. Some mothers' arms still held babies, or what was left of them. And all were hacked and mutilated. One room contained only heads, or half heads, as much as was unearthed. The excavators of the mass graves of the Murambi Technical School stacked the heads like firewood, in neat piles. Another room contained the corpses of children, twisted and brutalized children. One corpse in particular caught my eye. It lay in the fetal position. And when death came, he or she—I could not tell which—was still sucking a thumb.

There were about sixty classrooms at Murambi, and all were filled with corpses. Volunteers, all survivors of this slaughter, painstakingly dug up the mass graves on the school grounds and found the bodies. The Rwandan soil preserved some of the bodies well, like mummies. Others were heavily decomposed. The volunteers delicately cleaned the corpses. They treated them with a preservative powder. They laid the bodies in the classrooms—some on the concrete floor, others on strong wooden racks—where they would remain on display in memoriam of the most rapid, intense slaughter the modern world has known.

I visited Murambi in May 1998, four years after the Rwandan apocalypse that the world now records as genocide, when roughly 800,000 people were massacred. I visited because the repercussions of that genocide continued to shape events in both Rwanda and Congo-Zaire, just across the border. More war seemed certain to break out, and Rwanda, again, would be at the center of it, a tiny nation haunted by its killings and now hyperaggressive against any hint of their resurgence. To understand the turmoil of Central Africa in the 1990s, Rwanda was the place to start.

Murambi was but one of many sites where the killing occurred. By the time of my visit, precisely 27,148 bodies had been exhumed. In one mass grave dug by the killers, 650 bodies were found. Another had 3,000, another 18,000. No one knew how many pits of corpses would be found at Murambi. But there were more. I walked in silence from classroom to classroom. I held my hand over my mouth and nose. The scope of the death was sickening, the smell nauseating. Mary Braid of the *London Independent* traveled with me that day and she, too, was mortified. She, too, gagged quietly. Bosco, my friend and fixer from Bukavu, removed his ever-present hat and held it over his heart at the first sight of the corpses. Tears welled in his eyes, as did anger. He was a Tutsi, like all the Murambi dead. He'd lost family in slaughters just like this.

It struck me that the arms of so many of the corpses were still raised in struggle, as if they fought till the very end to save themselves. More likely, they were thrown into the pits still alive. I imagined them trying desperately to push away the bodies thrown in on top of them. I imagined them trying to dig for air, to carve out some space of life as the soil stole their breath away. After a while, I, like Bosco, could not take any more. I did not need to walk into every classroom. I understood. The objective fact of Rwanda's horror, a comprehension that had been only abstractly clinical until that day, sunk in. I felt chilled. The corpses frightened me. The dead children frightened me.

Outside, we walked along with Murangira Emmanuel. He'd survived what happened at Murambi in 1994, though just barely. A hole was still visible where a bullet had lodged in his forehead. Murangira remembered it vividly. He remembered those terrible days of 1994, when killings were under way all over the country, including the Nyamagabe village where Murangira lived in the Gikongoro district. Authorities urged people to flee to the Murambi school for safety. Murangira gathered his family and surged up a hill to the school grounds, in desperate hope for survival. But when the authorities and their troops disarmed the people, taking away their machetes and other farming implements that all Rwandans carried, Murangira knew something was terribly amiss.

Then truckloads of Hutu killers of the Interahamwe militia arrived, followed by the troops of Rwanda's Hutu army. They set fire to the main school building, where the doors were locked and people burned alive. They threw grenades and sprayed gunfire. They systematically hacked and shot just about everyone else on the Murambi grounds. Under threat of death, they forced people even to kill each other. Then they killed the killers they had made. The slaughter at Murambi lasted for three days, ending on April 22, the very day, back in New York, when the United States led the U. N. Security Council in a vote to withdraw most of the international peacekeepers in Rwanda rather than increase their numbers to stop the killing.

With a gunshot wound to his head, Murangira hid beneath bodies before the Murambi burials began. He dragged himself into the bush. As he moved south toward Burundi, he met other fleeing people, who helped him. Finally, he made it to a Burundian hospital. After he recovered and returned to Gikongoro, the dead of Murambi became his life. He worked to reclaim this killing field, he said when we met in 1998, because it was his duty to return to this place and nurture the national memory. It was his duty, he said, because he alone survived among the twenty-eight relatives who sought refuge with him at Murambi. His wife and his four children were among the dead, buried out there somewhere. He'd been looking for them.

There were virtually no Tutsis around Murangira's village anymore. He lived among the Hutus. Life—the grinding life of farming and grazing—resumed. But between the two groups, there remained a wariness that bordered on paranoia. Four years later, some Hutus still feared reprisals for the genocide, while Tutsis feared that among even the most moderate Hutu communities there could still be *génocidaires* awaiting a chance to strike again.

Many of the *génocidaires* of yesteryear were still hiding just across the border in Congo-Zaire and still made raids against Rwanda's new government. Living among this peril was made bearable, Murangira said in 1998, only because government troops of the Tutsi-dominated army remained on constant patrol in the area. They formed a barrier between life and certain death. "If they were not here," Murangira said of the troops, "the same guys would come back and kill me."

Stability and normalcy were absent from Rwanda, despite efforts by the government to foster justice and reconciliation. Rwanda's postgenocide government presented a multiethnic, multiparty lineup. The president, Pasteur Bizimungu, was a Hutu. The army had some Hutus in it as well. But that show of reconciliation, of democratic intent (if not actual practice), did not alter the Rwandan reality. The Rwandan Patriotic Front (RPF), whose army of minority Tutsi exiles had halted the genocide and overthrown the Hutu extremist regime of 1994, was firmly in control. The military command was largely Tutsi, as was the political power around the nation's true leader, Major General Paul Kagame, the vice president and defense minister.

Rwanda's very existence was a state of siege, and talk of postgenocide reconciliation, respect for human rights, and democratization took a backseat to militarization. By mid-1998, the *génocidaires* ensconced in bases inside eastern Congo-Zaire were mounting more and more raids into Rwanda. In an effort to stop the *génocidaires* from insinuating themselves into ordinary Hutu villages, Kagame's army forcibly removed nearly 500,000 Rwandans from their villages and placed them in military camps—over the howls of protest by human rights groups.

None of this was supposed to have happened. Kagame had installed Laurent Kabila as Congo's president in 1997 in the belief that Kabila would be both willing and able to contain the genocidal rebels. Kagame even sent some of his army commanders to help run Kabila's new army. But Kabila couldn't control the *génocidaires*—or, as Rwanda feared, he just wouldn't. By the spring of 1998, the solution of 1997 had all but unraveled. The big question in Central Africa was: how far would Kagame go?

I found my own answer at Murambi. I smelled the dead of 1994. I saw their mutilated corpses. I walked on ground once blood-red with the horribly systematic and efficient killing. At Murambi, the essence of postgenocide Rwanda crystallized for me: survival, at all costs. A nation that had suffered such a horror, and been abandoned by the world, would go to almost any length to prevent it from ever happening again. There would be more war. It was inevitable.

• • •

The situation in Rwanda had deteriorated so badly that when President Clinton arrived in March 1998, his security men would not let him venture farther than Kigali's airport. He stayed for only three hours, but that was long enough to pour on the "I feel your pain" empathy for which he was renowned as he spoke apologetic words to Rwanda about the U.S. inaction during the 1994 genocide. Rwanda haunted the Clinton administration's relations in Africa, for on his watch as the leader of the world's only superpower roughly 800,000 people were slaughtered. But of course, being the only superpower, U.S. support was now crucial to Rwanda's efforts to galvanize global guilt, so the Rwandans kept their resentment tamped down.

For me, as someone who wanted the United States to engage more effectively with Africa, Clinton's trip to Rwanda was offensive. I was not there in Kigali, but I followed it closely from Jo'burg. What Clinton said was an outrage, though the White House press corps traveling with him that day seemed to miss the president's utter revision of history.

"We did not act quickly enough after the killing began," Clinton said to Bizimungu, Kagame, and a crowd of genocide survivors. "We did not immediately call these crimes by their rightful name: genocide ... It may seem strange to you here, especially the many of you who lost members of your family, but all over the world there were people like me sitting in offices, day after day after day, who did not fully appreciate the depth and speed with which you were being engulfed by this unimaginable terror."

But the United States had been warned in advance. Months before the genocide, human rights groups as well as the U.N. peacekeeping commander in Rwanda warned the United States and the United Nations that Hutu extremists were compiling lists of Tutsis to be exterminated. Those Hutu killers were distributing weapons to Hutu civilians, and they broadcast bloodcurdling messages of anti-Tutsi hatred on Rwandan radio. As for not appreciating the depth of the crisis, we should all remember the dogged determination of Clinton's advisers not to acknowledge the genocide they knew was unfolding. But I suppose if the United States had no intention of getting sucked into another crisis, it made sense to behave as if no crisis existed. That way, obligations, moral responsibilities, even blame, could be kept to a minimum.

U.S. policy on African crises seemed to glide above reality, taking on a logic of its own that seemed to defy the facts on the ground. I'd seen it happen in Angola, where the United States kept declaring progress toward peace even as the combatants backslid into war. And Rwanda presented another classic example of willful American policy disconnect, when Clinton claimed the United States didn't know what it clearly did know.

After his brief stop in Kigali, Clinton flew to Entebbe, Uganda, for a regional summit. And again, the U.S. gloss was thick. Clinton met at Entebbe with a cabal of leaders his administration had dubbed a "new generation of African leader" or a "new breed." They were Yoweri Museveni, president of Uganda; Kagame of Rwanda, though he stayed in the shadows of President Bizimungu; Meles Zenawi, prime minister of Ethiopia; and Kabila of Congo-Zaire, a marginal and untested "new breeder." Not present, but very much a part of this cabal, was Eritrean President Isaias Afwerki.

These men were all in their forties and fifties and had risen to power after ousting an earlier generation of despots who had been the bane of Africa: Mobutu of Zaire, Habyarimana of Rwanda, Milton Obote of Uganda, and Mengistu Haile Mariam of Ethiopia. This "new breed" was largely market-oriented in its economic thinking. These leaders did not place their hopes on foreign aid, as had been an earlier generation's pattern for so long. And in the strategic vacuum left by the withdrawal of Cold War superpower rivalry, these men represented a growing tendency among African leaders to take matters into their own hands. Perhaps most important in fostering this new power bloc, the United States had its main strategic interest in Africa in mind. The "new breed" leaders represented a potential alliance of containment that could be brought to bear against the Islamic government in Sudan, which Washington had defined as a terrorist state. Sudan sponsored rebels in some of the "new breed" countries, and the new breeders, in return, were friendly with anti-Sudan rebels.

Despite all the soaring Clinton rhetoric, this U.S. alliance with the so-called new breed wasn't necessarily meant to help solve African problems. It was meant to solve American problems, both by forming a potential braking action on Sudan and by taking some of the moral heat off of Washington to do more in Africa. In embracing the new breed, the Clinton administration also pushed the notion of "African solutions for African problems." It became a favorite catchphrase for U.S.-Africa policy, and it sounded like an expression of American respect for African leadership. But as I watched it in practice, it seemed more like a code for disengagement when the going got tough.

Still, compared to the manipulative Cold War policies of Reagan and Bush, such as support for messianic rebel movements like Savimbi's UNITA in Angola or brutal dictators like the late Mobutu in Zaire, Clinton's approach was far less malevolent. In fact, Clinton elevated American commercial interest in Africa to a level previously unseen. He presided at a White House Conference on Africa in 1994 to raise the continent's profile and push American engagement with it. As a host of countries attempted democratization and economic reform, Clinton could legitimately point to the beginnings of political change that the United States had helped foster in Africa. South Africa's transition from apartheid provided the Clinton team with a central and positive focus. South Africa anchored a subregion that, at that time, was characterized by reform, stability, and economic development. And in 1998, when Clinton became the first American president to tour Africa, his cabinet secretaries and advisers hunkered down in meetings with their South African counterparts on trade, development, and security.

The trip brought intensive and largely positive coverage of the continent. Suddenly, policy makers, diplomats, and business executives who typically viewed Africa as marginal had to at least give it thought for a brief time while the global spotlight focused on Clinton. (And for Clinton, there were additional benefits. In the throes of his White House sex scandal back at home, he could hide out in Africa for a while, to bask in Mandela's radiance during his South Africa visit and to appear appropriately humbled and horrified at Gorée Island, a gateway for the transatlantic slave trade.)

Cynicism aside, I welcomed the trip and the new focus it would bring, even if only for a brief time, and even if only as an antiscandal diversion. As an African American, I thought it symbolically important for an American president to pay tribute to a continent so abused down through history and to which so many Americans like me claim ancestral links. The South African press, and lots of others, characterized the trip as a form of pandering to African Americans. But Clinton was in his second term. There'd be no more presidential elections for him. And anyway, he already had many black folk in the bag, as the author Toni Morrison would make clear in an October 1998 article in the *New Yorker* that dubbed Clinton America's first black president.

All the more reason for me to feel offended that this president in whom so much confidence and trust were invested was great style with little substance when it came to some of the continent's roughest places. In fact, when it came to U.S. policies on human rights abuses committed by Washington's friends, Clinton departed very little from the practices of U.S. administrations before his. When America's African friends ran regimes steeped in authoritarianism and human rights abuses, Clinton officials were largely silent. There they sat in Entebbe, Clinton with a group of leaders who shared strategic interests with Washington but who did not fit virtually any of the key democratic values the United States claimed to be pushing in Africa. To a man, these leaders did not actively promote multiparty electoral democracy. Museveni, the leading light of the group, ran a "no-party state," his explanation being that political parties would only inflame Uganda's fragile ethnic balance. When it came to human rights, in each country opposition figures were routinely arrested, along with journalists. Military repression—under the guise of national security—was a staple of reports on these countries by international human rights groups.

I often got the impression that the United States didn't know what to do in Africa—and didn't care to figure it out. Clinton's officials said all the right things, but, again, their words seemed disconnected from reality and their actions seemed sorely lacking. Secretary of State Madeleine Albright's December 1997 visit to see President Kabila in Kinshasa presented an alarming example. While she was there, Kinshasa's jails were filled with journalists, businessmen, human rights advocates, and opposition politicians. And Kabila's supporters and his troops harassed the U.N. investigators who were in the country to probe the massacres of the anti-Mobutu war. Clearly, a dire human rights situation had unfolded in the new Kabila regime, and Albright impressed upon Kabila in their private meetings the need to respect free political activity and freedom of expression.

But when the two officials held a joint press conference, Albright was surprisingly silent when presented with an opportunity to press Kabila publicly. During the conference, a journalist took Kabila to task for jailing his opponents. Kabila responded by railing against opposition politicians, accusing them of fomenting violence and vowing action against them. "If they incite people to violence, they will go to jail," Kabila declared. Then, in what sounded like a sarcastic afterthought, he added, "Long live democracy!"

Albright was caught completely off guard and looked embarrassed. She said nothing. She just stood there. Later that day, in obvious damage control, her State Department spokesman, James Rubin, said Albright would pursue the subject of political repression "vigorously" with Kabila. But it seemed to me she'd already let Kabila show her up rather badly.

So when I heard the results of Clinton's summit meeting at Entebbe during his March 1998 trip, I viewed them with skepticism. There was lots of talk at Entebbe about peace, security, and cooperation. The leaders even signed a communiqué about their common security interests. But even then, tensions between them were rising. And a few months after that high-flown summit, the new breeders took up arms against each other. Ethiopian and Eritrean troops went to war in May 1998 in a border dispute that laid bare a broader tug-of-war over regional dominance in the Horn of Africa. And in August, Rwanda and Uganda hit Congo yet again in fighting that would soon pit Rwanda and Uganda against each other and suck in a host of other nations. What a rebuke to U.S. policy. But all those slogans—the new breed, the new generation, African solutions for African problems—sure sounded good while they lasted.

• • •

KINSHASA, ZAIRE

I wasn't even on the continent in August 1998 when Rwanda launched its second Congo war. Covering for a colleague, I was way across the Indian Ocean on the tiny teardrop island of Sri Lanka writing about the nuclear race between India and Pakistan as well as the nasty ethnic Sri Lankan war that spooked me so, with its penchant for spectacular suicide bombings. Africa certainly did not have a lock on intractable mayhem, as raging conflicts in Asia, the Middle East, and the Balkans showed. But Africa that August of 1998 was my primary concern. I dropped everything in Sri Lanka and headed back to Congo in a series of flights—Colombo to Muscat to Nairobi to Kinshasa—that had my mind completely bent by the time I arrived.

I had no idea how wide a war this would become, how grave a setback to African progress it would prove to be. All I knew, when I arrived, was that this war was another chapter in the domino effect of the Rwandan genocide. Kagame of Rwanda decided he could no longer abide the presence of *génocidaires* hiding inside Congolese territory and, from there, attacking Rwanda at will. And he decided he could no longer abide Kabila's inability or unwillingness to help. The tension between Rwanda and Uganda on one side versus Congo on the other had been brewing for months. It reached a head when Kagame refused to attend Congo's liberation anniversary in May and when both Kagame and Museveni boycotted a regional summit that Kabila tried to host.

At the same time, Kabila had grown suspicious of his military commander, James Kabarebe, who had been the field commander of the Rwandan campaign in the last war and remained head of the Congolese army, on loan from Rwanda. When Kabila relieved Kabarebe of his command, paranoia swept through Kinshasa's Tutsi community. Tutsis began quietly packing up and leaving or taking trips on official business as cover for their flight.

The departure of so many Tutsis itself sparked paranoia for Kabila, who became convinced that a plot was afoot. By late July, he decided the game was up. He expelled all the Rwandan troops that Kagame had lent to the Congolese army.

In a matter of days, a new war exploded. Rwandan troops, their Congolese Tutsi allies, plus disgruntled multiethnic units of Kabila's army in the east launched a rebellion. In Kinshasa, government troops briefly battled among themselves when a Congolese Tutsi group in the army refused to be disarmed. The ethnic time bomb exploded, with Kabila's government launching a pogrom against all Tutsis in the capital, or against anyone who fit the stereotypical physical profile of a Tutsi.

Against this inflamed background, Kagame made a move that stripped his regime of substantial credibility, in my view, and set in motion a new phase of hateful ethnic fighting that would deepen his nation's ethnic insecurity. Led by Kabarebe, Rwandan and Ugandan troops hijacked three large commercial cargo and passenger planes from Goma in eastern Congo and ordered them flown all the way across the continent carrying hundreds of troops. They landed at the Congolese garrison town of Kitona at the Congo River's Atlantic coast estuary. Kitona was the site of an overcrowded Congolese army "reeducation" camp for at least five thousand troops once loyal to Mobutu. Many of those troops apparently threw in their lot with the Rwandans and Ugandans who'd suddenly landed there. The combined force of Rwanda, Uganda, and the newly freed Congolese soldiers mounted a steady push up from the Atlantic through the Bas Congo (Lower Congo) region, heading for Kinshasa. It made absolutely no sense. Rwandan Tutsi troops, imbued with the fire of an antigenocide crusade, were leading a march to take a city where Tutsis were being rounded up, tortured, and murdered in the streets, even by civilians. It made no sense, except for this: Rwanda had expected that its old ally Angola, from the last Congo-Zaire war, would enter the new war on Rwanda's side. But Angola played a different hand entirely.

Trapped in Kinshasa during that August, I realized the extent to which the United States had so completely receded from view in Central African affairs. When I'd call Washington for clues and information, my government sources more often than not could tell me nothing I didn't know already. In fact, sometimes they told me the information they did have came only from press reports, including mine. The State Department's main preoccupation was shutting down its embassy in Kinshasa for the safety of its employees and their families in a besieged city where paranoia and anti-Americanism were a combustible mix.

As embassy security gathered Americans at a U.S. diplomatic compound for evacuation to the airport, some Congolese troops monitoring the Americans' movements spotted some African Americans and believed they were Tutsis. Two dozen Congolese soldiers raided the compound one night. They shot off the lock on the gate and scaled the fence. Amid the dozen or so Americans huddled in the compound, the intruders found no Tutsis, so they reverted to form and stole cash and belongings. If this wasn't signal enough to speed up the embassy shutdown, the events of August 7 certainly were. On that day, terrorists linked to Osama bin Laden bombed the U.S. embassies in Kenya and Tanzania, killing 223 people and injuring thousands more. Embassies around the world went on alert, especially in Africa.

When U.S. diplomats shut the embassy and pulled out of Kinshasa, it hit me hard. On this stay in Kinshasa, I'd purposely shunned the Intercontinental, my usual haunt, and booked into the Memling Hotel in the city center in the belief that when Kinshasa finally exploded, I could make the short dash a few blocks to the U.S. Embassy for safety. Now, with the embassy closed, I had no backup plan. And when Congolese troops with rocket-propelled grenades and AKs invaded the Memling and burst into the rooms of a few of my journalist colleagues, I packed up my gear. Jennifer Ludden, my traveling buddy, did the same, and we headed over to the Intercon.

But the high-rise hotel made infamous by the Mobutuists' flight of 1997 soon became a strange netherworld of 1998. Food ran short. Housekeeping service disappeared. Roaches ran rampant. And as the Intercon's backup generators struggled to carry the load in the midst of a rebel-controlled blackout, the hallways and conference rooms were dimmed or went black.

My nightly struggle against the darkness descended into a tragicomic farce. Out of frustration, I flipped the light wall switches in my room one darkened night and discovered that my bathroom actually had electric power. To this day, I still cannot understand why the bathing area was lit while the rest of the room was not. But at the time, it struck me as an opportunity. I quickly devised a makeshift office. I snatched a pillow from the couch and stuffed it into the bidet. I hauled in a chair to place in front of the bidet to serve as a desk for my laptop computer, which I plugged into a wall socket next to the basin to maintain the battery's charge. The toilet seat sat within arm's reach of my new work area, so I used it as a side table for my notepads and cell phone. And after press conferences in a candlelit hotel conference room where Kabila's ministers tried to put a bold face on their meager defense of the city, I retreated to my bathroom office—when it was lit—and wrote fast and furiously, sinking into the cushioned bidet until the flickering lights sent me in search of my candles once again.

To make matters worse, I didn't have my satellite phone with me. I'd flown to Sri Lanka without it, for telephone connections there were superb—and I had no idea I'd end up in Kinshasa yet again, in dire need of communications. Luckily, the Intercon management set up a conference room with satellite telephone links for foreign correspondents—which was fine so long as we had candles and flashlights to see. That whole August was a logistics fiasco, but I reported and wrote day in and day out and managed to transmit my dispatches to Washington despite the hurdles.

During that time, I was waiting for one thing, as was everyone else in the know about Congo. We were waiting for Angola. If Angola threw in with Rwanda, Kabila's regime would be done with. No doubt about it. But if Angola decided to support Kabila, the putsch on Kinshasa would at least be forestalled. Kagame was waiting on Angola too, for his government thought it had at least tacit Angolan support for the war. Angola had been part of the Rwanda-Uganda coalition that ousted Mobutu and installed Kabila in power in 1997. And Angola's disaffection with Kabila's rule was widely known. But there had been hints around the continent that Rwanda had had contacts with the Angolan rebel movement, UNITA. Whether true or not, President dos Santos of Angola was obviously taking no chances. Whatever happened in Bas Congo—the backyard of the Angolan war—would happen under Angola's control and to serve dos Santos's anti-UNITA push. Period.

Whatever hope the Rwandans had harbored was dashed with the roar of Angolan jets over rebel positions in Bas Congo. The game completely changed. Rwanda was terribly, badly, and utterly mistaken. In its third intervention in African wars in less than two years, Angola threw its weight behind Kabila. It routed the Rwandans and rebels in Bas Congo and, along with Zimbabwe, saved the day for Kinshasa. Angola and Zimbabwe, with a token troop presence from Namibia, kept Kabila in power. Where Rwanda had once thrown a net around Kabila in the form of military assistance and alliance, now Angola and Zimbabwe held Kabila in their clutches. As a leader, Kabila would never be free.

The battles in Bas Congo and Kinshasa subsided, but the war in the east—where Rwandan and Ugandan troops were well entrenched—drags on as of this writing. The fighting ultimately sucked in nations from all regions of Africa: Angola, Chad, Namibia, Sudan, and Zimbabwe supported Kabila, while Rwanda, Uganda, and Burundi fought against him. At least a half dozen rebel forces from Congo's neighboring countries were fighting in the war as well. A massive swath of Africa was involved in a war whose origins could be found in the Rwandan genocide—more pointedly, in the international community's failure to intervene.

But the war reflected a far broader dynamic: a new scramble for Africa. Instead of Europeans carving up the continent as they did in 1885, instead of U.S.-Soviet rivalry creating spheres of influence in Africa during their Cold War, now African leaders themselves were fighting for their own strategic, ethnic, or venal interests, for better or for worse. Susan Rice, the U.S. assistant secretary of state for Africa, would call this conflict the first "world war" of Africa because of its continental proportions, the array of regional powers involved, and the high stakes at play. The war had the potential, if it ever ended, to produce a new regional balance of power and a new set of defining state interests. But that is, I admit, a charitable view. Before any new balance would be achieved, Congo and its contenders would plunge middle Africa into chaos in the extreme.

• • •

Zimbabwe was the most intriguing of all the combatants, and its involvement seemed the greatest folly. The other warring states at least had a plausible reason for intervening—rebels in Congo were a threat to them. But

Zimbabwe wasn't a neighbor. Zimbabwe wasn't even a power. Zimbabwe, frankly, was just a quiet, calm country that had hummed along in relative peace for much of its time since independence in 1980, with a respectable industrializing economy, a highly productive agricultural sector, and a relatively well educated population. South Africa's emergence from apartheid in 1994 had been a boon to southern Africa as a whole, and Zimbabwe reaped the benefits of regional peace.

But South Africa, apparently, was precisely Zimbabwe's problem. Not actually Zimbabwe's problem, but President Robert Mugabe's problem. A guerrilla fighter who led the former Rhodesia to independence, Mugabe had once towered in the region as leader of the "frontline states" opposing South African apartheid. Then Mandela was freed and South Africa's economic and political clout in the region took off, leaving Mugabe a junior player compared to the globally beloved South African president. The press in the region was filled with little stories about Mugabe's annoyance at Mandela, his allegedly intense jealousy.

Mugabe, clearly, sought opportunities to step out as a regional player in his own right, and Congo provided just such an opening. Though his troops did not fight in the first Congo war, Mugabe sent advisers and money to help Kabila's rebels oust Mobutu. After Kabila became president, Zimbabwean companies, most related to the defense industry, rushed into joint ventures with Kabila's new regime. Mugabe was crucial to the successful push to have Congo included in the nations of the Southern African Development Community (SADC), a regional body whose members had heretofore been strictly in the continent's southern cone.

Mugabe was chair of the SADC organ on defense and security, and he'd waged a rare public battle with Mandela in 1997 over that security organ's independence and the term limits of its chairmen. Mugabe wanted the organ to be autonomous and not answerable to the overall SADC leader, a post that Mandela then held. And to entrench himself as a regional leader, Mugabe wanted the security organ's chairmanship to be a permanent post, not a rotating one. So nasty did their tiff become that Mandela threatened to resign as overall SADC chairman if the organization bowed to Mugabe's demands.

Mugabe reportedly believed the SADC should become a sort of NATO-type body for the region, not just a development body. And he got his first chance to flex that kind of muscle when, in 1998, the second Congo war began. He couched the intervention of his own army, plus those of Angola and Namibia, as an SADC mission to rescue a legitimate president. But SADC itself did not approve of the intervention, and Mandela was furious, though ultimately he did publicly agree to the idea that intervening to save Kabila was a worthy goal. With his intervention in the continent's largest conflict, Mugabe was suddenly the man to watch in Southern and Central Africa.

As Zimbabwe's military involvement deepened, so, too, did the Congolese business deals of Zimbabwe's ruling elite. Reports of Congolese-Zimbabwean deals in cobalt mining, agriculture, diamonds, you name it, began to accumulate in the continent's press. The deals gave the impression that Zimbabwe had gone into Congo for purely monetary gain. But it seemed clear from Mugabe's clashes with Mandela that he was seeking power and prestige as well.

What Mugabe received, instead, was infamy. Over time, Mugabe's image would shift. The once-noble if somewhat eccentric and doctrinaire African leader came to be perceived as greedy, obsessive, strangely erratic, and dangerous. I wish I had met him. I visited Zimbabwe a few times, but came to know only a few of his ministers, not the president himself; and I came to know the country in the throes of a succession of crises whose blame critics lay squarely at Mugabe's feet. His economy was headed down the tubes even before the Congo war. Inflation was soaring and riots over price hikes hit the streets of Harare, the sleepy capital. Unrest over a new wage tax also rocked Mugabe's government. And veterans of the old liberation war started demanding more payouts from a veterans' disability fund that had been looted by corrupt officials.

In the midst of all this chaos, Mugabe fell back on his old standby method of pacification: to mollify restive blacks, he threatened to expropriate white-owned commercial farms and redistribute them to the landless. The threat didn't come out of the blue, for land redistribution had been under way in fits and starts since independence. In a nation where whites were 2 percent of the population but owned 70 percent of the arable land, both

Zimbabwe and Britain, the former colonial power, agreed on the need for reform, but on a willing-seller basis. But obviously, not enough owners had been willing to sell, which left land as an explosive and emotive issue that Mugabe could easily exploit. As in South Africa, whites in Zimbabwe remained—even twenty years after independence—an economically powerful minority. In late 1997, he declared that his government would simply seize more than fourteen hundred commercial farms for redistribution. His action set him on a collision course with the economy, in which white commercial agriculture was key, and with the international community, which did not support his hostile new measure.

With the economy on the skids and new racial conflict flaring over land, Mugabe's deployment of thousands of troops into Congo was greeted at home by angry protest. The country simply could not afford a war. Antiwar protesters took to the streets, where army troops were called in to quash the demonstrations. Journalists who wrote articles critical of the government—or even revealed details of the Congo war—were arrested and, in some cases, beaten and tortured. Mugabe's credibility reached such a low that for the first time since 1980, he looked potentially vulnerable to an opposition party challenge; and to secure power, he would revert to even more draconian measures that would reveal his claims to democratic leadership as false.

Congo's chaos found fertile ground in Harare. Worse, Zimbabwe's troubles began, because of simple geography, to spill into South Africa, its neighbor to the south. More Zimbabweans migrated in search of work, causing more competition for scarce jobs in South Africa, causing more xenophobia among South Africans already revealed to have a distinct distrust of their African brethren. Though it was thousands of miles away from the Congolese front, Pretoria was feeling the effects of that African world war. The momentum toward an African renaissance definitely was stalled, with wars raging from the Horn of Africa in the east, down through the heart of Africa in Congo, and into Angola on the southwest coast.

15

An African American Woman

Half-naked children toddled about the broad stone stairways that led from the street to the front door of the ancient mansion on the Rua Major Kanyangulo across from Angola's foreign ministry. The mansion was huge, with three stories and thirty-six rooms. Iron-railed balconies graced its arched windows, and its six double doors on the main floor were huge enough for a horse to walk through. Once upon a time, this mansion had been a place of significance and immense wealth. But by the 1990s, it had become a shanty. Luanda was like that. The old world and the new coexisted. Ancient buildings of the sixteenth and seventeenth centuries still stood, though mostly in a crumbling state, amid new shops and office blocks. Time seemed to loop and bend in Luanda, at least as I saw it, and nowhere did I get that sensation more than when I'd pass that ancient mansion.

On several trips to the city, the mansion fascinated me. By December 1998, I'd become obsessed. I needed to go inside, to learn more about the place, though it seemed foreboding. From the street, I could see shadowy movements in the huge foyer, crowded comings and goings, as if I were glimpsing the netherworld of Angolan suffering. The mansion's most recent occupants were destitute Angolans who'd fled fighting in the country's interior and squatted inside the mansion as if it were a refugee camp. The mansion was rumored to be a hothouse of prostitution and gunrunning, which made it a dangerous menace to the city fathers. Police had raided it many times.

Luandans knew it as the Palace of Ana Joaquina, also known as Ana Mulata. Her full name was Ana Joaquina dos Santos Silva, a mixed-race woman born in 1779 who became one of the wealthiest Luandans of the nineteenth century. The palace, as local people called it, was built in the 1700s, probably by the family of her Portuguese husband. From him, Ana Joaquina inherited a vast empire of sugarcane plantations, rum factories, and slaves. Thus, she became that rare breed in the annals of the slave trade: a female slave trader, running ships across the Atlantic to Brazil or to the islands of the Caribbean Sea.

Slaves brought in from the interior were kept in pens on her palace's ground floor, below her offices on the second floor and her living quarters on the third. History books describe her as quite a wily businesswoman and a force to be reckoned with among the merchants of her class. Even after Portugal, the colonial power, abolished the slave trade in 1836, Ana Joaquina continued in the business. And most fascinating of all, an ancient urban legend claims she skirted the antislavery authorities by having a tunnel dug beneath her palace courtyard to surreptitiously march her slaves out to the bay.

Learning all this, my imagination ran wild. Those could have been my ancestors, for all I knew, which actually was very little. I have no idea whatsoever of the precise region that produced the Africans whose bloodline runs through me. Somewhere in the neighborhood of 15 million Africans were captured from deep in the continent's interior and its coasts and shipped away in the terrible trade that lasted for well over three centuries. I had no clue where I fit into that torrent of humanity, and I'd grown comfortable just claiming it all. Maybe my ancestors were chained and loaded from Gorée Island in Senegal, or Elmina in Ghana, or even the Palace of Ana Joaquina in Luanda. Sure, it's a stretch. But maybe not. And my wonderings were fueled even more by the fact that I kept seeing faces in Angola that could have been faces of my relatives. People there sometimes mistook me for an acquaintance. They'd walk right up to me and start chattering, assuming I was one of their countrywomen. It was a charming way to meet people, though certainly uncanny.

As we drove around making appointments and doing interviews, the slave tunnel and my possible connection to it were my running commentary. My local guide and translator, Augusto "Gugu" Manuel, agreed that I looked kind of Angolan, though it was a question he thought strange. Even stranger, to him, was my mission to get into Ana Joaquina's mansion and find that tunnel. An unemployed clerk from a shipping firm, Gugu had grown up in Luanda and knew quite well the mystery and rumor that surrounded the old mansion. He didn't believe the legend of the tunnel. He flat out refused to go in with me. But I liked joking with Gugu that my slave ancestors could have been owned and sold by Ana Joaquina; that they could have walked through that legendary tunnel of hers. I even called it *my* tunnel, which really drove him up the wall. He knew I was angling to convince him to go inside with me, and I am certain that the very kind and patient Gugu thought his American friend had lost her mind.

Gugu was there when I visited Oscar Guimarães at the Instituto Nacional do Patrimônio Cultural. Guimarães told me that Ana Joaquina's courtyard had once been excavated and no tunnel ever found. Guimarães echoed Gugu's warning, saying, "It's not wise to go in there." Rosa da Cruz e Silva, a Luanda historian whose counsel I sought as well, debunked the tunnel story even more. She said that after the Angolan slave trade was outlawed in 1836, slavers stopped using the Bay of Luanda altogether and moved their suddenly illicit trade a bit south down the coast, to the inlet of the Capela do Morro da Cruz (Chapel of the Mount of the Cross). So off we went, Gugu and I, to the chapel.

Built in 1783, the chapel was in 1998 a somewhat decayed structure. It had been preserved as Angola's Museu da Escravatura (Museum of Slavery). Eerily silent, it was devoid of other visitors the day we were there. The place felt lonely and haunted. Bestial tools of the chattel trade were on display. They included rusted chains, spikes, neck restraints, metal mouth stoppers, yellowed ship's manifests of the human cargo, and descriptions of the slaves being blessed by priests as they were marched out of the chapel and down to water's edge. I ventured outside, following the slaves' path along the promontory, to the top of a few broken old stairs that led to the water. The inlet was calm. No vessels cruised its currents. I looked out to the sea, to the horizon, to my imaginings of the Middle Passage, and I stood for just a moment in silent tribute.

An elderly man appeared beside me, a sort of clerk/curator. Daniel Francisco was his name, and when I asked about the tunnel at Ana Joaquina's old palace, he said emphatically that it existed. In 1977, he told me, he'd been part of a cleaning crew sent down the stairs from the palace courtyard into an underground cavern. "Yes, I saw it. It went down the stairs and to the sea," he said excitedly. But really, he admitted, he could not say for sure where the tunnel went. He did not actually go beyond the cavern at the foot of the stairs. On the half-hour drive back up to Luanda, I told Gugu I'd be going into the palace for sure. And finally he relented. I suspect he, too, had become fascinated with finding the truth of the tunnel legend.

The next day, we pulled up in front of the palace and asked to speak to the man in charge. If the place was as criminal as we'd been told, it was wise to tread cautiously. Gugu explained that I was an American wanting to learn about the life of the palace. In short order, a man wearing a tattered old North Carolina Tar Heels T-shirt emerged from the entryway. His name was Abelino, he told us, and we again explained our mission. Though I had not come to hear more stories of hardship and war, about which I had written volumes on previous Angolan travels, out of courtesy I listened to the travails inside Ana Joaquina's old house.

Sixty families lived there, Abelino explained, most from the war-torn towns of Huige and Malanje in the interior. They toted water from taps nearby, for no water service came to the old palace. And they had only a bit of electricity in the rambling mansion, from lines rigged illegally. Abelino led us into the huge foyer. A gaggle of children followed us, beautiful little children despite the dirt and skin rashes that covered them. Flies filled the air. Women sat at rough-hewn wooden tables selling peanuts and beer and Fanta. The stench of sweat, soot, human waste, fish, and rancid food enveloped us.

A grand stone staircase wound upward, to the second story. Following its curve, I saw that the floorboards above me hung perilously. Yes, Abelino said, people did fall through from time to time. We walked through a long, wide hallway and out into the large courtyard where people had hung tarps and wooden slabs to delineate separate living quarters. Piles of buckets, pieces of mattress or foam—the possessions of a refugee life—were everywhere. More rooms ringed the courtyard at ground level and above, where an ornate iron railing hung on, draped with rags and laundry.

Men of the house gathered round me, shouting, smelling of beer, and airing their anger at this hellish life. My head swam—from the stench, from the shouts pressing in on me, from the stupidity of my tunnel mission. What right did I have to plunge into this place on my own selfish quest in the midst of such misery? None, obviously. But there I was. As Gugu tried to decipher the stories of the shouting men, I looked around to keep my bearings. My eyes fell on a little girl. She turned her angelic face up to watch me as she squatted on the ground to pee. And a few inches away from her lay a thick concrete slab, of modern make, about five feet square, clearly covering some hole in the ground. Oh my, I thought. That must be the tunnel. The men of the manor told me the concrete covered an opening to an old cavern. They believed it led to a tunnel, but of course, they didn't know. And really, I no longer cared.

The past and whatever it may have meant to me seemed not to matter. In that wretched palace of suffering, the present was choking me. But this, too, was my Africa. My affinity, I realized, resided not just in a hazy past to which I traced my ancestry, but in the ugly struggles of daily life that were as heartbreaking as a dusty child peeing on the ground.

* * *

My connection to Africa is a genealogic fact. I don't need regal African chiefs and legends of past greatness to make the connection; I don't need for history to be rewritten to make Africa seem more palatable, more worthy of my embrace. In all its splendor, its struggle, its horror, Africa is in me. I could reject it if I wanted to. I could recoil from its maddening ways and say that the place of my forefathers has nothing to do with me. I could say that the ties that once bound black people in Africa and the Americas have been severed by time and mean nothing now. Others have made that case. That is not where I stand.

I claim Africa as a political act, as an act of affirmation. It is my private way of staying true to the legacy of the struggles that link black people on both sides of the Atlantic. In our blackness, the Africans and the Americans are bound by a common experience. The construct of racism became, for both peoples, the pretext that Europeans used to justify their domination in Africa and in America. The struggle against such racism defined both peoples for generations and continues to define us still. That is why I call myself an African American, in honor of our common struggle.

But there's some tension on both sides of my compound identity. After all, Africans sold my people into slavery. That is an original sin and I do not overlook it. Nor do I overlook the fact that it was Americans who bought those slaves and held them in bondage for generations more. Some black Americans trip over the very phrasing of the term "African American." It's bulky as it rolls off the tongue, and it's the latest in a long string of group labels either forced on us or embraced by us over the generations. But it's the African part of the phrase that gives some people pause. Africa, even for many of its black descendants in America, conjures images of foreboding and menace, even backwardness. Ignorance about Africa runs rampant among us. I have heard one too many a black person refer to Africans as people who wear grass skirts.

Others, who perhaps know more of Africa, have been so repulsed by Africa's starving children, its murderous mobs, and its thieving dictators that they have decided they simply cannot claim the African part of their identity. Whole books have been written on the subject, mostly built on the false notion that Americanness and Africanness are somehow mutually exclusive, as if we are to make a choice. For me, it is not that complicated. My people became American because of what was done to Africa. The histories of both lands inhabit my consciousness and course through my veins.

It is a visceral bond that, for many people, is automatic. Even an old Zulu man who knew little of the outside world knew kinship when it confronted him. His name was Johannes Ndlovu and I met him in 1994 during South Africa's historic election. He lived deep in the Valley of a Thousand Hills, a rural area of the KwaZulu-Natal region, where he'd walked for hours in his rakish straw hat and dusty blazer to get to the voting booth to exercise his brand-new democratic voting right. I was traveling that day with Frank James of the *Chicago Tribune* and Sipho Khuzwayo, our guide and translator. When we introduced ourselves, Mr. Ndlovu became so fascinated with our blackness that he conducted an interview of his own after ours was through. We were the first foreign black folk he'd ever met. It was my honor.

"I am very happy to see black people from America, my own blood," Mr. Ndlovu said to us. "I used to hear people saying black people overseas left Africa a long time ago . . . I only know there are black people overseas. How they got there, I do not know."

We explained that we were descendants of people taken from Africa and transported on ships to America as slaves. With that, we immediately struck a familiar chord. The old man had spent his life as a sugarcane cutter on an apartheid-era farm. He knew a thing or two about repression. "Ah," he said when we told him of slavery. "We are the same."

Having said all that, let me now say this: The way I saw myself wasn't necessarily how Africans perceived me to be. And being an African American in Africa could, at times, be downright strange. Odd wedges and strange misperceptions kept cropping up, hitting me over the head unexpectedly in some of my encounters with Africans. Not that I expected everyone to rush up to me, arms outstretched, and call me "sister." But the level of dissonance I encountered did take me by surprise. I became hypersensitive.

At a packed, festive cocktail reception in Jo'burg, I ran into a prominent black South African journalist, Nomavenda Mathiane, whose work I'd admired in apartheid's final years. I'd met her before, but long ago, so a mutual friend reintroduced us. Mathiane repeated my name, making lighthearted fun of its very English sound. Yes, it is flat and monosyllabic. But she went a step further. She jokingly called it my slave name and suggested I should adopt an African one. I laughed at the clever, seemingly offhand comment. But it annoyed me. It seemed to suggest that I should shed the slavery part of my heritage, that I should want to obliterate it. It felt like one of those gratuitous jabs I'd heard before, between the lines, from Africans somewhat vexed by the African Americans in their midst.

In Lobito, Angola, I traveled with a guide named Joaquim Leiria, whom I hired through a contact at an aid agency. Resting at a seaside kiosk on the beach called the Restinga after a day of interviewing war refugees back in 1995, I lamented the fact that I hated to see so many people suffering, especially since they were black people like me. Leiria, who was of mixed African and Portuguese ancestry and had café-au-lait skin, did not understand. "But you are not black," he told me. To him, the notion of race was purely physical. He was mixed, and thus not black. So how could I, someone with his same skin color, consider myself black? He was adamant that I could not be black. I got the distinct impression that I had insulted him by calling myself black though I looked much like him.

What a strange conversation we had. I explained that blackness in America had evolved to become as much a cultural trait as a physical one. I told him that people who look almost physically "white" could still consider themselves black and be viewed that way by others. To him, in his postcolonial context, the Africans were black, the Europeans were white, and people mixed with the two were *mestiço*, or mulatto. *Mestiços* had been a distinct social group since early in Angola's contact with the Portuguese. They were middlemen during the slave trade and a merchant class in the capital's economy. The case was similar in America during slavery and just after it, when all kinds of twisted laws were written to subdivide black Americans based on degrees of mixture with whiteness. But I found Leiria's views startling. It was like the coloreds in South Africa who held fast to the identity given them under apartheid even after that old system ended. I chalked it up to colonialism and its vestiges, still digging trenches between the very people who were exploited.

I butted heads with odd perceptions of colonialism more than I expected as I traveled around my region. In the main, most folks with whom I discussed the colonial past understood fully how European rule had warped the African idea of governance and in many ways predisposed the newly independent nations toward authoritarian rule. After all, there was nothing whatsoever democratic about foreign domination. Rarely did I come across anyone who had anything good to say about the colonial days, which is why my encounter with an old man in the town of Goma, Congo-Zaire, made such a lasting impression.

I met Matabaro Mulihano while he sat in front of his small house holding a mirror in front of him as he shaved his white stubble with a pink-handled razor. He was seventy-three years old, with thirty children and several wives. And in his long life, he'd seen many, many things. He remembered the Belgian colonial days well. He worked in a colonial bank. He remembered the euphoria that greeted independence, and the letdowns that soon followed during the years of Mobutu's rule. He remembered how people from all walks of East African life felt like brothers.

Just to the north of Goma stands the towering Nyiragongo volcano, which erupted in 1977 and blanketed most of the town with the lava that hardened into rock and remains the town's strangest feature. People, including Mulihano, built their new houses right atop the old lava flows. He remembered the volcano vividly, even fondly. Those who fled across the border to Rwanda—including him and his family—were received well and given help, like brothers, by their Rwandan neighbors. In the ensuing years, repeated wars had roared through his town with a destructiveness that seemed as bad as the volcanic lava. When we met in October 1998, the second Congo war was well under way, as was the latest period of ethnic tension and cleansing.

I asked him what had been the best time of his life, and he took me quite by surprise when he said this: "Before the independence, that was the best period for me, because there was no tribal problem." But what about the *bazungu*, I asked him, using the colloquial Swahili word for whites or foreigners. "Everywhere where the *bazungu* have been in the colonial time, they were ahead in everything. But we were living a good life, even though they were ruling us," he said.

Knowing the depth of Congolese suffering during the wars, I found it hard to make the point that surely times were better than during colonialism. I didn't even bother. But Mulihano's view hit me like fingernails on a chalkboard. I hated to acknowledge the fact that things had degenerated so badly in some parts of Africa that it would actually seem understandable to me for someone to say that colonialism wasn't so bad. That was his reality. That is what he saw from his vantage point in the heart of the Congo-Zaire storm.

As we parted, I gave him my business card. He held it to his lips and kissed it. It seemed kind of charming and I did not mind. But he wouldn't have kissed the card of a man. That I know for sure, for my gender always had a bearing on how Africans perceived me. The fact that I am a woman added all sorts of interesting layers to my journalistic work, from small things like the kissed card to out-and-out sexual harassment. It all depended on context, of course, and on how I myself behaved. But being this African American woman journalist made me a walking, talking curiosity.

On top of that, I failed the basic test of tradition: I was single and child-less. People would ask, right up front: Do you have children? Nothing wrong with that. People all over the world expect women to have children. I expected it too, though it did not happen. But when I'd tell an African woman I had no children, it made me pitiable, somehow stigmatized. After all, whole divinities are devoted to fertility in many African traditions. To not bear children is to cut against the laws of the gods and the ancestors. I started getting a complex about that too.

I could get over the fact that folks in South Africa often mistook me as a maid. But I could not keep up with all the strange cultural noise coming at me over my many hyphens: single-childless-African-American-woman-doing-a-man's-job. When a black South African workman at my house in Jo'burg asked where my husband was and I replied that I was divorced, he actually stopped what he was doing, looked at me, and asked in all seriousness what I had done to him. Surely a woman who is divorced must have committed some marital crime.

In Zimbabwe, a security man eyed me suspiciously and had the nerve to ask me why I was sitting in the lobby—of a hotel where I was a paying guest. He didn't ask if I needed help; he didn't ask if I was waiting for someone. I think he thought I was a prostitute. During that same trip, a waiter in the same hotel asked me to pay up front for the meals at my table of three, where I was conducting an interview. I asked rather arrogantly whether the table next to mine—filled with white men—had paid up front. The waiter actually answered. No, he said, they did not pay up front. Well, I won't be paying up front either, I told him. And I didn't.

The list goes on and on. The doormen at my hotel in Lusaka, Zambia, would open the door for a white colleague of mine, but never for me. An immigration clerk at the Rwanda-Congo border crossing demanded to know why I was not married. A soldier in Saurimo, Angola, demanded my passport when he spotted me with two male colleagues, one white, one Indian. The soldier didn't ask for their passports, only mine; I learned later that local women were earning money servicing the mining men in that diamond region, so I guess the soldier thought I must have been practicing the trade too.

In my attire, I was careful not to show too much flesh, not to be suggestive. But even dressed conservatively, in a pantsuit during a summit of regional heads of state at Victoria Falls, Zimbabwe, I ended up having to read the riot act to a diplomat. I was sitting down with an Angolan ambassador, conducting an interview, when one of his aides reached over and started stroking my hair. I could not believe it. "Get your hand off my head," I hissed as I swatted his hand away. Then I turned to the ambassador and quietly berated him for having such unprofessional, ill-mannered staff that obviously needed training. The ambassador, who did nothing to stop his aide, suddenly seemed the epitome of decorum and apologized profusely.

The sexism seemed inescapable, no matter what I did. Even folks who should know better did not. A cabinet minister in South Africa once propositioned me during an interview, and the same thing happened in Congo a couple of years later when a comical Congolese official I had interviewed before suddenly declared to me, "You need a Congolese boyfriend." It cracked me up, but I kept a pretty straight face and told him to just forget about it, to which he responded, "No, no, no, I'm not talking about me!" Yeah, right.

But first prize in the sexism sweepstakes is awarded to the smarmy, condescending immigration official in Kinshasa who lectured me on the proper behavior of a woman. I had transgressed, you see, because I'd had the audacity to raise my voice above acceptable pitch to demand the return of my passport after it had been held for days for no reason. The female clerk on the receiving end of my American-style pushiness ratted me out to her boss. That's how I ended up in his office.

Actually, it was a little intimidating. He could have thrown me out of the country. This being Congo, he could have had me thrown into jail. I became my most mousy, humble self as he instructed me on the gender-appropriate qualities of quietness and politeness. In my most deferential tone, I thanked him for his guidance. Speaking softly, I requested the return of my passport. Satisfied that I had been successfully reeducated, he handed it over and we parted. I laughed like a hyena all the way down the hallway.

* * *

In lots of ways, my life in South Africa was quite different from that of most of the other African Americans on the scene. As a foreign correspondent, my mission wasn't to put down roots, so to speak, though I did consider it at one time. Nor was I there to find a niche, do a business deal, or assist in development or reconciliation, though I certainly supported those goals. My purpose was to be a chronicler and analyst of the big issues and broad dynamics unfolding in the new country, and in so doing I had to keep my fingers in many different worlds, not just the relatively narrow social niche of the expatriate American community.

But what I shared with most other African Americans was a passion to be part of South Africa's seismic shift from apartheid to democracy, to witness a freed African nation succeed where so many others were staggering or failing. That was the hope, and its lure struck universal chords not bounded by race. I knew many whites and others who'd been drawn by South Africa's new prospects too. Some foreign journalists who'd covered apartheid's end extended their stays to see the story through, and others who had left found ways to return, so compelling was the unfolding drama.

But the ties between black America and black South Africa were uniquely rooted in the similar experiences of both groups. At the turn of the twentieth century, the American branch of the African Methodist Episcopal Church established itself in South Africa, with churches and mission schools. During the civil rights struggles that for a time ran parallel in both countries, Martin Luther King, Jr., corresponded regularly with the ANC leader of that time, Albert Luthuli. Both men advocated nonviolent struggle, and both would go on to win the Nobel Peace Prize. Black Americans campaigned hard for South African civil rights, such as the Reverend Leon Sullivan, whose famous Sullivan Principles set forth measures on equity in the workplace that were adopted by many foreign firms in South Africa. And last but not least, African Americans successfully pushed for U.S. economic sanctions against apartheid-era South Africa as well as for Mandela's release from prison. The Free South Africa Movement galvanized U.S. public opinion against apartheid with the protest campaign it began in 1984, organized by Randall Robinson of TransAfrica. In protests at the South African Embassy in Washington, scores of people, even entire organizations like trade unions, offered themselves up for arrest in nonviolent protest actions. The movement caught on nationally, and similar protests and waves of arrest happened in the nation's major cities.

So among the Americans who began trekking into South Africa after apartheid, African Americans were prominent and in many cases still fired with the passion of the transatlantic antiapartheid struggle. They were academics, activists, architects, bankers, doctors, development experts, educators, entrepreneurs, lawyers, venture capitalists, you name it. Most were employed by American organizations, though some took up posts in South African firms. In many cases, they developed easy working relationships, business partnerships, and personal friendships. A whole social set developed between some black South Africans and their black friends from America in a comfortable social cocoon, like the group of black women from both sides of the Atlantic who hosted regular "Gumbo Society" lunches, which I enjoyed immensely the one time I was able to attend.

We Americans love to barbecue, and the Africans do too, though they call it by the Afrikaans word *braai*. Socializing over the patio grill became a ritual of my South African life. I went for *braais* to the homes of friends in Soweto, but I got the sense that few of the African Americans spent much time in the black townships. The township world was quite different from the world of the affluent northern suburbs, where the Americans were quite taken with the very comfortable standard of living they could enjoy amid swimming pools and tennis courts.

There, amenities were plentiful. Restaurants and cafés. Jazz clubs and multiplex movie theaters. Shops with very cool fashions, local and imported, though sometimes of dubious quality. I frequented restaurants and clubs owned by blacks, on those infrequent occasions when one would crop up. But in the main, when I went out—to dinner, the movies, the theater, to concerts—the range of availabilities was in the white world. Only at the shopping malls did you get that big broad panorama of South Africa's many cultures rubbing shoulders.

Out in the townships, on the other hand, entertainment amenities included backyard bars called *shebeens,* some dance clubs, and take-out food shops, including a butchery whose meat you could *braai* right there on the spot, on a communal grill. Some South African entrepreneurs had big plans to bring more "first world" amenities to the townships, like the black-owned cappuccino house that opened for business in Soweto. One of the early stories I wrote during my tour was a small feature on the opening of a Soweto bookstore. And why should this have merited news coverage? For this astonishing reason: it was the very first bookstore to exist in the only shopping mall in the most sprawling, vibrant, activist township in all of South Africa, home to more than 2 million people.

With its limits in services and amenities, plus its relative underdevelopment compared to the northern suburbs, Soweto saw its new black middle and affluent classes moving out and into the previously white communities that once had shunned them. And it was there, by and large, that blacks from both sides of the ocean socialized.

There was a range of types among the black Americans, from the righteous do-gooders who really knew the South African struggle, to the bona fide carpetbaggers who knew South Africa was wide-open terrain where a buck could possibly be made. In my clutch of friends who were development experts, lawyers, and a few journalists, we clucked our tongues at the silliness of an African American businessman who tried to launch a club for African Americans. We rolled our eyes at another prominent black American businessman who threw a massive party whose orgy of excess—its circus animals and dancers on pedestals—made headlines. I did not attend that party (I was not invited). At another party thrown by one of my male countrymen, I was stunned to see a throng of beautiful, young "colored" women who seemed to have been bused in to spice up the bash.

Oh, and lest I forget them, there were the African American types who showed up in the emotional throes of the "motherland," which tended to get on some black South Africans' nerves. Rather than arriving to assist South Africans in truly running their own country, these African Americans embraced the place for their own sense of freedom, as a place where they should be naturally accepted, as if blackness was their passport.

But truth be told, I had my fill of hearing African Americans complain— sometimes gently, sometimes crudely—about how Mandela's new black government was handling itself or about the lack of business acumen or aggressiveness among South Africans involved in business. This was more a cultural complaint, I thought, than a substantial complaint, for Americans tend to charge right into a meeting or a negotiation and get down to business, whereas South Africans tend to go more slowly, engage in pleasantries, observe protocols of respect, such as inquiring about the family. The African American attitude and lack of tact did not go unnoticed by those black South Africans who'd worked in close proximity with black Americans.

Shado Twala, a South African journalist and radio personality, was among those who noticed the American style and did not like it. When I interviewed her on the subject during President Clinton's trip to Cape Town, she complained: "Americans have almost taken over, not given us time to breathe after democracy. You guys have come in to be like Big Brother, in a very aggressive way as well, and condescending." And she said she meant Americans of all types, both black and white.

I'd gotten my first sense of this tension a few years earlier, back in Washington in 1993, during an ANC campaign fund-raising visit by Mandela. Approaching the watershed of South Africa's first all-races election, Mandela had been soliciting and receiving contributions from around the globe, including from figures who'd once been staunchly pro-apartheid. On the American leg of his travels, among his many stops was a luncheon hosted by Robinson at TransAfrica. Robinson invited me to attend as Mandela and his delegation met with a couple dozen African American lawmakers and activists of the Free South Africa Movement. The Americans were concerned, among other things, about Mandela accepting contributions from figures who had once been against black liberation. It seemed clear that the Americans feared that Mandela did not know from whom he was actually accepting money. I suspect Mandela knew full well. In fact, he seemed to take slight umbrage that the Americans were trying to steer his policy. He made it clear that the ANC was not open to sway on the subject, that it would raise money as it saw fit. He adroitly moved the discussion on to other matters, leaving some of the Americans miffed that their counsel was so thoroughly dismissed.

But of course, that bout of tension did not last. Many who were around the table that day also turned up in 1994 for South Africa's historic election. With the exception of Robinson, who stayed away, anybody who thought they were somebody flew from America to South Africa to be part of the jubilation at South Africa's most triumphant hour. And South Africans welcomed the world's attention.

Even then, some of the more astute observers were getting concerned about the boldness and prominence of these Americans who were sound-biting their way through South Africa. Far from simply supporting a new nation, some of these African American leaders sounded as if they were staking a claim. The issue exploded into public discussion years later with a tit-for-tat set of newspaper articles and a televised talk show on the subject, hosted by Felicia Mabuza Suttle, South Africa's answer to Oprah. The panel included a cross section of people from both sides of the Atlantic and aired the dirty little secret of black-on-black relations. All was not well in the "motherland."

"I've yet to meet an African American who is honest and says, 'I've come to work and make my own money and make my life comfortable.' They all say they are coming to help." That was William Malegapuru Makgoba, one of South Africa's premier scientists and something of an intellectual provocateur. He accused "foreign Africans, either from America or from the African continent," of taking positions that ought to be for South Africans and allowing themselves to be used as a "smoke screen against genuine affirmative action" for South Africans.

From the African American side, Charles T. Moses, a former journalist and management consultant from New York, shot back, "We are not dupes, Professor." He defended the contributions that many African Americans were attempting to make, by helping to train and finance black entrepreneurs, for instance. And that was a legitimate point. Lots of good work was being done in the alliances between blacks from both countries. But in the process, Moses said this: "Many of us have been lied to, misled and abused by our South African brothers and sisters, usually out of jealousy or ignorance. Deputy President Thabo Mbeki often talks about an 'African renaissance.' I'm sure that his definition includes Africans wherever they reside."

I felt his sentiments were misguided. The renaissance, for example, was very Africa-specific. But Moses had a more poignant reason for attempting to put down roots in South Africa. "Where is the hope for us in America?" he wrote. "We will never be in charge. We will always be 10 percent. We will always be fighting to keep some cop from shooting us in the back. But here, it's worth the battle. You can win this here."

When I read it, I cringed. "Win this?" "Be in charge?" But it wasn't our fight, it wasn't our country. We could assist the fight. We could give it our blessing. We could hold a sense of camaraderie in the struggle. But at the end of the day, I found that many African Americans in South Africa had to realize: it was someone else's battle. Our color and culture did not give us the right to claim ownership of someone else's victory, of someone else's society.

What I learned, and what made my experience in South Africa all the richer, was the extent to which I could look African, feel loyal to the African struggle, and remain an anomaly because I was American. It is similar for me in America, where I can look American, feel American, but remain an anomaly in many circumstances because I am black. That is my composite identity, my inheritance from the Middle Passage. It is a special way of being, and with it I am at peace.

16

Coffins and Whispers

UMZIMKULU, SOUTH AFRICA, FEBRUARY 1999

Busisiwe Chiya moved like a ghost, as if she'd already departed this world. A lacy yellow nightgown draped her body and fluttered lightly with each small step. She had been sick for several months. But when she awoke that February morning in 1999, she felt stronger than the day before, a day of convulsing pain. She'd wanted to be outdoors, to get a breath of air fresher than the stuffiness of her dingy room at Rietvlei Hospital, a place overrun with AIDS.

I walked a bit with her just outside the entrance to her ward. Best not to venture too far, I thought. She really ought to have stayed in bed. She may have felt stronger, but she didn't look it. Her sunken eyes seemed unfocused. Her voice sounded raspy, a mere whisper. Her arms quivered at her side. Suddenly, her knees buckled. She tottered sideways and collapsed against me in a swoon. I caught her beneath the arms before she hit the ground and steadied her while a nursing aide rushed over to help walk her back to her room. I hadn't noticed until I touched her that Busisiwe was wet all over. I could feel the moisture on my hands, a mixture of her perspiration and perhaps a bit of ooze from her rashes and lesions. As we settled her back into bed, I reminded myself not to touch my eyes or mouth until I could wash up. I sat with her for a little while, until I realized she was too weak to talk any more. She clenched her trembling fists to her chest as she dozed off to sleep.

"Blessed" is the English translation of her Zulu name. But in South Africa at that time, Busisiwe was among the stricken. AIDS was stealing her life away. She was forty-three years old, a third-grade teacher and mother of a six-year-old child she pridefully called her "handsome boy." The boy lived with his aunt, Busisiwe's sister, and would be starting school that year. She had wanted more children and felt stigmatized to have only one. But the wayward husband for whom she waited so many years never did return after he left her in 1985. And the new man with whom she'd taken up in 1992— the father of her child—stopped coming around when she fell ill. He turned out to be married. Busisiwe also learned that she was but one of a number of his outside women. "Men have no truth. They are liars," she complained as we talked when she had strength.

The end of her fertility confounded Busisiwe most when she'd received her HIV-positive diagnosis. Lulu Mqoothi, a nurse, delivered the bad news: "The results came back and we found that the results are positive, which means you have got this virus." Some fifteen hundred South Africans were receiving this news each and every day by 1999, adding to the mounting prevalence of HIV/AIDS that, by then, had doubled in just five years, push-ing toward 20 percent of South Africa's people. In KwaZulu-Natal Province, where Busisiwe lived, the prevalence of HIV was 27 percent, the highest in the nation. Rietvlei Hospital, which served both KwaZulu-Natal and the Eastern Cape Province, recorded one HIV-positive diagnosis in 1991. In 1992, there were six. By early 1999, there were fifteen to twenty per week.

Busisiwe was among them. She sat listlessly as she heard the news from Nurse Mgoothi. She folded her hands in the lap of her white cotton bathrobe. She was too weak to react very dramatically, and she'd been ex-pecting the diagnosis anyway. She was a smart woman. Even before the diag-nosis, she told me she knew it must be AIDS that caused her chronic diarrhea, her weight loss, her blurred vision, headaches, and pelvic inflam-matory disease. With Busisiwe's permission, I attended her counseling session, along with Susan Winters, a South Africa–based American photo-journalist, as part of our reporting on the AIDS pandemic.

Nurse Mqoothi continued: "The whole world is having this virus. But it's very much higher in Africa, especially this province, KwaZulu-Natal and Eastern Cape . . . So far we don't have a drug. It's incurable so far. They are still busy trying to get a remedy for this . . . You must use condoms whenever you are doing sex . . . You must try by all means to eat a high-protein diet" with lots of milk, vegetables, and beans, among other foods. "To elevate, to stimulate, to maintain your health, you must have these nutritious meals."

She tried to explain that there should be no stigma attached to AIDS. It is deadly, she explained, but so are other diseases. What matters most, Mqoothi counseled, was to ready oneself to fight it. "You must accept this and take yourself very close to God."

Busisiwe asked one question and one question alone: would she be able to have more children? "Now I am worried about this because now I am having only one," she said softly.

Mqoothi answered unequivocally: "You have this one. Thank Jesus for that. You cannot have another child because it's going to be infected . . . You must accept this. Take it to Jesus. Accept that this will be the first and the last."

The diagnosis, once it sank in, was confusing to Busisiwe. Her mind began racing into various forms of misperception and denial. I realized after we talked later that the very concept of a virus running rampant in her body was something she did not grasp. She understood things like TB, like pneumonia. Those were illnesses that attacked and then were treated. But AIDS? Something utterly incurable? Like so many women I met at Rietvlei, the notion of a virus that produced other diseases made no sense. Rather, the only way some of them could understand it was in the context of their traditional beliefs. Something this powerful, they surmised, must have been sent by someone, must have been a kind of poison cast on the sufferer via *muthi*, in other words via a combination of spells and herbs. How else to make sense of this terrible disease?

Busisiwe tortured herself trying to figure it out. One day, as I sat at her bedside, she reasoned that if AIDS came from sex, then maybe sex was key to its cure. Would she get better if she had no more sex? Or would sex itself be an antidote? Could she get rid of it by passing it back to the man who gave it to her? This last thought struck her as morbidly funny. "He's the one who's given me this sickness. I want him to take it and go to the other women and give it." She chuckled weakly and just stared at the ceiling. I suppose it had not occurred to her that the other women were probably just like her already—sick, and dying.

"It's a pity and very funny [strange]," she mused again, "that some women have many boyfriends and don't get AIDS, and I have one boyfriend and I have gotten AIDS."

• • •

AIDS could not have hit South Africa at a worse time. Of course, there could never be an opportune time for such a deadly epidemic, but at least a society with more stability, less poverty, a better developed health care system, greater social tolerance, and fewer superstitions and myths would have been better able to fight the disease. South Africa was not such a place.

Instead, it was a society in flux. The conflicts and upheavals of the apartheid era had shattered the black family structure in many communities: the forced removals, the jailings, the killings, the flights into exile, and the migrant labor. And the apartheid-era policy of planned impoverishment left much of the country languishing in third-world conditions out of reach of the first-world hospitals, clinics, schools, and other amenities once reserved for whites.

The only good thing that the apartheid system did against AIDS was keep it out, for a while. As the epidemic deepened in Botswana, Zimbabwe, and other neighboring countries in the 1980s and early 1990s, South Africa's closed borders and pariah status served as a wall against the disease. When AIDS did begin to surface in South Africa, it was confined largely to white homosexuals, who lived extremely closeted lives amid the macho white South African culture. And when AIDS began surfacing among blacks in the early 1990s, well, health officials of the old white-minority era paid it little mind. A regime whose scientists once researched methods for the mass sterilization of black women was not a regime you'd expect to become alarmed by a viral scourge hitting black communities.

That is the backdrop for any understanding of the South African epidemic. But there were deeper reasons, more difficult-to-discuss reasons, that made the virus spread so rapidly. When men returned home from their migrant-labor jobs in the big cities or on the diamond and gold mines, HIV went home with them. In KwaZulu and other regions, men had for decades traveled to Jo'burg and elsewhere to work on the gold mines or to labor as municipal street cleaners or ash collectors, even as gardeners in the homes of wealthy whites. Most often, these men left their families back home in the village and visited them a few times a year. Often they kept at least two sets of women: their home-ground women back in the villages and their city women where they worked, not to mention the prostitutes who serviced the male-only mining hostels. The taxis and buses that brought these men to and fro between the cities and the rural areas of KwaZulu-Natal and the Eastern Cape were like conveyor belts of HIV.

But the culture itself helped to carry the disease along. This is the part that many black South Africans did not want to discuss openly, for the combination of culture, race, and sex was a volatile topic. The realities of gender relations in South Africa too easily fed the Western stereotype of a sexually promiscuous Africa. In a society whose leaders felt they needed to prove that black South Africans were sophisticated enough to lead, to govern (and of course they were), discussing the ugly side of the picture seemed almost like selling out, as in the old days of the struggle.

The fact is this: within black South Africa there were vast segments of society still locked in a culture of traditional practices that proved deadly, even suicidal. And it all centered on male dominance and the second-class status of women that was deeply woven into the culture. In customary law in South Africa and many other African countries, women had no rights as adults. This was especially the case in rural areas that still held to the old ways. For instance, women could not inherit land left by their husbands. Instead they, like the land, were passed on to a male relative, most commonly the deceased husband's brother. Women had no say, and this diminished status extended to sexual affairs as well. In some deeply traditional or impoverished communities, women were viewed as fair game for sex at any time. Rape was all too common. But even in consensual sex, a woman had no rights. She had no right even to suggest that her partner or husband use a condom. Such a request was complicated. It could suggest the woman had more sexual knowledge than her man deemed appropriate. It could suggest, in his mind, that she'd been running around. It could suggest the woman was getting too big for her britches and needed to be brought down to size. The mere suggestion of condom use could risk verbal thrashing or physical beating. People just did not discuss sexual affairs in South Africa. Mothers did not discuss it with their daughters, nor fathers with their sons; nor husbands with wives or vice versa. Talking about sex was taboo.

Likewise, to complain about the "other women" was futile. Traditional culture encouraged men to have numerous sex partners, whether through polygamous marriages or through mere girlfriends. A man who had only one woman was deemed insufficiently male, in some areas. This was a fact of life that women had to accept, unless they intended to remain celibate, single, and childless, all of which could get them tagged as strange, beyond the pale, perhaps even witches requiring punishment or people cursed by a bad *muthi*.

When AIDS began appearing in noticeable numbers in KwaZulu, in fact, bewitchment and accursedness became the ready explanations. Traditional healers, known as *inyangas*, diagnosed the disease as a particular curse. Some *inyangas* sold the false hope that their purgative brews would get rid of the disease. Or people would believe that God was angry—that's why he targeted someone with the illness. Or maybe the spirits of the ancestors had a gripe against the person. Only prostitutes got AIDS, some people would say. Only people with no morals got it. Or poor people who were unclean. Maybe it was the white people—that's what some folks assumed. Maybe the white commercial farmers poisoned the oranges and bananas they sold to the local folk. Maybe the whites angered by apartheid's end had finally found a way to get rid of the blacks, like they'd tried with that old condom ploy, trying to keep the black population down. Even in urban townships, some black youths said "AIDS" stood for "American invention to discourage sex." The myths went on and on. And so did the dying.

AIDS was so stigmatized, in fact, that some people who suspected they had it refused to get tested. They could not bear to know. Men feared revealing the disease, for it would show them as weaklings. And women feared revealing their HIV-positive status to their men, though their men gave it to them in the first place. To be afflicted with AIDS was to be ostracized, even put out of the family home. To be ill with the disease was to be a walking insult to one's community, deserving of ridicule. With AIDS sufferers wasting away into skeletal thinness, some young men decided that fat women must be safe. For a time, fat girlfriends were in vogue. If they were fat, so the warped thinking went, they couldn't be sick with AIDS.

And babies were raped. Some men, no doubt deranged, believed that sex with a baby would cure them of HIV. A variant on this was just as horrific: that sex with a young virgin was the cure. Even before HIV, sex was driven by strange myths, like the one about unreleased sperm backing up into the brain and causing insanity, or the one that said a man must be impotent if he could not become erect three times in a night.

Mandela's government tried to counteract all these myths, all this deadly disinformation among the uneducated. But it was completely unprepared for the AIDS onslaught and the paranoia and superstition the disease unleashed. The first-world methods of AIDS prevention that worked elsewhere had little resonance in a third world where deep denial and entrenched sexual patterns, as in South Africa, were fertile ground for HIV. As one AIDS policy maker told me in frustration, how do you effectively preach abstinence or monogamy in the traditional cultures that virtually require men to have several women? How do you convince women to demand that their partners use condoms in a culture where such assertiveness risks a beating? Politicians and health officials urged condom use and mounted condom distribution campaigns. But in a culture in which talk of sex was verboten, how do you teach young men the skill of rapidly applying a condom in the dark? South Africa was slow to marshal radio and television into the effort, and most South Africans could not afford cable or satellite TV and see the anti-AIDS campaigns of other countries.

Even the well-educated and worldly-wise folks in Mandela's government seemed to be in denial about AIDS or, at a minimum, deeply ambivalent about it. Virtually no prominent member of government, with the exception of Mandela himself, spoke out loudly about AIDS. How could a victorious liberation movement admit that the scourge of AIDS was subverting its triumph? With great difficulty, if at all. Even as officials attended funerals and buried the dead, the denial continued—and grew increasingly irrational.

"We all whisper after the coffin has gone down, but nobody will say it," Nono Simelela lamented. A senior health official in the anti-AIDS campaign, she seemed especially despondent. Efforts to break through the wall of silence, she said, weren't working. "We are dancing with death all the time." That is why some folks in South Africa had given sex a new name: African roulette.

One such campaign that appeared, at first, to be a sure winner in raising AIDS awareness fell apart under the weight of corruption and controversy. Mandela's health minister, Nkosazana Zuma, a physician, mounted a $3-million campaign in 1996 to stage an AIDS-prevention musical that would travel the country to educate young people. Modeled on South Africa's internationally acclaimed antiapartheid musical called *Sarafina*, the anti-AIDS play would be called *Sarafina 2* and would be the centerpiece of the prevention policy. But the production never flew. Investigators bogged it down after it was revealed that proper tender procedures were not followed when the contract for the musical was awarded to one of Zuma's friends.

And there was the oh-so-strange 1997 episode over Virodene. Zuma pushed for government funding for development of this supposed anti-AIDS drug, produced by a South African company in which, it was later revealed, some ruling party politicos held shares. But the government's own Medicines Control Council nixed the idea, calling Virodene dangerous and toxic.

Finally, in the first salvo of what became an AIDS war that rages to this day, Zuma canceled a government pilot project to distribute the drug AZT at public hospitals to HIV-positive pregnant women. Studies had proved that AZT could dramatically reduce the transmission of HIV to newborn babies, and private-paying patients who could afford the drug were able to get it. But Zuma said the government couldn't afford to subsidize it for the poor, even though at least one pharmaceutical company had already said it would provide the drug at a discount.

Quietly, some of my shocked and alarmed South African sources began speculating about a cynical government gamble: that it would be more cost-effective to let these babies become infected and die along with their sick mothers than to be socked with the huge social costs of raising a generation of orphans. By the time Mandela departed from his legendary propriety and reserve on intimate issues and boldly called in 1998 for national condom use, the pandemic was well entrenched. By the time his deputy president, Thabo Mbeki, sat before a national TV audience that year and pleaded for people to change their behavior to thwart the epidemic, people were already beginning to wonder about his and the government's actual commitment to the cause.

There seemed a clinical hollowness to Mbeki's appeal. He called for people to accept the AIDS-afflicted and to help them, not shun them. But as his words were broadcast live to the nation, he looked unmistakably ill at ease with the cute little healthy-looking toddlers playing at his feet. They were HIV-positive. They smiled and played and tugged on his knees and shoulders, but he did not reach out for them at all, as you'd expect someone to do when besieged by toddlers. His behavior sent a chilling message. Not even the deputy president seemed willing to touch a child with HIV.

After Mbeki's appeal for tolerance, an ordinary woman stepped forward on World AIDS Day a couple of months later. Gugu Dlamini publicly revealed her HIV status. She was an activist in KwaZulu with the National Association of People Living with AIDS, and her heroic action remains largely unparalleled in frightened South Africa. People there just don't tell, especially not black people. But Gugu did. And two weeks later, youths in her community of KwaMashu stoned her to death. People in KwaMashu said that Gugu had brought their community into disrepute.

Gugu's death shocked the AIDS activist community. Even more shocking was the reaction to it. The association of people with AIDS received 435 international messages of condolence in response to Gugu's death. It received only 12 such messages from people in South Africa. "We have developed a modern-day leper syndrome," Mark Decker, an association official, said of South Africa.

It seemed no accident that so much of the trauma of AIDS was unfolding most intensely in KwaZulu. A deeply rural and traditional region,

KwaZulu proved extraordinarily resistant to AIDS awareness. It is an impoverished and illiterate region, meaning it was ill prepared to confront the plague of HIV that descended on its towns and villages with full force. Rietvlei Hospital, located on the border between KwaZulu and the Eastern Cape provinces, served this hard-hit region. I had never heard of this remote hospital until Susan Winters, the photographer, suggested it as a place I must visit if I was to understand AIDS. She knew the hospital well from her AIDS-awareness research. Using photographs she shot over weeks spent with several AIDS-afflicted families in the region, Susan published an educational photo-journal, called *Ubomi* (Living), and distributed it in the Xhosa and Zulu languages.

Like hospitals all over the country, Rietvlei seemed to stay filled with HIV-positive people suffering from tuberculosis. TB was the most prevalent of the AIDS-related diseases in South Africa; also common were pneumonia, chronic diarrhea, rapid weight loss, lymphatic swelling, pelvic inflammatory disease, extreme dermatitis, and lesions. Half of Rietvlei's three hundred beds held patients suffering from AIDS-related diseases. For the first time, the hospital had become so overcrowded in early 1999 that some patients had to sleep on mattresses on the floor.

South Africa's clinics and hospitals were barely able to cope with ordinary illness, let alone something as staggering as HIV/AIDS. The saddest part, to me, was this: these hospitals were filled to the rafters with thin, gaunt, wasted people brought down by a syndrome they were still hard-pressed to understand even as they died from it. As I walked the grounds at Rietvlei one day, I felt I'd entered a purgatory. I looked through the open windows and curtains of the male TB wards and felt a terrible sadness at seeing the hopeless, hollow eyes of proud men made stick-thin with disease. I could see the goatskin bracelets some of them wore as protective amulets against the bad spirits that many believed caused their illness. The men peered at me as I passed. I waved hello to be polite. I felt so very sorry for them.

Clinically speaking, these men would die from AIDS. Culturally speaking, they would die from their own ignorance about the disease, and their own chauvinism. Politically, they would die from their nation's shameful denial and its benign neglect. No one had effectively warned these men how deadly their way of life would be—the multiple sex partners, the eschewing of condoms as unmanly, the browbeating of women into sexual submission, the demands for the "dry sex" achieved with herbs inserted into the vagina, giving men more pleasure but easily tearing their partners' skin and leaving them even more susceptible to infection.

I had tried talking to some of the men, to hear their stories. But they were reluctant—maybe out of shame, maybe out of embarrassment to discuss it with a woman. One hospitalized man, a long-distance bus driver between KwaZulu and Jo'burg, told me he was petrified of his community's reaction if they found out he had AIDS. "When you get this disease, they treat you like animals."

* * *

Rarely had I seen such a beautiful baby. Her skin was the color of cinnamon, her eyes the shape of almonds. Her name was Zimbini and she oozed the giggly charm of an eight-month-old. A laughing smile dimpled her pudgy cheeks as she bounced happily on her mother's knee. While I interviewed Thenjiwe Dzanibe, I knelt down to play with baby Zimbini. I did not expect what I saw when the baby opened her mouth. It hurts to even remember the patches of cottony thrush that grew on the baby's tongue. I feared it was a sign of AIDS. This work, this journalism, was too sad sometimes. And what I saw at Rietvlei Hospital overwhelmed me day after day.

Thenjiwe loved her baby girl. She held her gently and cooed to her. And despite the absence of any reason to hope, Thenjiwe did what any mother would: she clung to the possibility that her child would be spared. Thenjiwe was a good mother. In a world without AIDS, her life would have remained hard, no doubt, for she was a widow raising five children on her late husband's pension. But there'd be no death sentence from disease, without AIDS. There'd be no reason to foresee the near-certain demise of her family.

Nothing that the thirty-seven-year-old Thenjiwe knew before had prepared her for HIV/AIDS. She was a simple rural woman with only a little education. She had absolutely no idea what AIDS really was until she found herself confronted with it. A month before I met her, she arrived at Rietvlei Hospital too weak even to walk. Once a chubby 170-pound woman, she weighed only 88 pounds. Doctors diagnosed her with tuberculosis. It was her second bout with the disease; she'd had it three years earlier as well. The Riet-vlei doctors also tested her for HIV, the results of which she still awaited when we first met. While in the hospital, surrounded by all this talk of AIDS, Thenjiwe began to seriously put two and two together. It happened even as she told me her story.

Her husband, a migrant worker and ash collector who lived in Jo'burg most of the time, died from TB in 1995. Maybe that was actually AIDS, she now thought. Her new man—a relative of the husband, as is the tradition—was sick now too, losing weight and coughing up blood. Maybe that was AIDS too, she said. "Aye! All these men of mine are sick," she said apologetically. But her new man, who also lived in Jo'burg, did not wish to be tested.

"He's afraid some other sickness may be there." To cut through the euphemism, "some other sickness," I had to ask for her to complete that thought. "He's afraid that he might be having AIDS," she said. "But sometimes he becomes better. He goes to private doctors and seems to get better. But it comes back again . . . Yes, he is sick. He's just well for a short time."

In the hospital, it also dawned on Thenjiwe that little Zimbini was at risk of AIDS. Thenjiwe admitted that both she and the baby's father were ill when they conceived the child. And Thenjiwe remained sick during the baby's birth. In the months since, the baby developed a terrible cough. Then came the vomiting and diarrhea. Medicine had eased both problems, but test results on the baby were still outstanding. I asked Thenjiwe if she thought Zimbini might have AIDS. She looked lovingly at the baby. "Sometimes I doubt this AIDS," she said. "I often tell myself sometimes it is only God's will that people die."

Thenjiwe was a patient in the women's TB ward, where bright pink curtains added a spritz of cheer to the drab, faded walls, dull wood floor, and metal cots that sagged despite their light human loads. The women of the TB ward were wasted and thin. They could have been plucked from any refugee famine anywhere in Africa. Susan and I explained to the women that we were news reporters visiting to learn of their struggle with diseases like HIV/AIDS. They were desperate for any information. One of the patients blurted out, "If we've got TB, does that mean we are going to have AIDS?" I thought to myself: Oh, my Lord. These women haven't figured out or haven't been told that they may have AIDS already.

Philipina Mabuntana, a retired counselor from the hospital, translated and helped me conduct my interviews. Thenjiwe's was especially difficult because of the confusion she harbored about the disease and the many questions she posed, some of them valid and well reasoned. In her understanding at that time, TB was the source of AIDS, not vice versa. Nurses had told her that because she had TB she might also have AIDS, and that suggested to her a cause-and-effect relationship. Following that line of reasoning, she returned to the question of baby Zimbini and told me matter-of-factly, "It could happen that the child doesn't have it." I did not want to show any agreement. I merely wrote down her words and muttered something neutral like "let's hope so."

I asked her if she knew that many people die from AIDS. "I have never heard that," she said. "Even in TB, you have people dying and some people getting well . . . I've heard that sometimes the only difference in AIDS and TB is a person can get sick [with AIDS] without really showing, and when he starts to show, he shows many different diseases . . . I am afraid of AIDS, but in another way I am not afraid, because I read in the paper that TB is related to AIDS."

Her confusion was disturbing. At one point, she asked, "Can I be cured of AIDS and these different diseases that come out?" I hadn't expected a question so difficult and fundamental. It was a hard moment for all of us. I asked Philipina, the translator, to respond for me, since she had been a health counselor and knew better than I how to tell someone that there was no cure. Philipina told her that no cure had been found so far.

A few days later, Thenjiwe received her diagnosis. "I have understood," she told Susan. Despite the tangle of denial and misperception in which these women were trapped, many knew deep down, even before their diagnosis, that AIDS had gotten them. But right away, in discussing her diagnosis, Thenjiwe also volunteered this: "The one thing I know for sure is I'll never tell the father of my child." The man, she said, would not even consider that he gave her the disease. Instead, he would accuse her of running around. He might shout at her, even beat her. What struck me as saddest of all was that she thought she'd soon be well enough to travel to Jo'burg.

"I will continue to go to Jo'burg to see him, because now I can't start with anyone else. If I don't go to Jo'burg, he will think I am bewitched."

She felt safe enough to tell her younger sister and her *umfundisi,* or priest, at her Catholic church. But otherwise she would keep her AIDS a secret as much as she could. She did not want to become a victim of her community. Thenjiwe knew firsthand the cruelty meted out to AIDS sufferers, though she said she herself had never laughed at and ridiculed a person with AIDS.

"According to people's belief, we ridicule and laugh at people who've got AIDS. It's better that you know yourself and just take care of yourself... They make you lose hope and lose respect ... Even TB they ridicule. Some don't even want to come near me. They are observing me with a special eye to find out about this TB.

"It [AIDS] has become an insult to people. Instead of fighting to get some form of prevention, they say it's an insult... If it happens that they know, your heart can stand still. Especially the in-laws. To have AIDS among people, it's a disgrace."

Thenjiwe died that spring. Busisiwe passed away as well. Baby Zimbini languished in the hospital for several months, then finally was retrieved by her extended family for a fate unknown. And as of this writing, the South African denial of AIDS has itself become the disgrace.

17

Madiba's Twilight

CAPE TOWN, SOUTH AFRICA, FEBRUARY 1999

ape Town's beauty seemed melancholy. The steep slopes of Table Mountain curved down to the bay, while the pastel stucco buildings, including mosques and their minarets, climbed up toward the sky. Africans, European settlers, and Asian slaves had blended in this, the fairest Cape, producing a city that felt global and yet strangely parochial. I loved the Cape environment, though I wasn't too enamored of Cape society. Apartheid had been most perfect, most ugly, in this town known as the Mother City because it was South Africa's oldest.

In the deepest days of apartheid, blacks weren't even allowed to work in Cape Town, let alone be on its streets without their racial pass books or a provable cause for being afoot. Mixed-race coloreds were given legal employment preference over their darker countrymen. And the Afrikaans language that the coloreds shared with their Afrikaner rulers smothered out all others. In those days, police could stop a suspected black posing as a colored and test him on the spot to see if his command of Afrikaans would exonerate him of his Africanness. If he failed, he'd be loaded onto a truck and sent packing.

In the new system of one person, one vote, the National Party of apartheid won a majority in the Western Cape Province. Coloreds were a significant plurality among the Western Cape voters, but whites led the National Party, to which the coloreds were loyal. And the region's leaders were proud that Cape Town remained South Africa's most Europeanized city, for that meant it remained a popular tourist destination. It seemed that westerners loved to visit Africa without getting too African, and the city's most popular hotels tended toward a faux colonial splendor that the well-heeled foreign tourists seemed to relish. The hotel in which I awoke that February morning was of the hip new variety that sported an Afro-Euro fusion. The rooms were even outfitted with guest telescopes, which is what I liked most.

I could look out over Table Bay and see South Africa's most hallowed ground peaking up from the swells in the sea, out where treacherous shoals and rocky outcroppings piled the ocean floor with centuries of shipwrecks. I could see Robben Island, a piece of land that had incubated a nation. I'd been to the island many times, to write of it and to show it to my family. And each time I saw it, the island offered a precious reminder of how far South Africa had come. The island, as it was called, had been a fortress, a leper colony, and, mostly, a prison. The British had banished nineteenth-century Xhosa warriors and chiefs to the island, and history repeated itself in the twentieth century when the Afrikaners jailed generations of black activists who suffered, yes, but emerged as towering leaders. And the island's most beloved former inmate, President Nelson Mandela, topped my agenda that morning.

I caught a quick peek through the telescope to see Robben Island's lights flickering in the purple of a predawn sky as I rushed to get ready for my day with the president. I'd been trying for four years to secure a one-on-one interview with him. I'd been with him many times, at press conferences, group interviews, aboard the *Outeniqua* during the Zaire peace talks. But never with the sustained, focused attention that a one-on-one interview can bring. His office once gave me a date back in 1997, but I happened to be in Zaire in the midst of war at the proposed time. Now, in 1999, with his presidency winding down and my days in his country numbered as my tour came to a close, I'd finally get the much-coveted presidential interview. Better still, I'd spend the day flying with him through the Cape region. I was jittery with excitement, hoping that all would go well.

I'd been through the same ritual the week before in Pretoria, when a scheduling snafu caused me and Mandela's press secretary, Parks Mankahlana, to arrive at Waterkloof Air Force Base just after the presidential jet, the *Falcon*, took off. Mandela had left me behind. I could think of nothing more humiliating in all my life as I watched his plane high overhead while a clutch of crisply uniformed guards chuckled at my expense. I knew my Washington editors would fall out of their chairs laughing too when they learned that Mandela had ditched their intrepid Africa correspondent. Embarrassed that his boss had ditched him too, Parks told me not to feel too bad: Mandela had once flown off and left his own foreign minister behind.

When I recovered from the shock of it, the Pretoria calamity made sense. Mandela had spent twenty-eight years as a political prisoner, most of it on Robben Island, with time out of his control and in the hands of his jailers. Now, in his twilight at eighty years of age and with the clock running down on his presidency, time was his to use as he saw fit. For that, I could not begrudge him. Still, the Pretoria fiasco stung, and in a more personal way than it should have. I desperately needed to absorb some of that Mandela hope and wisdom after all the troubling developments I'd witnessed in South Africa and beyond. Through my four years on the continent, Mandela had been my personal talisman: when I felt especially hopeless about Africa's fate, I needed only to remember one of its most remarkable sons.

In Cape Town, I wasn't about to let him leave me behind again. I'd been instructed to arrive at the Cape's Ysterplaat Air Base by 6:00 A.M. But I planned to arrive at least an hour earlier. I arrived so early, in fact, that the sleepy soldier at the gate barely examined my official letter of invitation before waving my taxi through. And no one answered at the VIP lounge that was our rendezvous point, until I gave up knocking and started banging on the door. A surprised kitchen worker let me in and brought coffee. I settled onto the sofa and watched the sun rise over this most lovely African terrain, well pleased with the very thought of what my day had in store.

* * *

Shortly after dawn at Ysterplaat, a trio of businessmen arrived, executives of the liquor industry. Mandela rarely made trips into the country's rural areas without taking business leaders along. It was his way of prying commitments from the corporate community to build a school here, a clinic there, and help the government meet the country's pressing social needs. He wasted no opportunity to try to correct apartheid's legacy.

Finally, at 6:30 A.M., Madiba himself made his charming grand entrance. That is what many people called him, Madiba. It was his clan name, and his closest friends used it so often in public that it took on a general, respectful, affectionate usage. His arms outstretched, his gold-printed shirt billowing, Madiba boomed, "Ah, good morning!" like a man happy to see another day. I felt a swell of excitement, laced with dread as I watched him carefully totter on those bad knees. His unsteady gait struck universal fear. It constantly reminded the nation of his dangerously advanced age. Mandela's health was such a touchy issue that when rumors circulated in 1996 of an ambulance at his official residence, the currency took a nosedive. (The ambulance wasn't there for him.)

But on that lovely Cape morning, nothing about Mandela suggested decline. He was the gracious host, the national nobleman, saying, "Okay, let us go," as we fell in behind him for the short walk outside to the tarmac where the presidential jet (and his traveling physician) awaited. He situated himself on a specially padded seat and began poring through the day's newspapers. A cabinet minister, Geraldine Fraser Moleketi, was traveling with us; she held the social welfare portfolio. There were also three security men as well as the traveling secretary and the spokesman, Parks, who'd managed, like me, not to be left behind again.

As we were flying inland from the Cape, the Great Karoo unfolded beneath us. A semidesert flatland, the vast expanse had been home to the Khoikhoi and San people commonly known as Bushmen before the European conquest, but now was dotted by farms and small towns dominated by the Afrikaners. Life was harsh and spare for most of the Karoo's people, meaning the coloreds and blacks who still lived in the apartheid-era conditions bereft of proper housing, plumbing, schools, and clinics. The new government was slowly bringing such development to their region, and seeing Mandela up close and in the flesh would also bring an infusion of hope to a region so long hopeless.

All day, the eighty-year-old president raced against time—trying to be in as many places as he could, to spread his message of unity and development to as many ears as would hear, and wearing himself out perilously in the process. He delivered four speeches in three languages—Afrikaans, Xhosa, and English—in four remote towns. He got on and off the plane a dozen times, clutching the arms of an aide for support on each climb. At one point, we had to transfer to a military craft to fly to a very small town with only a gravel landing strip. And at each stop, Madiba danced his trademark shuffle for the adoring crowds as they sang songs of praise. His feet rarely left the ground. His legs did not bend much. But his magic still shone through as he pumped his arms briskly and smiled so genuinely he seemed to have invented joy.

Through the day, I'd had only small talk with him. At one point as we stood on a tarmac, he jokingly asked me, "Are you keeping up?" I spent most of the time scurrying with his small entourage, outside his heavy security cordon, trying not to get trampled by the adoring throngs that greet Mandela wherever he goes. At a couple of the stops, I ended up onstage with him, seated at the back with his staff. It felt odd to see from his vantage point the upturned faces of adoring crowds hungry for word, any word, from their national patriarch. He moved through the Karoo that day, through towns called Prieska, De Aar, Colesberg, and Williston, as a kind of messiah trying to coax his people out of the desert of their old ways, their old chains, and onto the rich terrain of reconciliation, national progress, and hope.

"None of you should fear serving your own country," he bellowed from the stage inside the town hall of Colesberg. His audience there was mostly Afrikaner, with a large minority of coloreds and a sprinkling of blacks. It was to the Afrikaners that he addressed his words. Especially in the rural regions, Afrikaners continued to labor under a fear of black-majority rule. That crime had spiked since apartheid's end seemed to confirm, for them, that old shibboleth of the "black peril." Many Afrikaners had retreated from national life into their own sullen worlds after their people lost power in 1994.

"You have no other country," he told them. "This is your country. Don't sideline yourselves. You have the advantage of education. You went to schools. You went to university. We want you. Don't be on the sidelines, because white supremacy in this country we have destroyed. It will never come back."

Then, in his classic evenhanded style, he turned his attention to blacks, even though, in this crowd, only a smattering of blacks was on hand. "Now, to you blacks, you Africans. We are in the majority and the majority tends to abuse, tends to have contempt for the minority. One of the greatest mistakes is to try to abuse the minority." I am certain that his words, though addressed to blacks, were meant as much to reassure the whites, for whom the issue of minority rights remained, even four years after the transition, a source of insecurity.

Parks, the spokesman, told me it was necessary for Mandela to tailor his remarks for specific racial groups because of the huge gulfs between them and the different material realities in which they lived. At the same time, though, Mandela pressed the point over and over that South Africans were one people.

"Every day I go to bed feeling strong like a young man of twenty because I can see this rainbow nation rising in front of my eyes and that is what inspires me," he told the adoring crowds. "As far as I'm concerned, there is no colored, there is no Indian, there is no white person. There are only human beings, all of whom I love."

Mandela's corporate guests tagged along through the day, meeting with him on the plane but otherwise just being there. One of them told me they came to see firsthand the kinds of needs of which Mandela so often spoke. Gary May of Gilbey's explained his own understanding of Mandela's corporate appeal: "What he's saying is there's a big backlog of development. There are communities that have been left behind. And so he's trying to take people there and say, 'Can you, as a businessman, put some resources in?'"

But Mandela did not seem to be asking. Quite frankly, he seemed to be talking these potential business commitments into reality, locking them in by presenting them as done deals. At Williston, a desperately poor community that did not have a clinic, Mandela told the crowd, "Ever since I came out of jail in 1990, I have gone right around the country with business—not as part of any organization, not as part of government, but as an individual old man to say to business 'I want you to deliver services to our people.' Last year alone, I took thirty different businessmen to various parts of the country . . . In each place, each one of these individual businesspeople is going to build a modern clinic, a modern school."

At Prieska, Mandela introduced May and his colleagues to the crowd. It was clear that he was pulling them along faster than they had planned to go. "They have come to see for themselves what is required and to meet those whose needs we must all address together," Mandela told the people of Prieska, a largely colored town. "They are eager to play their part in the reconstruction and development of our country and to share their resources with those who were disadvantaged in the past. They are acting in the true spirit of reconciliation, a practical partnership to overcome the legacy of our divided past."

Not much wiggle room there. And May seemed bemused, but slightly worried. "He must just be careful not to overpromise, because we can't do every town," May said to me later. But Mandela was famous for getting just what he wanted from the nation's corporate barons: schools, clinics, playgrounds, and houses. Parks, the spokesman, told me that no one ever turned him down.

• • •

When we boarded at De Aar for the final flight to Pretoria, I worried. This was the time set aside for my interview, and if Mandela felt as tired as I felt, I knew the interview would be rough. But as it turned out, I would have to wait longer still. An emergency back in Cape Town had captured the president's attention. A senior police antiterrorism official had just been shot in a highway ambush, the second such attack in recent weeks. Rocked by a spate of bombings in Cape Town, Mandela's government had made a priority of getting to the bottom of the terrorism. Officials believed a Muslim vigilante group formed to combat crime had taken to combating the police as well. Mandela decided—despite the length of his day—to return to Cape Town. "I must go to the hospital to see him," he told his secretary on the plane. And so we flew back to Cape Town.

The injured officer was Western Cape Police Superintendent Schalk Visagie, who'd narrowly escaped death in a pipe-bomb blast only a few months before. Mandela knew the man more than in passing, for Visagie was the son-in-law of one of the apartheid era's most notorious presidents, P. W. Botha. In his efforts back in 1997 to cajole Botha into cooperating with the reconciliation effort, Mandela had hosted Visagie and his wife twice at the presidential residence in Cape Town, called Genadendal.

By going to join Botha's family at the hospital, perhaps Mandela wanted to make a symbolic gesture, the kind that had been trademarks of his presidency: that he was a leader concerned about all South Africans, no matter their race or past. No doubt he also wanted to send a message to the criminals: that the president's full weight was behind the antiterrorism effort. But as we flew back to Cape Town, he was so tired. A flight attendant named Michele Williams knelt before him and gently removed the heavy shoes from his swollen feet. With some effort, Mandela elevated his legs and stretched them out in a facing seat as Williams fluttered a soft-fringed blanket over them. The attendant treated him with reverent precision, for he was, after all, the nation's most precious passenger.

Once at the Milnerton Medi-Clinic in Cape Town, we plunged into a media circus. Television cameras surrounded the clinic entrance, and heavily armed cops outfitted for battle took up position for Mandela's arrival. Inside, hospital workers lined the hallways to glimpse and greet their president. He moved somberly among them. This was not a jovial occasion. While Mandela met behind closed doors with the officer's wife (Botha's daughter), whispers filled the hallway outside the private room. It seemed that the woman, Rozanne Visagie, was emotionally overcome, as would be expected. But she also wanted to make some political hay of the ambush that had nearly taken her husband's life. Crime was flourishing in South Africa, and many conservative whites and some blacks believed the abolition of the death penalty in 1995 had given license to the criminals. His critics had accused Mandela of being too soft on crime.

There in the hallway, I was in earshot of the sotto voce deliberations of Visagie's Afrikaner friends and family. They debated the merits of Mrs. Visagie's desire to release a statement blaming the government's stand on the death penalty for the ambush of her husband. In that idea, some in the small hallway crowd apparently saw the fingerprints of Botha himself, still trying to play politics. "If P.W. wants to send a political message, he mustn't do it under these circumstances," a worried white man said to another. The hallway was filled with apprehension.

In the private room where Mandela met with Mrs. Visagie, lamplight cast their figures in silhouette against thin mini-blinds. Mandela sat. She stood. She paced in front of him, flailing her arms, gesturing excitedly. At one point, it looked to me as if Mrs. Visagie was angrily and disrespectfully pointing her finger in Mandela's face. I know she was upset, but this was the president! It galled me to see such arrogance. No black person, not even in the throes of grief, would ever have behaved with such disrespect for Mandela.

He emerged from their meeting moving more slowly than ever. After he made a brief, formalistic statement to the press, the entourage fell in behind him for the plodding walk to the motorcade, to head back to the airport, for the last leg of a full day's journey.

• • •

Parks called me forward. Finally, my time had come. But the arrangements aboard the *Falcon* were awkward. I was directed to a seat across the aisle from Mandela's. To see eye-to-eye, we'd have to strain our necks. And though renowned for never wanting to admit he was tired, Mandela looked like the weight of the day, the nation, the world, bore down upon him. It was 8:30 P.M. Fourteen hours had passed since we first took off that morning. Out of concern for him, I almost wanted to offer that we do the interview another time. But I'd waited four years already, and my June departure from South Africa loomed as the greatest of deadlines. So I made the best of an uncomfortable situation and began delicately and slowly.

I explained the kind of piece I planned to write, a portrait of a day in the life of a revered national icon as he winds down his tenure toward retirement. It had been conventional wisdom that Mandela was tired, ready to take on a slower pace, to retreat to Qunu, his home village in the Transkei, and spend time with his new bride, Graça Machel. The widow of Mozambican President Samora Machel, Graça Machel had been Mandela's companion for many months before they actually wed in 1998, and their romance brought a certain giddiness to public events as people saw them hold hands, blush, and softly whisper to each other. Tutu, the archbishop, had repeatedly prodded them to tie the knot to set a good moral example. And finally, in a private wedding that was South Africa's worst-kept secret after days of press speculation, the couple exchanged vows at Mandela's large Jo'burg home. After being fed lies all the previous week by Mandela's aides, who denied a wedding would take place, the press corps, including me, descended on Mandela's street and joined the veritable festival of well-wishers from the neighborhood, both wealthy whites and their domestic workers, who sang praise to the new couple.

Also in 1998, Mandela seemed to signal a desire to change the presidential pace. Though he had already assigned many executive duties to his deputy president, Thabo Mbeki, Mandela announced that he wanted "to be relieved of all government duties," as he put it at the time, to focus on the coming election campaign. Of course, that was not possible, and Mandela's chief of staff reassured the nation that President Mandela would continue on as required by the law. I had all these indicators in mind when I opened my interview on the plane by asking if he looked forward to retiring into private life.

"What is the relevance of that?"

Whoa. He snapped at me. I had hit some nerve I didn't even know was there. I struggled to maintain my composure, for when I'm nervous in interviews, my hands shake. I did not want him to see how badly he'd rattled me already. So I pandered. I called upon every scintilla of my interviewing agility and found novel ways—though probably quite transparent ones—to ask the same question less objectionably. I explained that the world, including my readers, had watched his presidency with inspiration and surely were interested in his life to come and how he perceived his retirement. And he eased his resistance a bit.

"I've gone so far to say Thabo Mbeki is the de facto president of the country and I am the de jure president. It's not a question of being eager, but in that sense I am looking forward to it."

But I hit that edgy nerve again when I asked what his ideal day would be like after he retires. "No, I don't think we should talk about ideal worlds. I am in South Africa, here."

This is not an interview, I thought; this is some kind of combat. I persisted, though gently and despite my mouth going dry from nerves. I could tell he was just tolerating me. This interview will penetrate nowhere, I thought. It is doomed. The day has been too long, too full, to expect him to now sit back and be amiable. I could feel my heart sinking, for I knew I came seeking something, some personal affirmation that I would not get. And forget about the journalism of it. Mandela wasn't playing along.

But he softened. He offered up a gem of a glimpse into his thoughts. His twenty-one grandchildren came to mind, and everyone in South Africa knew how much delight he found in them, in contrast to the guilt he felt at missing most of the lives of his own children, who'd had to live without their father while he was in jail.

"I have got grandchildren," his gravelly voice said. It sounded dissonant with so soft a subject. "I miss the opportunity of listening to them, to their dreams. I have vowed, whatever else I do, I must give space to my grandchildren and be able to help them to grow and formulate."

He said he would split his time between his party duties and his grandchildren, either in Jo'burg or back in Qunu. "My knees are bad," he explained, so he wouldn't be able to walk the hills of Qunu as he once did. Still, he said, "I will enjoy being in my country village."

Then he shut that door completely. No more personal thoughts. The only subject he wished to discuss was the day's mission: getting corporate South Africa to finance school and clinic construction. It was a form of reconciliation, a central theme of Mandela's presidency. I knew all about this investment effort. He'd been doing it since day one. It was an inspired policy, but old news. Still, to keep the interview going, I had no choice but to ask him questions about it, why it's so important, whether his entreaties are ever refused (never, he said). On these issues, he was expansive and even-tempered. Thank goodness. I relaxed a little. And anyway, I could think of nothing I'd like better than listen to Nelson Mandela explain to me his philosophy of reconciliation in that formal, old-world cadence of his.

"There is a realization that the community which has got advantages as a result of the history of the country must now share those resources . . . Insofar as getting business to deliver services, it's something which I have to do because the need is there."

It occurred to me as I listened to him that I'd been asking the wrong questions, missing the man completely by not adequately grasping his essence. I asked him if he enjoyed days such as the long one just finished, and he said, "It's not because I like it. But I have to do it." It was, you see, his mission. Between Mandela and his mission—his country's liberation and its upliftment—there was no separation. It wasn't emotion that drove him, but a single-minded and unswering commitment, and that commitment defined his entire being. I think that is why my questions about his feelings, his desires, struck a nerve. Those things were beside the point; they had no bearing on his mission. How he felt about his work was immaterial. When I asked how he felt about the huge, surging crowds he routinely faced, the people with outstretched hands trying to touch him, he said he regarded them with a sense of respectful duty. "I don't regard it as proper, when people are a close distance from you, to spurn their hands."

He also would not discuss his tenure as president, his disappointments and successes. If I wanted to talk about those things, he said, I'd have to make another appointment. On this, he was firm. He sat back and nestled in his seat, as if signaling the interview's end. I would never know precisely why he was so brusque, not displaying an ounce of the personal charm for which he was known. But the day had been a Mandela marathon, a love fest between Madiba and the nation he had tried so valiantly to create. From the moment he walked free from prison in 1990, that had been his mission: to build a new nation from the brutal human failures of apartheid. And so much had gone so very, very well.

South Africa was a legal democracy underpinned by a brand-new constitution that guaranteed individual rights and equality before the law. New institutions to support the transitional democracy were up and running, including a new Constitutional Court, the highest court in the land. From the national Parliament to the smallest town council, government was, for the first time in modern South African history, representative of the people.

Even the armed forces were being integrated into one unified force amalgamating the old black liberation armies with the white troops of apartheid. It didn't happen easily, but that it happened at all was a source of national strength, for those who could see beyond their own narrow interests.

The political violence that had racked parts of the country had subsided. Education was being reformed to strip it of the racist teachings of the past and bolster it for a modern economy. Houses, clinics, and schools were slowly going up in towns and villages that needed them. The new class of black capitalists was listing companies on the stock exchange, sitting on corporate boards, and slowly filling the management ranks of industry. And the backdrop to it all had been Mandela's tireless work. He had been the glue—not alone, but certainly in the main. He'd brought South Africa's disparate people together as never before and showed the nation, by his own example, what dignity and forgiveness looked like.

But his push for reconciliation had foundered somewhat on white defensiveness and on black bitterness. And politics had tripped up reconciliation, as well, with de Klerk's chronic assaults against the Truth and Reconciliation Commission. Even the ANC, under the leadership of Mbeki, not Mandela, had taken the Truth Commission to court in late 1998. Proving itself a dangerously defensive party, the ANC tried (but failed) to stop publication of a final Truth Commission report that branded some ANC actions during the liberation war as human rights violations. Mbeki in effect led the ANC in opposition to the very institution that the party had created to lead the push for reconciliation. It was, for me, an unnerving display of the strangely schizophrenic tendencies that would mar Mbeki's coming term as president.

Mbeki, a generation younger than Mandela, would be a very different kind of president, leading South Africa at a very different time. He seemed, back then, a man up to the task, an economist by training, an intellectual by bent, even a visionary. Other characteristics would emerge later—autocratic tendencies, political paranoia, devastatingly extreme denial on the AIDS crisis—that would send a chill through me as I recalled the wonderful halcyon days of promise and progress under the beloved Mandela. As he prepared to step down, the aging president's mission was only partly fulfilled, but he'd started the evolution of a new society that would continue to grow for years to come. I found it hard to imagine what South Africa would have become without a man like Mandela at its helm.

Even as cantankerous as he was with me on the plane, I still held him in awe. Unfortunately, I also still had the silly idea that I could crack through to some personal reflectiveness. I took one more stab at the retirement question and kept my game face on. Surely, after fifteen-hour days filled with speeches and motorcades and flights and huge heaving crowds—surely there is reason to look forward to some relaxation in retirement, I said to him. But I was, again, just misleading myself. He offered an odd answer that felt like the verbal equivalent of swatting a fly.

"Well, if you are talking about the fact that I keep in mind that in May or June of this year I will step down, in that sense I'm looking forward to it. It's just an ordinary event like the other events which take place in my life."

Oh please, I wanted to say. Yours, Mr. President, could hardly be characterized as an "ordinary" life. But I let it go. I let him go. My time was up. I was, effectively, dismissed. Shaken and exhausted, I walked back to my appointed seat in the cabin's rear. I felt queasy. I felt mystified at the absence of magic in a moment I thought I'd hold and savor.

And yet the magic of the day itself had been intense. His was a Herculean task, and he never faltered. His nation's needs knew no bounds, and he pushed himself beyond all human limits to try to fulfill them. People repeatedly urged him to slow down. Tutu, the archbishop and old friend, chided Mandela for his exhausting schedule. But he would not slow down. He could not slow down. Mandela and his mission would keep marching forward as long as it remained humanly possible to do so. The mission was the magic, and I'd spent four years under its spell.

I leaned out into the aisle, just watching Mandela, regarding him. The father of the nation reclined beneath his fringed blanket and closed his eyes, resting at last from this oh-so-ordinary day in an undeniably extraordinary life. I sat back and relaxed too, savoring this moment of flight with Mandela across a starlit African sky.

Epilogue

ith a lump in my throat, I sat through a luncheon in Pretoria that May of 1999, where Mandela said farewell to his press corps. The first term of South Africa's democratic era had been a remarkable time, and all of us in attendance, whether South African or foreign, knew how blessed we had been to witnesses Mandela's new world unfold. When the luncheon was over and Mandela circulated through the crowd, I held his hand in mine ever so briefly and wished him Godspeed.

Leaving South Africa, leaving Africa, proved far more wrenching than I'd have ever imagined. I'd embraced so fully the many stories that had unfolded on my beat that they'd become my reality. But I had to go. That is the foreign correspondent's lot: to immerse oneself in a time, in a place, and then to move on. So I said my own farewells to friends, to sources, and, tearfully, to Bernard Gumede, my rock of stability at the Jo'burg house. And then I flew home, back to America.

But really I didn't leave Africa. And Africa didn't leave me. The continent infused my sensibilities and viewpoints. For many months that stretched into years, I grappled in America with a more crystal clear perception of the culture's general whiteness—its sense of blackness, of Africanness, as something abnormal and apart, as has defined the national character since its founding. It troubled me less than it had before I lived in Africa, for I returned to America as if part of a secret society, more cognizant and appreciative of the unique identity bequeathed to me from the land of my ancestors.

And that is why for many, many months after my return to America, I still raced in the African current, at least in my mind, still lived and relived all I had experienced and learned. Writing this book helped to keep those times alive for me, to memorialize the many people who taught me so much by the simple practice of their humanity and the exercise of their hope. More than their words, they gave me a taste of Africa's essence—the surging aspirations and the crushing struggles I was fortunate enough to know and able to cherish in all their bittersweetness.

From the U.S., I have watched events in my old region move beyond where I left them. I have watched as Mandela, even in retirement, has continued as an elder statesman, still traveling South Africa with businessmen in tow, still trying to bring development to regions that have gone without it. He continues to mediate in continental conflicts, and he remains a voice of morality and vision for South Africa and beyond.

His successor, President Thabo Mbeki, who'd comported himself as a progressive pragmatist while Mandela's deputy president, stepped into the presidential shoes and became an enigma. Mbeki is hailed globally for his forward-looking development and economic policies, encompassing both South Africa and the continent as a whole. His visions of African economic unity and political accountability are laudable, at least in theory and perhaps, with time, in practice. But the early years of his presidency also were defined by a strange official denial regarding the AIDS pandemic sweeping South Africa and the region. He has confounded scientists and diplomats, not to mention South Africa's own people, by questioning the origins of AIDS and its accepted treatments. Though Mbeki's government finally relented in providing the AIDS drug AZT to its people, his odd dabblings on the subject have diminished South Africa's credibility and made Mbeki the subject of much suspicion at home and abroad—quite a step down from the heroic mantle he inherited from Mandela.

In Congo-Zaire, the "world war of Africa" continues even as of this writing, with a death toll estimated near 2 million. In January 2001, an assassin shot down President Laurent Désiré Kabila. His son, Joseph Kabila, assumed the presidency. Various attempts at peace have floundered, leaving the country in de facto partition and strangled by fits and starts of fighting. From Paris and the Moroccan capital of Rabat, Mobutu Sese Seko's son, Mobutu Nzanga, watches Congo-Zaire's travails and waits—if not for his own return, then for the return of his father's remains, for burial on his home ground. From time to time he phones me, just to say hello.

In Rwanda, Paul Kagame, the Tutsi guerrilla leader who had been the defense minister and vice president, has become president of the tiny nation. Pasteur Bizimungu, a Hutu who had been president, was removed from office and fell into political opposition. Rwanda's efforts to reconcile its ethnic divisions continues to falter. And so treacherous has the Congo war been for Rwanda that it even fell into battle in Kisangani for a time against its old ally, Uganda, led by President Yoweri Museveni, who also remains in power.

In Zimbabwe, President Robert Mugabe's once-placid nation has been thrust into chaos because of a downward economic spiral and an explosion of political repression. In the first serious electoral challenge to Mugabe in the twenty-two years he has been in power, an opposition leader looked set to take the presidency in balloting in March 2002. But Mugabe's ruling party manipulated voting rules, repressed free expression, and intimidated voters so totally that the long-time president held on to power, his iron-fisted grip tighter than ever.

In Angola, the infamous UNITA rebel leader Jonas Savimbi died in a battle with Angolan government forces in February 2002. Another peace accord was signed shortly thereafter, and Savimbi's troops, pounded and starving, began turning themselves in. Fighting in the long Angolan war, begun at independence in 1975, had finally stopped.

While writing this book, I returned to Africa—to South Africa, Angola, and Congo—to see old friends and sources and places. I went to Ngobila Beach, in Kinshasa, to see that old Congo River ferry. I thought I wanted to see its color, its rust, and to hear the cacophony of the port once again, even the memory of the drummers who carried me across those troubled waters. But really, I just wanted to feel Africa's charge, its rush; to feel the dizzying sensation that defined my old life, a life I lived between fear and freedom.

Acknowledgments

Without Tom Tshibangu, Mbongo Mamanisini, Pierre Mabele, Augusto Manuel, Felisberto Machava, Jean Mafurebo, Alec Muhoho, Vita Matundo, Benedito Diogo, Nickson Bahati, David Alcock, and Sipho Khuzwayo I would not have had the rich travels that are the fiber of this book. In South Africa, Angola, Rwanda, Congo-Zaire, and Mozambique, these men were indispensable as "fixers," translators, and drivers who got me where I needed to go and kept me safe in the process. To them, I owe my humblest thanks.

In South Africa, I was fortunate to be embraced by a close network of colleagues. Though the list is long, my heartfelt thanks go especially to Liz Sly of the *Chicago Tribune*, Marcus Mabry of *Newsweek*, Judith Matloff of the *Christian Science Monitor*, Tina Susman of the Associated Press and *Newsday*, Mary Braid of the *London Independent*, Dele Olojede of *Newsday*, Jennifer Ludden of National Public Radio, and Charlayne Hunter-Gault of CNN. Several of these colleagues read my manuscript and offered important insight and memories that helped shape this work.

A host of friends in South Africa were touchstones of normalcy during my very abnormal life in South Africa, and to them I am eternally grateful: Noluthando Crockett-Ntonga, Jerri Eddings, Lori Waselchuck, Ellen Brown, Alison Brown, Amma Ogan, Fazela Hanif, David Himbara, Yoon Park, Roland Pearson, Bernadette Moffet, Michael Giles, Alice Brown, Oyama Mabandla, Gayla Cook, Tommy Mohajane, and especially Moeletsi Mbeki for his affection and wisdom.

There are numerous Africa analysts and academics to whom I turned for context and historic analysis while covering Africa. Without them I would have been blind to some of Africa's many complexities. They include: Khehla

Shubane and Thomas Friedman of the Center for Policy Studies in Johannesburg; Tom Lodge of the University of the Witwatersrand; Mahmoud Mamdani of the University of Cape Town and, now, Columbia University in New York; William Malegapuru Makgoba of the University of the Witwatersrand and, now, South Africa's Medical Research Council; Georges Nzongola Natalaja of Howard University; I. William Zartman of Johns Hopkins University; Herbert Weiss of the City University of New York and Columbia University; Gerald Bender of the University of Southern California; and Salih Booker of the Council on Foreign Relations and, now, Africa Action in Washington.

Numerous international aid organizations facilitated my work and travel, and to them I offer my gratitude: the World Food Program, World Vision, the International Medical Corps, Médicins sans Frontières, Refugees International, and the International Rescue Committee.

At the *Washington Post*, I am grateful for the support and encouragement I have received through the years from Leonard L. Downie, the paper's executive editor, and Donald E. Graham, chairman and CEO of the Washington Post Company. My African journey would not have been launched without Michael Getler, the senior foreign editor who first dispatched me to South Africa in 1990, and Jackson Diehl, who selected me for the paper's foreign service in 1995. My thanks also to Eugene Robinson, Ed Cody, and Andy Mosher, all foreign editors who tolerated my telephonic tirades and trusted my journalistic judgment.

My agent, Faith Childs, proved indispensable at the beginning of this project, when she helped me bring order to a riotous mass of memories and impressions that seemed hardly able to form a book. For her patience and guidance in shaping the final product, I am also grateful to my editor, Janet Hill, at Doubleday.

I am most deeply thankful to my husband, Phillip Dixon. He was my sounding board for this project, and heaven knows I sounded off a lot. His incisive editor's eye, caustic wit, and keen intellect kept me sharp during the writing of this book. I am blessed by his support and love.

Index of Names and Places